Social Perspectives in Mental Health

of related interest

Good Practice in Adult Mental Health
Edited by Tony Ryan and Jacki Pritchard
Good Practice in Social Work 10
ISBN 1 84310 217 X

Racism and Mental Health
Prejudice and Suffering
Edited by Kamaldeep Bhui
ISBN 1 84310 076 2

Spirituality and Mental Health Care
Rediscovering a 'Forgotten' Dimension
John Swinton
ISBN 1 85302 804 5

Ethical Practice and the Abuse of Power in Social Responsibility
Leave No Stone Unturned
Edited by Helen Payne and Brian Littlechild
ISBN 1 85302 743 X

New Approaches to Preventing Suicide
A Manual for Practitioners
Edited by David Duffy and Tony Ryan
ISBN 1 84310 221 8

Surviving Post-Natal Depression
At Home, No One Hears You Scream
Cara Aiken
ISBN 1 85302 861 4

Deliberate Self-Harm in Adolescence
Claudine Fox and Keith Hawton
Child and Adolescent Mental Health Series
ISBN 1 84310 237 4

Mental Illness
A Handbook for Carers
Edited by Rosalind Ramsay, Claire Gerada, Sarah Mars and George Szmukler
ISBN 1 85302 934 3

Social Perspectives in Mental Health

Developing Social Models to Understand and Work with Mental Distress

Edited by Jerry Tew

Foreword by Judy Foster

Jessica Kingsley Publishers
London and Philadelphia

Chapter 1 incorporates material from Tew, J. (2002) 'Going Social: Championing a Holistic Model of Mental Distress within Professional Education' in *Social Work Education 21*, 2, 143–155, and is reproduced with permission from Taylor and Francis.

First published in 2005
by Jessica Kingsley Publishers
116 Pentonville Road
London N1 9JB, UK
and
400 Market Street, Suite 400
Philadelphia, PA 19106, USA

www.jkp.com

Copyright © Jessica Kingsley Publishers 2005
Foreword copyright © Judy Foster 2005

Library of Congress Cataloging in Publication Data
Social perspectives in mental health : developing social models to understand and work with mental distress / edited by Jerry Tew ; foreword by Judy Foster.— 1st American pbk. ed.
        p. cm.
Includes bibliographical references and index.
ISBN-13: 978-1-84310–220–5 (pbk.)
ISBN-10: 1-84310–220–X (pbk.)
    1. Mental health—Social aspects. 2. Mental illness—Social aspects. 3. Psychiatric social work. I. Tew, Jerry, 1955-
    RC455.S5975 2005
    362.2'042—dc22

                                        2004030317

British Library Cataloguing in Publication Data
A CIP catalogue record for this book is available from the British Library

ISBN-13: 978 1 84310 220 5
ISBN-10: 1 84310 220 X

Printed and Bound in Great Britain by
Athenaeum Press, Gateshead, Tyne and Wear

Contents

Foreword

It is a cause for celebration to be able to introduce this thought-provoking book to a wider public. Each chapter is the tip of an iceberg of knowledge and experience, perfectly replicating the sense of discovery of the original study day that inspired the book.

The Social Perspectives Network (SPN) is a network open to anyone who is interested in looking at mental distress in terms of people's social experience – how social factors may both contribute to people becoming distressed, and play a crucial part in promoting their recovery. It grew out of a need to find space to explore the common ground between those who use services and those who work in them. One shared view is that a disease model of mental distress – which treats someone's 'illness' apart from their life events, social relationships and place in the community – has inevitable limitations.

There have been recent moves to relocate social care practitioners within combined health and social care trusts. This has led to concerns that reshuffling the pack of how services are delivered might be at the expense of what is valued by those using the services. If social perspectives became marginalised, the overall impact of reorganisation might be to reduce people's opportunities for recovery – particularly if social care workers moving over into joint trusts were to lose their community links into housing, employment, benefit knowledge and leisure opportunities. There were worries that the relationship basis of much of this type of work was less 'evidenced' than the psychopharmacological approaches of twenty-first-century practice. However, set against these concerns, the new structures for 'joined-up' working offer real opportunities for crossing professional boundaries and promoting social perspectives within the practice of all mental health workers.

SPN debates policies and presents the results back to the creators and implementers. It campaigns for increased attention to be paid to social and user-focused research, and is committed to a consideration of issues of equality and diversity. It has published a series of papers that record the formal contributions made at each of its study days and the discussions that took place. Being easily accessible (www.spn.org.uk), with a shared membership across professions and hierarchies and a respect for individual experience, it encourages a diverse range of people to be heard by policy formulators and service leaders.

SPN is an independent organisation that currently receives funding and support from the National Institute for Mental Health in England (NIMHE) and the Social Care Institute for Excellence (SCIE), where it has its administrative base. To be accessible to a wider membership and to influence policy and practice locally, SPN is developing networks in each English region, working closely with the NIMHE Regional Development Centres.

This book marks a new stage on SPN's mission. Read it with pleasure. It may show you a way forward.

Judy Foster
Co-chair, Social Perspectives Network

Introduction

Jerry Tew

By its very nature, mental distress may be a profoundly confusing and frightening experience, both for those going through it, and for those close to them within their social and professional networks. Part of the attraction of the biomedical model has been that it seems to provide answers, meanings and certainties. However, for many people, it does not always provide the most helpful 'pegs' on which to hang their experience.

As a result, a range of more socially oriented viewpoints and knowledge bases have emerged, both from practitioners and academics from a variety of mental health disciplines, and from service users, family members and other allies. While medical technologies may make a valuable contribution in enabling people to manage specific vulnerabilities and reactions to stress, it is increasingly being recognised that mental health promotion, crisis resolution and longer-term action to support recovery may need to be underpinned more explicitly by social perspectives.

However, although there may be a groundswell of interest in social perspectives, what has *not* so far happened is for the various strands of alternative 'social' thinking to be brought together as a coherent model, or set of perspectives, in its own right – one that can, in its own way, be as influential on policy and practice as is the medical model.

This book brings together a range of social perspectives that may be useful in understanding mental distress and the social and personal issues that may connect with it. It is important to develop a repertoire of concepts and models that may help to move us beyond the territory of just treating symptoms, and may be useful in giving meaning to experience, and in enabling and supporting recovery.

This book may be seen as determinedly pluralistic. There is no assumption that there will be a single coherent 'social model' into which the complexities of people's experience will be shoe-horned. Instead, there is a need for a lively and creative dialogue, in which the perspectives of those with direct personal experience of living with, or working alongside, mental distress may be seen as having as valid a contribution to make as those perspectives that are more grounded in established social and psychological theory.

The inspiration for this book arose out of a study day, organised by the Social Perspectives Network in November 2002 (SPN, 2003). This was deliberately set up as a 'melting pot' of diverse ideas and experiences – and it is the aim of this book to take this exploration further. Contributors come from diverse backgrounds, including various combinations of lived experience of mental distress and/or experience of working in academic, policy or practice settings. They also reflect a variety of disciplinary orientations. It is hoped that the ideas, concepts and models that are developed in the various chapters of this book will provide a useful range of 'pegs' on which service users, carers and practitioners may be able to 'hang' elements of experience that may previously have seemed confusing or problematic. Having ways of *making sense* that work for us is a crucial foundation for personal recovery and for enabling the recovery of others.

The primary focus of the book is on exploring different ways of understanding mental distress from a social perspective. It is hoped that much of the material within it will be seen to be of direct relevance to the development of policy and practice in the mental health field.

Chapter 1 offers an overview of social perspectives and provides pointers to the emerging knowledge base that already exists in this area. Alongside this, it seeks to identify core themes, particularly in terms of values and orientations, that underpin and define any social perspectives approach.

Writing from a service user perspective, Peter Beresford reviews, in Chapter 2, the current political and policy context within mental health, and the emergence within this of 'survivor knowledge' that draws on the standpoints of those with first-hand experience of mental distress and of the impact of services upon them. He charts how this is beginning to challenge dominant medicalised understandings of distress, and draws parallels with the disability movement's campaign to redefine disability from a social perspective.

Duncan Double gives an insider perspective on competing models and traditions of practice within psychiatry in Chapter 3, showing how more holistic and socially oriented models have played, and continue to play, an important role within the development of practice.

In Chapter 4, I explore aspects of social theory which may be relevant to developing social understandings of mental distress – in particular, frameworks for understanding how both distress itself, and social responses to it, may be shaped by the operation of power relations. This may be at the micro-scale of interpersonal interactions, and also in terms of the structures, ideologies and attitudes that characterise modern societies.

Martin Webber, in Chapter 5, focuses on one set of approaches to looking at social resources and opportunities: exploring the usefulness of different conceptions of 'social capital'. These ideas are currently generating a lot of interest in the wider field of health and social care, but have yet to be applied to any great extent within the field of mental health itself.

Drawing directly on her experience as a practitioner, Sally Plumb sets out in Chapter 6 a comprehensive model for explaining a wide range of experiences of mental distress in terms of how they may be understood as perfectly logical and sensible responses to forms of trauma such as sexual abuse.

In Chapters 7, 8 and 9, Peter Ferns, Jennie Williams and Sarah Carr explore the impacts of discrimination and inequalities on the mental health experiences of, respectively, Black people, women, and lesbian and gay people. They show, on the basis of personal experience and research evidence, how these factors may contribute to causing distress and breakdown in the first place, and how they may also permeate professional practice and modes of service delivery, to such an extent that experiences of systematic unfairness and oppression may actually be reproduced and exacerbated. Out of this emerges an agenda for change which must be central to any social perspectives approach.

Within the current political and professional discourse around risk, user-centred perspectives can easily become split off or marginalised. In Chapter 10, Shulamit Ramon offers a wider social perspective on the current discourses of risk which can be so disabling to service users, and argues that risk taking should be seen as at least as important as risk management in promoting people's mental health.

In Chapter 11, Jan Wallcraft draws on her own research on service users' 'recovery narratives' in order to provide a critical overview of international and British developments of the concept of 'recovery' in relation to mental health. A focus on 'recovery' rather than 'illness' offers the potential to re-orientate services in a way that is both empowering to service users and embraces much more of a social perspective.

Finally, in Chapter 12, I draw together some of the key strands that have emerged from the preceding chapters, and look at how to start putting social perspectives into practice.

Reference

SPN (2003) *Start Making Sense… Developing Social Models to Understand and Work with Mental Distress*. London: Social Perspectives Network.

CHAPTER 1

Core Themes of Social Perspectives

Jerry Tew

Over recent years, there has been a resurgence of interest in the social aspects of mental health, both in terms of seeking to understand what may contribute to mental distress, and what forms of support and intervention may be most helpful in assisting people to reclaim meaningful and socially valued lives (Duggan, 2002; Karban, 2003). This interest has come from users, their families, friends and allies, and from practitioners and academics from across the spectrum of mental health disciplines. This has been reflected in government policy initiatives such as the National Service Framework (Department of Health, 1999), strategies and guidance for services for women, Black and ethnic minorities, and for personality disorder (Department of Health, 2003a, 2003b, 2003c), and a wider recognition that mental health should figure within the overall social inclusion agenda (Office of the Deputy Prime Minister, 2004).

Although currently topical, there is nothing new about social perspectives – in different ways, understanding the interrelation of 'mental distress' and 'problems of living' is something that has been on the agenda of:

- *sociology* – for example, studying the impact of poverty, discrimination and social labelling on mental distress
- *psychology and psychotherapy* – for example, exploring links between trauma and mental distress
- *social work* – focus on anti-oppressive practice and empowerment
- *social psychiatry and behavioural family therapy* – for example, looking at 'expressed emotion' and communication in families

- *transcultural psychiatry* – how problems of living and mental distress may be expressed and dealt with differently in different cultural contexts

- *women's movement and lesbian and gay movements* – how systematic forms of oppression and discrimination may link with particular mental health issues

- *disability movement* – applying the social model of disability to mental health

- *mental health user networks* – understanding 'symptoms' as having meaning, and valuing people's own strategies for resolving or managing their distress

- *recovery movement* – proposing that recovery is more about claiming (or reclaiming) a socially valued lifestyle than becoming 'symptom-free'.

However, although there may be a groundswell of interest in social perspectives, there remains a lack of clarity as to what exactly is meant by social models in practice. There are no generally accepted social approaches that have had the same influence on current thinking and practice as the biomedical model. Within multidisciplinary teams, there can be a tendency to see a social perspective as simply a concern with the practical issues that may impact on a person's life, such as welfare benefits and housing. While these may be important, there can be much more to a social approach – both in terms of developing frameworks by which to make sense of mental distress, and in devising strategies for promoting recovery and positive mental health.

The domination of biomedical approaches to mental health has so far offered relatively little space for the articulation of alternatives (see Chapter 3). However, there is currently little evidence that a primary reliance on bio-medical strategies for working with people with mental distress has been successful in promoting longer-term recovery, as, for example, rates of recovery from schizophrenia have not improved in any consistent way over the last 50 years, during a time of rapid medical advance (Harding *et al.*, 1987; Harding and Zahnister, 1994; Sargent, 1966). Instead, socio-economic variables, such as unemployment rates, appear to show a far closer correlation with overall rates of recovery (Warner, 1994). From long-term longitudinal studies undertaken in areas with similar demographic characteristics in New England, there is some evidence that recovery rates *may* improve significantly where there is a more socially oriented service – for example, Vermont has achieved around a 15 per cent better recovery rate than neighbouring Maine (Deegan, 1999; see also Brier and Strauss, 1984).

Research shows that it is social factors, such as substance misuse, unemployment, unstable family circumstances or poor education, rather than any categories of psychiatric diagnosis, that correlate more closely with risks such as violence (Monahan, 1993; Murray, 1989; Taylor and Gunn, 1999). However, there has been a tendency to follow an overly medicalised model of risk assessment, with the implicit assumption that people are intrinsically dangerous due to their 'illness', rather than engage in a more holistic dialogue which may 'encompass the full spectrum of risk impinging on the lives of people in the mental health system' (Walton, 1999 p.384; see also Langan and Lindow, 2004, and Chapter 10).

This evidence suggests a need to re-evaluate the knowledge base underpinning mental health practice across all professional groups (including psychiatry itself):

> For 150 years, psychiatry has fanned the flames of public hope and expectation, holding out promises of 'cure' and treatment for an ever-wider range of complex human and social problems. But these promises have failed to materialise… We believe that psychiatry should start a 'decolonisation', a phased withdrawal from the domains that it has laid claim to, including psychosis, depression and PTSD, by admitting the limited nature of its knowledge. (Bracken and Thomas, 2000 p.20; see also Michaelson and Wallcraft, 1997)

Such a 'decolonisation' does not imply an abandonment of what medicine may have to offer – in terms of helping people to manage specific experiences that may be problematic for them – just a process of reclaiming the whole person as a social being from the partiality of a purely medical definition.

Values

Central to the work on values currently being carried out by the National Institute for Mental Health in England (Fulford, 2004) is the notion that values and knowledge are inextricably linked, and that multidisciplinary mental health practice must acknowledge and respect a plurality of knowledge bases – with particular primacy being given to those held by service users and carers themselves.

Carrying this logic through, it is important that the value base underpinning the development of social perspectives must itself be able to embrace diversity. The aim of the project must not be to hone down one singular and internally consistent 'social model' – somewhat in the image of the current construction of the biomedical model – by which the complexities of people's experience could be reduced to some simple formulation. Instead, there is a need for a plurality of overlapping perspectives that reflect the complexity and diversity of experience based on a range of factors such as gender, culture, economic status, age, personal biography, and family and social relationships. Nevertheless, alongside this acceptance and valuing of plurality, there are certain core values which should be seen as fundamental in any development of social perspectives.

First of all, a social perspectives approach requires an end to 'them' and 'us' thinking that imposes (or reinforces) splits between 'normal' people and those suffering distress. Mental distress must be seen as situated within a continuum of everyday lived experience, and not constructed as some alien entity which separates out some people as fundamentally 'different' and starts to define their identities in terms of their 'pathology' (see Bainbridge, 1999).

Second, there needs to be a commitment to a holistic approach – always seeking an integrated understanding of people in their social contexts, rather than just focusing on *either* the 'inner' *or* the 'outer' aspects of their experience in isolation. As part of this, there must be a willingness to engage honestly with all the fractured and contradictory elements that may constitute a person's experience and social relationships. People's lives are not always reducible to simple or consistent patterns – and the dominant medical discourse of diagnostic categories can fail to recognise this. Often, it may be tensions and inconsistencies that can provide the 'spark' which ignites a process of change and recovery.

Closely linking to the first point, a third foundation of a social perspectives approach must be a commitment to hear and take seriously what people may have to say about their mental distress: the content of their experiences, and the meanings, histories and aspirations that *they* attach to them. This implies a shift away from a discourse of 'symptoms' in which the content of people's experience or behaviour is only seen as important in as much as it may help to locate a person within a system of diagnosis. Instead, it demands a much deeper engagement with the many layers of feeling and meaning, concerning a person and their social experience, that may be bound up in their expression and acting out of their distress. In order to do this, it can be important to be open to the unconventional 'intermediary languages' (Lefevre, 1996) by which people may be trying to express themselves, through metaphoric speech patterns, disembodied voices or self-harming behaviours.

However strange or difficult this may be to engage with, it nevertheless represents part of 'the meaning of our lives' (Plumb, 1999 p.471), and may contain important messages about difficult aspects of people's social experience – for example, loss, injustice or abuse.

This quality of listening to people *on their terms* is something that users have consistently identified as lacking within current service provision (Mental Health Foundation, 1997; Rogers, Pilgrim and Lacey, 1993), and explicitly challenges those approaches to mental health which have sought to classify, diagnose or interpret such experiences *for* people. Within many conventional medical, psychological *and* social approaches, there has been a tendency to impose frameworks *upon* people in ways that deny their own knowledge and expertise. Under the guise of 'objectivity', academics and practitioners have put a distance between themselves and those whose situations they ultimately seek to comprehend (Beresford, 2003). If we are to home in on, and start to make sense of, what is really important to people, we must value and engage with the 'standpoint' knowledges of those with lived experience of mental distress. These are understandings that are grounded in direct experience, and may often be developed most effectively through research conducted by, or in partnership with, service users and survivors (Beresford, 2000; Tew *et al.*, 2000; see also Chapter 2).

This suggests a move away from a conventional medical paradigm of evidence-based practice, in which knowledge is gathered in a way that assumes uniformity of experience and aspiration across populations, and is designed to enable professionals to develop ever more potent technologies by which to treat people as passive subjects (or 'patients'). Instead, it suggests a partnership approach to research and explanation, in which it is the active participation of those with direct experience that is seen to give validity to findings (Social Perspectives Network, 2004). Such a social perspectives approach may be seen as explicitly emancipatory in its purpose, aiming to support a practice of working together that enables people to recover a meaningful degree of control over their lives, live in greater safety and participate more fully within social, economic and community life.

Finally, any social perspective should be informed by principles of anti-oppressive and empowering practice. This involves an awareness of power differentials and maintains a concern with those factors which may diminish people's sense of self-esteem or value, or constrain their personal, social or economic opportunities (Tew, 2002). It places questions of stigma, discrimination, inequality and internalised oppression firmly on the working agenda.

This implies a very different language from that of the biomedical model: one that situates the person with mental health difficulties no longer as a 'patient', but as someone who is active and is assumed to have the capacity to be involved in all decisions affecting their lives, including their care and treatment. Such a language needs to draw on the terminologies that have been proposed and negotiated by service users and survivors. A shift from a discourse of 'mental illness' to one of 'mental distress' signals a move away from an emphasis on some objective disease entity (and the tendency to conflate the person with their hypothetical illness) to a more 'full-on' appreciation of the subjective pain, unhappiness or confusion that a person may be experiencing. Instead of inviting people into the essentially passive role of 'patient', waiting to be 'done to', other terms, such as survivor, consumer or service user, may offer identities that may enable people to reclaim some sense of control over their lives – although, in practice, many people with lived experience have not been entirely comfortable with some of these terms.

Foundations for social models

Social model of disability

Perhaps the most far-reaching instance of people reclaiming a holistic appreciation of their experience has arisen out of the analysis and campaigning of the disability movement. People rejected the stigmatising reductionism that went along with the medicalisation of their entire identities as, say, 'spastic' or 'Down's Syndrome'. Medical diagnosis fed into wider social attitudes which constructed them as a 'tragedy' both in terms of their own self-perception and in how they were to be viewed by those around them. Their failure to be 'normal', despite any possible medical interventions, was ultimately to be blamed on their own genetic or biophysical inadequacies: the problem was situated, fairly and squarely, with the individual her/himself.

The social model of disability turns this way of thinking on its head (Oliver, 1996). While impairments may be recognised, and medical interventions may be seen as having a useful part to play in maximising certain aspects of people's potential, the focus is shifted onto what may make the greatest difference in terms of people's quality of life, aspirations and opportunities for social inclusion. For many people, what is experienced as most disabling is not the impairment itself, but societal responses to it. Disabled people face a wide range of barriers to their full social and economic participation that are to do with stigma, discrimination and prejudice. Discriminatory social attitudes and practices may be seen to be underpinned by power-laden assumptions: what is constructed as 'normal' is taken to be unproblematic and is not seen as needing to be challenged or changed, whereas those who are constructed as (medically) 'abnormal' are seen as marginal, second-class and 'other'. They may be shut away or segregated through a form of social apartheid, so that their very existence cannot pose a challenge to dominant constructions of 'normality'; or they may be required to jump through whatever 'hoops' may be deemed necessary in order to achieve the possibility of some limited degree of assimilation.

This analysis and critique may be seen to apply equally well – and, in some ways, even more so – to the lives of people experiencing mental distress. For many people, living with mental distress may be difficult, but this may be nothing compared with dealing with the 'double whammy' of hostility, vilification, rejection and exclusion that they may face from society at large, and sometimes from friends and family. And it is very easy for negative attitudes and exclusionary classifications to become internalised. However, through the impact of user-run organisations such as the Hearing Voices Network, people are beginning to reclaim their identities from medicalised labels such as 'schizophrenic' and to see themselves as people who, *among other things*, hear voices – but whose primary identities may be around family, work, community, spirituality and so on.

Perhaps more radical still is a shift from being situated within a discourse in which it is up to the psychiatrist to make people 'normal' again, to one in which people feel empowered to accept their mental distress and start to expect that same acceptance from others. This also brings about a shift of focus in which it may be seen that what will make the biggest difference to people's lives is not necessarily any form of medical treatment, but a shift in social attitudes and practices that promotes social inclusion (Office of the Deputy Prime Minister, 2004). Rather than having to wait until medical treatment renders one 'normal' again before re-entering the social mainstream (a wait that may go on for ever), many people have found that being able to take on meaningful and socially valued roles has, of itself, resulted in a diminution of the severity or intrusiveness of their distress, or has given them greater capacity to live with it. And their social participation may, in smaller or greater measure, also have some influence on redefining the narrow and exclusionary nature of what may be seen as 'normal' or mainstream.

Rethinking mental distress from a social perspective

Social models explore the ways in which mental distress may be understood as, in part, a response to problematic life experiences. At the heart of this, there are two complementary ways in which mental distress may be viewed. It may be understood as:

- *The internalisation or acting out of stressful social experiences* that could not be resolved in other ways. The particular 'content' of a person's distress may be seen as an expression (usually indirect) of unresolved issues in relation to what has happened, or is currently happening, to them. Stressful experiences may include loss, discrimination, injustice, abuse or subjection to oppressive expectations made by powerful others. Typically, what may make these hard to resolve is a person's powerlessness and lack of personal and social support.

- *A coping or survival strategy* that a person may be using in order to deal with particular painful or stressful experiences. The specific form taken by someone's distress, such as voice hearing or self harming, may therefore be understood as their best available strategy for coping with life circumstances – both past and present – that may seem threatening and unliveable in some way. In this sense, manifestations of mental distress may be seen not as some unfortunate impairment, but as a reflection of people's resourcefulness and ingenuity.

Thus, at one and the same time, mental distress may represent both an awesome story of survival in relation to an oppressive or unliveable situation, and a desperate cry for help and understanding. Whether viewed as a coping strategy or as an expression of extreme disquiet, it may nevertheless be seen as potentially dysfunctional within current life circumstances. It may represent a way of being that is lived out at some considerable cost to the person, and may pose difficulties or risks both to them and to those around.

Certain aspects of this approach connect back to the libertarian anti-psychiatry movement, in that it argues that what may conventionally be labelled as 'illness' may perhaps be better understood simply as unresolved conflicts or 'problems of living' (Szasz, 1961). However, by locating the problem just in societal reactions to unconventional coping mechanisms, and in psychiatry's complicity in the social control of 'difference', anti-psychiatry has tended to overlook the profound sense of subjective distress, confusion and inability to cope that may come with many experiences of emotional or mental breakdown. A social model of understanding should take this seriously and be open to hear mental distress as a desperate plea that things as they are may be almost unbearable. This suggests a professional agenda which is *both* about supporting people in repairing their internalised 'damage', *and* challenging any inability of family, professionals or communities to accept and accommodate coping strategies which may be an important part of people's survival.

Social factors that may contribute to mental distress

Rather than taking the extreme position that 'mental illness' does not exist, social models may accept the possibility that some people may have greater innate vulnerabilities to particular experiences due to medical, nutritional, genetic or other factors. Within social psychiatry, mental or emotional breakdown has often been conceptualised using a stress/vulnerability model (Zubin, Stuart and Condray, 1992), and this may be a useful framework through which we can see how there may be interplay between genetic and biological factors on the one hand, and social and environmental factors on the other. Some of us may have less in-built resilience and greater vulnerability to particular forms of social stress due to our genetic and biochemical inheritance.

However, over and above any physical or biological predisposing factors, evidence suggests that a variety of social factors can play a major role in contributing to longer-term vulnerability to breakdown or distress. There is a considerable body of research and narrative which has correlated membership of social groups that may be subject to systematic oppression or disadvantage with various indices of mental distress (Bruce, Takeuchi and Leaf, 1991; Fernando, 1995; Gomm, 1996; Pilgrim and Rogers, 1999; Prior, 1999). The specific experiences of Black people, women, and lesbian and gay people are discussed in greater detail in Chapters 7, 8 and 9.

Alongside such generalised structural factors, there is increasing evidence that many people suffering mental distress are able to link its onset with problematic social events or experiences. Research with voice hearers indicates that the majority of people with diagnoses of schizophrenia and dissociative disorder could relate the onset to some previous and specifiable trauma (Romme *et al.*, 1994). Physically and psychologically invasive acts such as sexual or emotional abuse – particularly when there was little support available to the victim at the time – would seem to be particularly frequent precursors of experiences of mental distress (Ensink, 1992; Mullen *et al.*, 1993; Staples and

Dare, 1996; Williams and Watson, 1996). Other events, such as abandon-ment, bereavement or witnessing domestic violence may also be experienced as traumatic in this sense (see, for example, Brown, 1996; Perry *et al.*, 1990).

What may be seen as common to all these forms of trauma is that they ren-der the person a powerless victim of circumstances or forces beyond their control, unable to negotiate their boundaries and relationships with others. It is this that may be seen to construct the social (as distinct to any physical) aspect of a traumatic experience, and may come to have a profound impact on a person's sense of self and attachments with others (see Chapter 6).

At a theoretical level, it may be possible to chart how people's social expe-riences following on from a trauma may (or may not) lead individuals towards manifestations of mental distress that are conventionally given a range of medical diagnostic labels from anorexia to psychosis (Brown, Harris and Hepworth, 1995; Perry *et al.*, 1990; Zerbe, 1993; see also Chapter 6). Where this approach differs so markedly from the medical model is that what would have been seen just as clusters of 'symptoms' come alive as meaningful responses to sequences of often horrendous life circumstances. This sets the foundations for new forms of alliance and dialogue between practitioner and service user, one that starts with a validation of the user's immense expertise in living with and surviving situations that may be well beyond the direct experience of the worker.

For some people, vulnerability would not seem to stem from some identi-fiable trauma (although there may be evidence of trauma as well), but from difficulties in relationships with powerful others during critical periods such as early childhood. Research on attachment has shown how children may adapt when faced with situations of no one being there for them in any real sense, or just as potentially problematic, situations when key figures may be inconsistent and unpredictable (Ainsworth *et al.*, 1978). Some, giving up on external care-givers, may look to develop their inner resources to find the basis of hope or, at least, survival – creating complex and idiosyncratic worlds of fantasy, distraction, rationalisation and inner guidance in order to find their best way of surviving. Others may seek to develop techniques and strategies (often at some considerable cost to themselves) whereby to try to 'manipulate' powerful and unpredictable others into being there for them more consis-tently. Identifying such patterns and strategies may be a key to understanding and working with certain ways of living that have conventionally been char-acterised as different forms of personality disorder or mental illness (see, for example, de Zulueta, 1998).

These perspectives may be seen to link with a nearly forgotten tradition of work looking at how communication styles and patterns of relationships within families might relate to the development of psychosis. The seminal work of pioneers such as Bateson *et al.* (1956), Lidz (1975) and Laing (1965), albeit based on largely anecdotal evidence, suggested that having to respond to logically conflicting or emotionally intrusive communications from powerful others could lead to the developing of 'thought disorder' as a way of functioning in an otherwise unliveable situation. Interestingly, the more systematic work conducted subsequently which has linked the effect of intrusive communication patterns ('expressed emotion') with higher probabilities of schizophrenic relapse (Leff *et al.*, 1983) has baulked at any exploration of how these patterns might also precipitate *initial* breakdown – although this would seem to be the logical extension of such research (Johnstone, 1999; Tew, 1999). However, any development and updating of this work would need to place problematic communication and relationship patterns within a more sophisticated analysis of power relations. There is a need to move beyond, say, the potential blaming of the 'schizophrenogenic' mother for her apparent over-involvement as if it were her conscious choice, with a recognition that she, in turn, may have been trapped by wider constructions and oppressive expectations upon women within contemporary forms of social and family organisation.

A consistent thread that may be seen to run through much of this discussion is that of oppression, exclusion and powerlessness. Whereas an illness model suggests 'bad luck' in terms of genes, viruses or biochemical disorders – something that could befall anyone indiscriminately, and where no one external to the person has any responsibility – a social model locates experience within an understanding of social relations in which power plays a determining role, both in terms of 'macro'-scale structural inequalities in relation to gender, 'race', class, age, sexual orientation and so on, and in terms of the 'micro'-scale dynamics of conflict, exclusion or abuse that may take place within families or other intimate social contexts. As Jennie Williams argues:

> Behaviours defined as symptoms and disorders are best understood as creative responses to difficult personal and social histories, rooted in a person's experience of oppression(s). (1999 p.31)

Crisis and breakdown

As with other forms of crisis, mental health crises may often be seen to have histories – processes of build-up of conflicts and tensions leading up to some recent 'trigger' event or precipitating circumstance (see Tew, 2002). The vulnerability factors discussed above may typically be understood in terms of unresolved issues of injustice, powerlessness, oppression, abuse and loss, coupled with well-rehearsed (if sometimes rigid or dysfunctional) strategies for keeping these issues under some sort of control. What may then lead to a crisis or breakdown may be some combination of events and changes in external circumstances, and problems associated with a person's current repertoire of coping strategies.

Often the most potent 'trigger' events are those whose dynamics connect in some way with previously unresolved issues. Stressful life events or circumstances, such as relationship breakdown or unemployment, may be seen to have a wide-scale impact on levels of mental distress (Brown *et al.*, 1995; Fryer, 1995), and these may link with earlier experiences of discrimination or loss. A common aspect of many 'trigger' events is an enforced sense of powerlessness. In his research on the life events that may provoke the onset of depression, George Brown found that they were often characterised by 'devaluation in one's own or other's eyes, experience of defeat, entrapment, [or] lack of a sense of control' (1996 p.41).

Research on stress suggests that any form of life transition, whether imposed on the person (such as, for example, redundancy), or chosen shifts in lifestyle and affiliation (such as leaving home), may be destabilising for someone already vulnerable. Life transitions typically involve the renegotiation of personal relationships and social identities. Where these are already fraught with unresolved conflicts and internalisations of oppression, such processes may become problematic. There may also be resonances with previous experiences – perhaps earlier memories of having elements of familiarity or security taken away arbitrarily by powerful others, or being subject to oppressive processes of having unwanted identities forced upon one.

Contradictory pressures associated with social roles, such as caring or work responsibilities, may constitute a form of stress (as can losing, or being excluded from, such roles). What may be crucial can be the often conflicting patterns of expectations that may attach to these roles when they are located within oppressive patterns of power relations. For example, many women may have little ability to control or negotiate taking on caring responsibilities –

and may also find that the importance and difficulty of this work is devalued within prevailing social and family structures (Finch and Groves, 1983).

Theorising the social impact of mental distress

Arising out of the previous discussion, mental distress may be conceptualised as both a response to, and an implicit revolt against, experiences of injustice, enforced loss or abuse. Viewed from the outside, it may appear as either a failure, or a refusal, to perform the image of a rational, consistent and responsible subject that may be expected in order to fit within a modern social order (Foucault, 1967; Tew, 2002; see also Chapter 4). Appearances of breakdown may be seen as signalling a disturbing reality that must be 'hushed up' and denied respect within both professional and everyday discourses (Barnes, 1999).

As was discussed earlier, the disability movement has argued that it is not physical impairments that are hardest to live with in themselves – it is society's responses, in terms of stigma and discrimination, that can be most damaging. The attitudes and practices of both the community in general, and of professional services, may be prejudicial in that they can promote social exclusion through the establishment of segregated services and by failing to open access to mainstream facilities – thereby marginalising people's access to crucial forms of social capital (Duggan, 2002; see also Chapter 5).

These issues apply similarly to people who are experiencing mental distress. However, in many ways, the stakes would seem to be even higher in mental health. Both at an individual and at a societal level, there may be vested interests in avoiding the uncomfortable truths and testimonies of those whose social experiences may be re-enacted through their mental distress. Particularly where this may touch on their own (similar) experiences, 'ordinary' people may choose to project their anxiety and disquiet on to a segregated category – the 'mentally ill' – who may then have to deal, not just with their own issues, but with being 'dumped' with the issues that others are not prepared to face in their own experience. It is this that may start to explain why, although not posing a greater physical threat than any other group of citizens (Taylor and Gunn, 1999), people with mental distress may continually come up against exaggerated reactions of fear, exclusion or repulsion throughout their daily lives (Barnes, 1999; Foster and Zagier Roberts, 1998).

In turn, such social responses of stigmatisation and 'scapegoating' may feed into the very experiences of oppression or exclusion that may have contributed to people's original experience of mental distress, thereby instigating a potentially vicious circle of increasing victimisation, powerlessness and distress. Over time, people may lose their social and family networks and become either socially isolated or ghettoised within mental health services. And continual subjection to negative stereotyping may lead to shifts in identity, with a loss or distortion of any positively valued sense of self.

Social models and recovery practice

There has been a sustained critique of current service models from sections of the user movement. First, as medicine is not, in fact, able to deliver any 'cure' for mental distress – only long-term management of symptoms – medical diagnosis may actually serve to deliver a 'life sentence' of dependence on services (Coleman, 1999). Medical treatment tends not to be located within a paradigm of hope and recovery, although longitudinal research indicates that a substantial proportion of people do recover from psychosis – interestingly with much higher recovery rates recorded in some Third World settings (World Health Organisation, 1979), where biomedical practice is less dominant and cultural expectations may be more socially inclusive – for example, in the assumption that people should return to meaningful participation within the economic and domestic tasks of family life as soon as possible.

Second, users have also questioned the usefulness of medical definitions of recovery which are couched purely in terms of remission of symptoms. Users have argued for more holistic definitions in terms of the ability to 'get on with life' in a way that seems appropriate and meaningful to them (see Chapter 11). This may involve accepting and living with parts of themselves or their experience that had previously appeared frightening or shameful – such as finding ways of valuing and negotiating with voices rather than seeking to eradicate them (Coleman and Smith, 1997). It may involve challenging structures or relationships which have been oppressive, discriminatory or abusive, and establishing new social networks of support and mutuality. It may simply involve reclaiming aspects of ordinary life, such as decent housing and employment opportunities.

Research indicates that a crucial pre-requisite for recovery is not some form of 'expert' professional intervention, but for the person to find a way of understanding their experience that makes sense to them, and which returns to them some sense of personal value, together with the responsibility (and potential capability) for working it through (Deegan, 1999). Writing from the perspective of her lived experience, Helen Glover argues that 'people who experience the distress of mental illness have the right to understand their distress and develop the understanding that one can grow from the experience' (2001 p.7). Here, for some, the medical model on its own can be problematic in that it can hand over this responsibility to the physician, leaving people waiting passively for a cure to come. A holistic approach which helps to make links between what may seem bewildering thoughts, feelings or behaviours, and the realities of people's social and personal experience, may be more helpful in contributing to such an understanding.

In practice, if a person is to be enabled to own their experience and chart their unique journey of recovery, then they will need to make their own connections. Therefore workers may need to use a social model more as a basis of asking questions, than as a way of delivering insights or answers. Their most important role may be one of taking seriously and being the 'enlightened witness' to people's past and present experiences, and being particularly sensitive to any themes of loss, oppression, trauma and subjection to the expectations of powerful others that may emerge. A key difference between the recovery paradigm from that of rehabilitation is that recovery cannot be 'done to' people; it cannot be led by 'experts' who claim to know both the destination and the route by which this is to be reached (see Chapter 11).

As well as helping people to make connections between their mental distress and how it may relate to their social experience, there may be other important roles for professional involvement. In a very real sense, family, friends and social networks may also need to recover from their own elements of distress – a breakdown can involve relationships as well as individuals, leaving legacies of confusion, blame, guilt, anger and sadness. Whereas the medical model tends to focus primarily on the individual whose 'illness' is to be treated, leading to a potential marginalisation of family and friends, an approach which locates distress in its social context should seek to include all significant others as part of the 'action system' working towards recovery. This would suggest an important role in supporting the renegotiation or rebuilding of social and family networks (or in establishing new ones), and in seeking to challenge any tendencies towards oppression or exclusion that may be present within them.

Conclusion

This exploration of a social perspectives approach starts to clarify the links between mental distress and a range of social circumstances – from more generalised factors such as subjection to structures of discrimination and inequality, to more individualised experiences such as loss and trauma. It is underpinned by a value base that is somewhat at odds with that of the more reductionist approach of biomedical practice – which may result in some difficulty in the two paradigms talking to one another. However, a more holistic perspective may not be so alien to psychiatric practice as may sometimes be suggested (see Chapter 3), and approaches such as the stress/vulnerability model may provide a useful basis for dialogue and integration between perspectives.

Central themes within a social approach are a concern with issues of power and powerlessness and a focus on the connectedness of inner and outer worlds. While it uses the social model of disability as a starting point, the framework of understanding that is required in mental health is necessarily more complex: not only are many of the disabling factors associated with mental distress socially constructed, but, to a significant extent, the very distress itself may be seen as an effect of, and a way of coping with, people's past and present social experience. Finally, a social perspective is important in avoiding the tendency to over-individualise both mental distress and the process of recovery. The dynamics of people's distress may connect with, or resonate through, a range of personal, social and economic relationships. Working through these dislocations, tensions and breakdowns may be seen to be a crucial part of enabling recovery for many people.

References

Ainsworth, M., Blehar, M., Waters, E. and Wall, S. (1978) *Patterns of Attachment.* Hillsdale, NJ: Erlbaum.

Bainbridge, L. (1999) 'Competing paradigms in mental health practice and education.' In B. Pease and J. Fook (eds) *Transforming Social Work Practice.* London: Routledge.

Barnes, H. (1999) 'Exclusion and mental health – the relationship context of mental health practice.' *Social Work Education 18*, 4, 401–416.

Bateson, G., Jackson, D., Haley, J. and Weakland, J. (1956) 'Towards a theory of schizophrenia.' *Behavioral Science 1*, 4251.

Beresford, P. (2000) 'Users' knowledges and social work theory.' *British Journal of Social Work 30*, 4, 489–503.

Beresford, P. (2003) *It's Our Lives: A Short Theory of Knowledge, Distance and Experience.* London: Citizen Press.

Bracken, P. and Thomas, P. (2000) 'Prison wardens or mental health professionals?' *Openmind 101*, 20.

Brier, A. and Strauss, J. (1984) 'The role of social relationships in the recovery from psychotic disorders.' *American Journal of Psychiatry 141*, 8, 949–955.

Brown, G. (1996) 'Life events, loss and depressive disorder.' In T. Heller, J. Reynolds, R. Gomm, R. Muston and S. Pattison (eds) *Mental Health Matters.* Basingstoke: Macmillan.

Brown, G., Harris, T. and Hepworth, C. (1995) 'Loss, humiliation and entrapment among women developing depression: a patient and non-patient comparison.' *Psychological Medicine* 25, 7–21.

Bruce, M., Takeuchi, D. and Leaf, P. (1991) 'Poverty and psychiatric status: longitudinal evidence from the New Haven Epidemiologic Catchment Area Study.' *Archives of General Psychiatry 48*, 5, 470–474.

Coleman, R. (1999) *Recovery? An Alien Concept.* Gloucester: Handsell.

Coleman, R. and Smith, M. (1997) *Working with Voices: From Victim to Victor.* Gloucester: Handsell.

de Zulueta, F. (1998) 'The borderline personality disorder as seen from an attachment perspective.' Paper delivered to Mind Conference on Personality Disorders, London.

Deegan, P. (1999) Presentation to Recovery Conference, Birmingham.

Department of Health (1999) *National Service Framework for Mental Health.* London: Department of Health.

Department of Health (2003a) *Mainstreaming Gender and Women.* London: Department of Health.

Department of Health (2003b) *Inside Outside: Improving Mental Health Services for Black and Minority Ethnic Communities in England.* London: Department of Health.

Department of Health (2003c) *Personality Disorder: No Longer a Diagnosis of Exclusion.* London: Department of Health.

Duggan, M. with Cooper, A. and Foster, J. (2002) 'Modernising the social model in mental health: a discussion paper.' London: SPN Paper 1.

Ensink, B. (1992) *Confusing Realities: A Study on Childhood Sexual Abuse and Psychiatric Symptoms.* Amsterdam: VU University Press.

Fernando, S. (1995) 'Social realities and mental health.' In S. Fernando (ed.) *Mental Health in a Multi-Ethnic Society.* London: Routledge.

Finch, J. and Groves, D. (eds) (1983) *A Labour of Love: Women, Work and Caring.* London: Routledge.

Foster, A. and Zagier Roberts, V. (eds) (1998) *Managing Mental Health in the Community: Chaos and Containment.* London: Routledge.

Foucault, M. (1967) *Madness and Civilisation.* London: Tavistock.

Fryer, D. (1995) 'Labour market disadvantage, deprivation and mental health.' *The Psychologist 8*, 6, 265–272.

Fulford, B. (2004) Presentation to Mental Health in Higher Education Conference, Bristol.

Glover, H. (2001) *Challenging Mental Impotence.* Birmingham: Centre for Mental Health Policy, University of Central England.

Gomm, R. (1996) 'Mental Health and Inequality'. In T. Heller, J. Reynolds, R. Gomm, R. Muston and S. Pattison (eds) *Mental Health Matters.* Basingstoke: Macmillan.

Harding, C., Brooks, G., Takamaru, A., Strauss, J. and Breier, A. (1987) 'The Vermont longitudinal study of persons with severe mental illness.' *American Journal of Psychiatry 144*, 6, 718–735.

Harding, C. and Zahnister, J. (1994) 'Empirical correction of seven myths about schizophrenia with implication for treatment.' *Acta Psychiatrica Scandinavica 90* (suppl 384), 140–146.

Johnstone, L. (1999) 'Do families cause schizophrenia? Revisiting a taboo subject.' In C. Newnes, G. Holmes and C. Dunn (eds) *This is Madness: A Critical Look at Psychiatry and the Future of Mental Health Services.* Ross on Wye: PCCS Books.

Karban, K. (2003) 'Social work education and mental health in a changing world.' *Social Work Education 22*, 2, 191–202.

Laing, R. (1965) *The Divided Self.* Harmondsworth: Penguin.

Langan, J. and Lindow, V. (2004) *Living with Risk: Mental Health Service User Involvement in Risk Assessment and Management.* Bristol: Policy Press.

Lefevre, S. (1996) *Killing Me Softly. Self Harm: Survival not Suicide.* Gloucester: Handsell.

Leff, J., Kuipers, L., Berkowitz, R., Vaughn, C. and Sturgeon, D. (1983) 'Expressed emotion and maintenance neuroleptics in schizophrenic relapse.' *Psychological Medicine 13*, 799–806.

Lidz, T. (1975) *The Origin and Treatment of Psychiatric Disorders.* London: Hutchinson.

Mental Health Foundation (1997) *Knowing Our Own Minds: A Survey of How People in Emotional Distress Take Control of Their Lives.* London: Mental Health Foundation.

Michaelson, J. and Wallcraft, J. (1997) 'Alternatives to the biomedical model of mental health crisis.' *Breakthrough 1*, 3, 31–49.

Monahan, J. (1993) 'Dangerousness: an American perspective.' In J. Gunn and P. Taylor (eds) *Forensic Psychiatry.* London: Butterworth-Heinemann.

Mullen, P., Martin, J., Anderson, J., Romans, S. and Herbison, G. (1993) 'Childhood sexual abuse and mental health in adult life.' *British Journal of Psychiatry 163*, 721–732.

Murray, D. (1989) *Review of Research on Re-offending of Mentally Disordered Offenders.* London: Home Office.

Office of the Deputy Prime Minister (2004) *Mental Health and Social Exclusion: Social Exclusion Unit Report.* London: Office of the Deputy Prime Minister.

Oliver, M. (1996) *Understanding Disability: From Theory to Practice.* Basingstoke: Macmillan.

Perry, J., Herman, J., Van der Kolk, B. and Hoke, L. (1990) 'Psychotherapy and psychological trauma in borderline personality disorder.' *Psychiatric Annals 20*, 1, 33–43.

Pilgrim, D. and Rogers, A. (1999) *A Sociology of Mental Health and Illness (Second Edition).* Buckingham: Open University Press.

Plumb, A. (1999) 'New mental health legislation. A lifesaver? Changing paradigm and practice.' *Social Work Education 18*, 4, 459–478.

Prior, P. (1999) *Gender and Mental Health.* Basingstoke: Macmillan.

Rogers, A., Pilgrim, D. and Lacey, R. (1993) *Experiencing Psychiatry: Users' Views of Services.* London: Macmillan.

Romme, M., Pennings, M., Buiks, A., Escher, A., Honigs, A., Corstens, D. and Ensink, B. (1994) 'Hearing voices in patients and non-patients.' Paper presented at World Congress of Social Psychiatry, Hamburg.

Sargent, W. (1966) 'Recovery rates from schizophrenia prior to the introduction of neuroleptic medication.' Paper delivered to the Royal College of Psychiatrists.

Social Perspectives Network (2004) 'Where you stand affects your point of view: emancipatory approaches to mental health research.' SPN Paper 4. London: Social Perspectives Network.

Staples, E. and Dare, C. (1996) 'The impact of childhood sexual abuse.' In K. Abel, M. Buszewicz, S. Davison, S. Johnson and E. Staples (eds) *Planning Community Mental Health Services for Women.* London: Routledge.

Szasz, T. (1961) *The Myth of Mental Illness.* New York: Harper and Row.

Taylor, P. and Gunn, J. (1999) 'Homicides by people with mental illness: myth and reality.' *British Journal of Psychiatry 174*, 9–14.

Tew, J. (1999) 'Voices from the margins: inserting the social in mental health discourse.' *Social Work Education 18*, 4, 433–449.

Tew, J. (2002) *Social Theory, Power and Practice.* Basingstoke: Palgrave.

Tew, J., Gell, C., O'Rourke, A., Glynn, T. and Saddal, S. (2000) 'Finding a better way… Constructing user evidence about experiences of compulsion under the Mental Health Act.' Paper presented at 'Why Theorise Social Work Research?' Conference, Manchester.

Walton, P. (1999) 'Social work and mental health: refocusing the training agenda for ASWs.' *Social Work Education 18*, 4, 375–388.

Warner, R. (1994) *Recovery from Schizophrenia: Psychiatry and Political Economy.* New York: Routledge.

Williams, J. (1999) 'Social inequalities and mental health.' In C. Newnes, G. Holmes and C. Dunn (eds) *This is Madness: A Critical Look at Psychiatry and the Future of Mental Health Services.* Ross on Wye: PCCS Books.

Williams, J. and Watson, G. (1996) 'Mental health services that empower women.' In T. Heller, J. Reynold, R. Gomm, R. Muston and S. Pattison (eds) *Mental Health Matters.* London: Macmillan.

World Health Organisation (1979) *Schizophrenia: An International Outcome Study.* London: Wiley.

Zerbe, K. (1993) *The Body Betrayed: Women, Eating Disorders and Treatment.* Washington: American Psychiatric Press.

Zubin, J., Stuart, R. and Condray, R. (1992) 'Vulnerability to relapse in schizophrenia.' *British Journal of Psychiatry 161*, 13–18.

CHAPTER 2

Social Approaches to Madness and Distress

User Perspectives and User Knowledges

Peter Beresford

Acknowledging complexity and contradiction

This is a time of enormous change and *contradiction* in mental health policy, practice and thinking. It seems to be characterised by the energy of *opposed* developments. On the one hand, are those initiatives which seem to be breaking new ground and pointing to a different future. This book, for example, is itself one small sign of the search for new approaches to making sense of and responding to 'madness' and 'distress'. It embodies and reflects a renewal of interest in social approaches to 'mental health' (Duggan, 2002; SPN, 2002). It connects with the recent political enthusiasm for 'evidence'- or 'knowledge'-based policy and practice. We do not yet know how far such government enthusiasm extends beyond rhetoric, but it is undeniably explicit and service providers, commissioners and analysts are under increasing pressure to sign up to it. Organisational changes stress the importance of connecting related policies including employment, benefits, disability, education and so on and developing a more holistic approach to 'mental health'. There is an almost unprecedented interest in service user perspectives. The buzz words are 'involvement', 'inclusion', 'empowerment' and 'partnership'. These terms were all highlighted in the government's key National Service Framework for Mental Health (Department of Health, 1999).

On the other hand, and certainly more visible in the public and political domain, are counter pressures to regulation, control and surveillance. The dominant approaches to 'treatment' continue to be chemical. The trend has been towards an increase, not a reduction, in the number of compulsory hospital admissions. The emphasis has been on keeping 'severe and enduring mental illness' in check, rather than on prevention and supporting people experiencing distress and stress-related problems. This approach has been framed in regulatory terms of 'assertive outreach' and (drug) 'compliance'. There has been a renewal of interest in bio-chemical and genetic explanations of 'mental illness' which emphasise the 'otherness' of mental health service users/survivors and offer the disturbing promise of revisiting bio-ethic/ eugenic approaches to dealing with 'the problem' (Coppick and Hopton, 2000; Rogers and Pilgrim, 2001).

During this same period, we have also seen increasing importance attached to the dustbin diagnostic category, 'personality disorder'. More generally there has been an increasing medicalisation of socially related experience, distress and difficulties, particularly among children and older people, through the creation of new diagnostic categories and the increasing use of chemical 'treatment' responses.

But perhaps most important and most visible has been the emphasis on the 'threat' posed by mental health service users. The political and media focus has been on the 'dangerousness' and 'risk' represented by mental health service users. Often racialised and associated with the commission of homicides by mental health service users, it has resulted in government prioritising of the concept of 'public safety' in mental health policy. This has become a key policy and presentation concept. Yet the evidence base has indicated that the number of homicides linked with mental health service users is small and diminishing (Taylor and Gunn, 1999).

This preoccupation with violence in the public debate about 'mental health' has resulted in pressure for the extension of compulsory powers and increased restrictions on the rights of mental health service users. This has particularly related to the extension of compulsion beyond the hospital and the incarceration of people labelled as having 'severe personality disorder' prior to conviction for any offence. The government is currently committed to such proposals in forthcoming mental health legislation (Department of Health, 2002).

Opposition to such government proposals has been on an unprecedented scale. It has also been broadly based and included church, community, civil rights, Black and minority ethnic, mental health, charitable, service users and professional organisations, including the Royal College of Psychiatrists. Proposals for extending compulsion have probably led to more campaigning activity, including pickets, demonstrations and marches than any previous issue. What has also distinguished this campaigning is that it has involved both service users and non-service users (Mental Health Alliance, 2002).

However, the alliance which has come together in opposition to government proposals for mental health legislation, is potentially a fragile one. It disguises many long-standing differences in perspective, philosophy and goals. It should not be assumed that it reflects a more deep-seated consensus, rooted in fundamental concerns that proposed legislation is impractical *and* unethical. There is a very real gulf between the concern of psychiatrists, that they will be expected to operate what they see as an unworkable system, and of service users, who fear further restrictions on their civil liberties and the extension of the net of compulsory 'treatment' to an even larger number of people. The alliance conceals broad fears about the continued dominance of psychiatry in mental health policy and practice as well as the latter's politicisation.

The mental health debate is a heavily politicised and controversial one. But, as we have seen, it is also a complex and *ambiguous* one. It is difficult to see how many of the components included in this debate can be reconciled, but so far this issue does not seem to have been addressed seriously. Thus, on the one hand, government is highlighting in its National Service Framework for Mental Health and in other documents and guidance, the importance of advancing the social inclusion of service users and their empowerment and involvement. On the other hand, it emphasises the risk from service users to 'public safety' and the need for greater public protection and control of service users. This is likely to marginalise, exclude and stigmatise them generally. The question is: can mental health policy and practice truly be facing in two such opposed directions at once? The view of many service users and their allies, clearly, is that it cannot (Shaughnessy, 2002).

Questioning the construction of 'mental health' policy: part one

The architects and advocates of current mental health policy do not yet seem to have faced up to its inherently contradictory nature. It is these internal conflicts that make it both untenable and unacceptable. They will need to be addressed and resolved if this is to change. It is difficult to see how policy can be constructed as both empowering and regulatory at the same time. However, in this author's view, such internal division may only be a reflection of a much broader issue. This issue is the essentially *medicalised* nature of mental health policy and practice.

For some, this may not seem to be a problem. To claim it as one may appear partisan, trivialising and unhelpful. It is not intended to be so. But critics may argue that to deny the individual has a 'mental health problem' is to deny the difficulties they face, the issues they 'present' with, and the support or 'treatment' they may need. It is not this that is intended. What is being called into question here is the *construction* that is being placed upon the individual and their situation and experience. The inherent problem with a medicalised approach to 'mental health' – and even the descriptor is itself medicalised – is that it is based on a *pathologising* construct. The underlying construct that dominates 'mental health' policy, provision, practice and service users is that of 'mental illness'. It is possible to be persuaded that this is not the case, because terms like 'mental illness', 'mental disorder' and 'psychopathology' are less often and less explicitly used nowadays. Instead a range of euphemistic terms like 'mental health', 'mental health problems' and 'issues' are used. But their origins and meaning are the same. Their legal base is the same. Something is wrong with the person. They are 'ill'. Their experience, behaviour, perceptions – they *themselves* – are pathologised. This is how we come to understand ourselves as mental health service users.

Through this model, it is hardly surprising if mental health service users have come to be associated with violence, threat and danger. Violence is medicalised as in the following examples.

- Common (physiological and psychological) responses to extreme threat and danger are reconceived as a form of mental disorder: 'post-traumatic stress disorder'.

- 'Mental disorder' is offered without reliable or consistent independent criteria or evidence to support it as an explanation for violence.

- 'Mental illness' and 'mental disorder' are routinely introduced as legal defences for criminal and violent behaviour.

- Committing violent acts without remorse is identified as a form of 'severe and dangerous personality disorder'.

- Being subjected to sexual and other violent abuse or assault (especially in childhood) is offered as a sufficient predictor or explanation for an individual's own subsequent abusive or violent behaviour.

- The perpetration of child sexual abuse is identified as a category of 'mental disorder'.

The dominance of medicalised individual approaches

These worrying developments can be traced to the trend in the twentieth century to interpret and reconstruct madness and distress in predominantly medicalised individual terms. Such a medicalised approach has shaped theorising, policy, provision, practice and 'treatment' (Coppick and Hopton, 2000; Rogers and Pilgrim, 2001; Sayce, 2000). Strongly influenced and encouraged by developments relating to violence and trauma in two world wars (Holden, 1998), this has fundamentally influenced professional, political and public understandings of the phenomena included as 'mental illness'. Most recently, this reliance on medicalised approaches to understanding has been highlighted by the renewed international interest placed in the idea of 'recovery'. This has now been taken up by the newly established government National Institute for Mental Health in England (NIMHE).

It is important to remember that other broader influences have also been at work. We should not forget that there has long been a 'social' psychiatry and psychology. Other professions like social work have sought to inject wider social understandings into their professional approach and understanding. But generally these have taken as given the over-arching medicalised framework of 'mental illness', although differing in the extent to which they saw it as a consequence of nature or nurture.

'Mental health' policy and thinking continue to be based essentially on a medical model. The dominance of psychiatry in the field, in terms of status, legitimacy and power, continues, even though it may be argued that it has been subjected to increasing managerialist and political pressures in recent years. It still plays a dominant role in shaping provision as well as individual mental health service users' experience and outcomes and its influence has been felt by all related mental health professions and occupations to a greater or lesser extent; from nursing to social work, occupational therapy and occupational health, to housing support.

Questioning the construction of 'mental health' policy: part two

The dominance of psychiatric thinking and the 'mental illness' model is becoming increasingly anomalous. There have been relatively few (successful) challenges to psychiatric dominance during its lifetime. The most conspicuous challenge came from the 'anti-psychiatrists' in the 1960s and 1970s (Laing, 1965). While they may have left an important cultural legacy, it is debatable whether they had a deep-seated effect on mainstream mental health services and people's day-to-day experience of them. They have been succeeded by groupings such as 'The Critical Psychiatry Network' which looks 'beyond psychiatry'. While this is an energetic and visible grouping, which has sought to build wider alliances, it still only represents a minority of professional opinion.

We might have expected, though, that the emphasis on user involvement, which entered mental health policy and practice from the late 1980s, would represent a major challenge to *'psychiatryism'* in policy and thinking.

User involvement became one of the guiding formal principles of mental health policy. Requirements for it have been built into mental health guidance and processes. It is meant to operate at individual and collective levels. Provisions for user involvement have been at the heart of assessment procedures established with community care 'care management' and the 'care programme approach'. State interest in user involvement led to a massive expansion in market research and consultation initiatives in mental health as in other areas of health and social care (Beresford and Croft, 1993). The consumerist commitment of former Conservative administrations to user involvement became embedded in New Labour managerialist/consumerist 'third way' variants which have followed (Beresford, 2002; Giddens, 1998).

Thus the emphasis on user involvement in mental health policy and practice means that we should be hearing from other voices and accessing different viewpoints and understandings. To some extent this has happened. But mostly people as mental health service users have internalised the dominant mental illness/health model of understanding. They are often under enormous personal pressure to do so. It offers some kind of explanation which, at times of great individual difficulty and pain, may seem helpful. It is likely to be the only framework for understanding that many people are offered or can access. Service users also express concerns that much user involvement has only been able to operate within existing frameworks of policy, analysis, organisations, 'treatment' and so on, thus restricting the opportunities service users have had to generate their own ideas on equal terms.

This leads us to the second major challenge to the construction of mental health thinking and policy. If the first problem that has been identified with current mental health policy and thinking is its profound internal contradictions ('empowerment' versus subordination), the second relates to the nature of the process of its construction. While the accent on partnership, participation, inclusion and empowerment predicates a new social process of development, involving *all* key stakeholders, the distribution of power between service providers and recipients seems little changed. Traditional professional groupings continue to be in control (Barnes *et al.*, 1999).

The shift to 'user involvement' seems to have made relatively little difference to this situation, but a challenge has nonetheless emerged with the development of service user/survivor organisations. It is important not to treat the two – user involvement and user-controlled organisations – as the same. Clearly there are links and overlaps, but if user involvement is an initiative that has come from the state and service systems, service user/survivor organisations come much less ambiguously from us as service users ourselves.

While the 1990s emphasis on 'user involvement' can be seen as an expression of changes in political ideology and new 'mixed economy' approaches to public and welfare services, the emergence of 'user-controlled' organisations and 'self-organisation' can be traced to different political origins. At its heart, this development represents a strong collective reaction from people included in health and social care categories to their negative experiences of welfare and associated professional responses to them. It is also related to a number of other broader social and political changes over the same period (Croft and Beresford, 1996). The survivors/mental health service user movement is only one manifestation of this trend. The disabled people's movement is perhaps the most strongly established and visible of these movements, with the most well worked-out philosophy (Barnes, Mercer and Shakespeare, 1999; Oliver and Barnes, 1998; Shakespeare, 1998), but this should not divert attention from the collective action of other groups, including people with learning difficulties, older people, people living with HIV/AIDS and of course mental health service users/survivors (Beresford, 1999). What these movements have in common is that they have been:

- based on self-identification, relating to long-term use of or interventions from health and welfare services
- self-organised and self-run: organised around local, national and international groups and organisations based on their own identities, which they themselves control, developing their own ways of working, philosophies and objectives
- committed to both parliamentary and direct action: the latter reflected, for example, in the activities of the disabled people's

movement's Direct Action Network (DAN) and psychiatric system survivors' Reclaim Bedlam campaign and Mad Pride grouping.

These characteristics significantly distinguish such movements from traditional challenges to state social policy and associated social and economic inequalities, reflected still, for example, in anti-poverty and un-employment campaigning. This has primarily come from organisations and groups which have *not* been controlled by the people directly affected by the problem, but which have instead acted on their behalf – generally without any agreed mandate from them. This is not to say that the latter have not struggled and sought to be at the heart of such activity. Ironically such a traditional approach has often made this difficult (Beresford *et al.*, 1999).

These new movements have developed their own cultures, arts, ways of organising and working, histories and their own *knowledge*. Of course, as long as there have been formal welfare arrangements for people identified as dependent or vulnerable – whether religious, charitable or state provided – there has been 'users' knowledge' about it. This has followed from people's role, status and experience. It is only very recently, however, that this knowl-edge has begun to be recognised by state and social policy organisations. In 2000, the government established a 'Quality Strategy for Social Care', which included service users' knowledge and experience as a key source of evidence. The recently established Social Care Institute for Excellence, charged with responsibility for developing the knowledge base of social care, includes ser-vice user knowledge, alongside practitioner and other knowledge, as a core constituent of that knowledge base.

The emergence of 'survivor knowledge'

The knowledge of mental health service users/survivors is both individual and collective. It has developed both formally and informally. It has grown through the contact that service users have with each other, both within and beyond the service system; in self-advocacy and user groups and organ-isations; at meetings and in campaigns. There is a massive body of unrecorded and hidden service user knowledge, which remains alive in the memories of service users. In recent years such knowledge has increasingly been recorded in the form of service users' accounts, testimonies, critiques and discussions (Beresford, Stalker and Wilson, 1997; Campbell and Oliver, 1996; Read and Reynolds, 1996). These are to be found in users' newsletters, journals and other publications and now increasingly in professional publications and mainstream print and broadcast media. In addition, service users are now producing and contributing to their own histories (Campbell, 1996; Campbell and Oliver, 1996; James, 2001; Wallcraft, 2003).

One key quality distinguishes service user knowledge from that of all others involved in the field of health and social care. Their knowledge alone is primarily based on direct *experience* of such policy and provision from the receiving end. Service users' knowledge grows out of their personal and collective experience of policy, practice and services. It is not based solely on an intellectual, occupational or political concern. As in all identity-based groupings and movements, it is experientially based. Thus the introduction of service users' knowledge into the discussion, analysis and development of 'mental health' policy and thinking brings into the arena a crucially different relationship between experience and knowledge and between direct experience and 'mental health' discourses. As we shall see, the importance of this cannot be over-stated. It is likely to have fundamental implications for the understanding of 'mental health'.

As has been said, modern understanding of madness and distress is still dominated by medicalised frameworks for analysis and 'treatment' which have their origins in nineteenth-century science. Mental health service user/survivor knowledge can now also be seen to offer an additional basis for interpretation. The potential scale of this contribution is also reflected in service users' increasing role in the production of research (Faulkner and Layzell, 2000; Faulkner and Nicholls, 1999; Lindow, 2001).

Service users' role in research takes two forms. First, there is their involvement in mainstream research, encouraged by wider pressures towards this, linked with government agendas for public, patient and service user participation. Second, there is the development of their own research approaches and findings. For many service users, including mental health service users, research has been part of a structure of discrimination and oppression: an activity which is both intrusive and disempowering in its own right and which serves the damaging and oppressive purposes of a service system over which they can exert little or no influence or control. Mental health service users/survivors have particular concerns about the influence of the pharmaceutical industry on research and its effects in dictating a predominantly drug-based 'treatment' response to mental health issues.

The development of their own research by the disabled people's movement, mental health service users and other user movements has been coupled with their increasing demands for changed social relations in mainstream research, with a more active and equal role for research participants. This has led to an increasing interest in the degree of control that service users have in research (Evans and Fisher, 1999). Thus alongside participatory and emancipatory paradigms, discussion has developed about user-led and user-controlled research. This discussion focuses on the degree of user involvement and control in all key aspects of research including:

- the origination of research
- who gains the benefits of research
- the accountability of the research
- who undertakes the research
- research funding
- research design and process
- dissemination of research findings
- action following from research.

Mental health service users are now involved in commissioning, peer reviewing and identifying priorities for research. Organisations such as the Sainsbury Centre for Mental Health, Service User Research Enterprises at the Institute of Psychiatry and Strategies for Living at the Mental Health Foundation, have established strategic initiatives to undertake and develop user-led and user-controlled research. The latter has developed practical guidance to support 'survivor research' as well as running a national programme supporting local research projects and training survivor researchers. Meanwhile local and regional groups of survivor researchers are increasingly undertaking their own research initiatives. There has been considerable progress in a relatively short space of time (Beresford, 2003; Beresford and Wallcraft, 1997).

Service user/user-controlled research faces particular obstacles, because it has challenged traditional positivist approaches to research, with their emphasis on values of 'objectivity', 'neutrality' and 'distance'. It has also generally made clear that as well as having a strong intellectual base in 'new paradigm' research, it does have an allegiance: to the empowerment of service users and social change in line with their rights and needs. Its rationale is to bring about change, rather than solely to act as an instrument for knowledge production.

Thus there is now a large and growing body of identifiable mental health service user knowledge, based both on formal research and evaluation and on the individual and collective experience and ideas of mental health service users and their reflections on these. This knowledge, which addresses issues of difference, both within the constituency of mental health service users, and in comparison with wider populations, offers both service users' perspectives and their interpretations and analysis.

There can be no doubt that the views of mental health service users, and their knowledge and experience, are beginning to enter the professional world and service system of 'mental health'. It is difficult to know what effect they are actually having. Certainly it is important neither to over- or under-state the significance of this development. However, large obstacles still stand in the way of user knowledge exerting a substantial impact. Its structures, including, for example, service users' organisations and their research activity, command less credibility, fewer resources and are more insecure than those of other professional stakeholders. Mental health service users are also fundamentally disadvantaged by dominant understandings of them. Since the idea of 'mental illness' inherently challenges the rationality and intellectual capacity of those who have been 'diagnosed' with it, the knowledge of mental health service users and their understandings and interpretations of their experience, are always liable to challenge as potentially inferior and defective. Such prejudice still operates both in relation to mental health service user/survivor knowledge generally and with regard to survivor involvement in research (Faulkner, 2003).

Thus service users' knowledge and analysis is beginning to impact upon the professional and academic world of mental health. But the process is at a relatively early stage and there are significant identifiable obstacles in its way. These seem most pronounced in one key domain. It has, so far, perhaps had least impact on the medicalised individual framework which still predominates in mental health.

The persistence of a medicalised conceptual framework

Several reasons for this may be suggested. First, the medicalised individual model of 'mental illness' represents a powerful belief system in which enormous legitimacy has been invested. It not only forms the basis for 'mental health' policy and practice in western societies (and is increasingly being exported to have global impact and significance). It is built into legislation internationally, is institutionalised in powerful professions and is still seen as a benign influence, which can challenge traditionally superstitious and punitive responses to madness. The mental illness model still plays a central role in defining understandings of and responses to madness and distress. It is the cornerstone of the system.

As yet the mental health service user/survivor movement (both in the UK and internationally) does not seem to have developed any kind of agreed alternative to this model. There do seem to be a set of shared values and beliefs underpinning the mental health service user/survivor movement, for example, in the UK. However, the movement does not seem to have developed explicit philosophies or theories comparable to those of the social model of disability or independent living developed by the disabled people's movement. The reasons for this appear to be various and complex. They seem to relate to two concerns which mental health service users/survivors appear to have. The first of these relates to challenging the underpinning medical model of 'mental illness' when service users'/survivors' intellects are inherently perceived as 'defective' or 'pathological' and there is a fear that rejecting a medicalised individual model of their situation and identity would lead to them being ruled out and discounted as simplistic and irrational (Campbell, 1996). The second relates to service users'/survivors' worries about signing up to any kind of monolithic theory or set of principles (particularly one dependent on the social model of disability) for fear that these dominate and subordinate them and demand an orthodoxy in the same way as professional psychiatric thinking has done for so long (Plumb, 1994). There is a strong libertarian strand in much mental health service user/survivor thinking.

New survivor-led understandings of madness and distress

While mental health service users/survivors may not have developed an agreed and discrete theory or philosophy so far, there is no doubt that they and their organisations have developed different ways of understanding their experience, feelings and perceptions and, as a result, different approaches to and understandings for support and services. There can be little question that these are based on a thought-through ideology, albeit one that is frequently not articulated in any depth. This ideology follows from their own experiential knowledge and is strongly suggestive of an implicitly social approach.

For example, as long ago as 1987, Survivors Speak Out, the pioneering organisation of psychiatric system survivors, at its founding conference in Edale, produced a 'Charter of Needs and Demands' which were agreed unanimously. These demands prioritised the provision of non-medicalised services and support, the value of people's first-hand experience, the rights of service users and the ending of discrimination against people with experience of using mental health services (Survivors Speak Out, 1987).

Significantly, the understandings that mental health service users/survivors have developed about their 'illnesses' have generally followed less from knowledge production through research, than from knowledge production through collective action and reflection.

Such survivor understandings have developed from people trying to make sense of their own experience by sharing, collecting and analysing it. This has been reflected in discussions of their individual experience, their history and their 'treatment' (Campbell, 1996; Chamberlin, 1988; Craine, 1998; Mental Health Media, 2000; Read and Reynolds, 1996). Most important, perhaps, it has also emerged from efforts to reinterpret and make better sense of their experience than they feel that the psychiatric system and the predominant medical model have done. This is a common theme, in all the key areas where mental health service users/survivors have renewed thinking about the psychiatric categories into which they have been placed. They have challenged (and rejected) medicalised understandings of the experience as pathological and only negative. They have implicitly challenged the 'illness' model.

Instead they have placed an emphasis on people's first-hand understandings of themselves and their situation. This is exemplified by the development of the international hearing voices movement and in the UK of the Hearing Voices Network. Instead of accepting the diagnostic category 'schizophrenia' and victim status as a sufferer, the emphasis has been on trying to make sense of hearing voices both at a personal and at a societal level. There is no denial of the phenomenon or attempt to minimise the difficulties it may cause individually or socially. Instead the accent is on acknowledging and exploring the experience, recognising its power relations and learning to comprehend and deal with it better (Coleman, 1999; Coleman and Smith, 1997; Romme and Escher, 1993).

The same has been true of developments relating to self-harm and eating distress. Even the language has been altered. This seems to be part of a commitment to rejecting assumptions of 'neurotic' inadequacy or deficiency in the individual. Instead of being dismissed as an irritating nuisance activity, self-harm has been reconceived as a coping strategy and a frequently appropriate response to difficult, hostile and inappropriate experiences, like childhood sexual and domestic violence (Arnold and Magill, 1996; National Self-Harm Network, 1998; Pacitti, 1998; Pembroke, 1994; Trump, 2001).

Similarly, survivor activists like Louise Pembroke played a pioneering role in reconceiving 'anorexia nervosa' from a medicalised syndrome, to 'eating distress', demedicalising the phenomenon and highlighting its social, cultural and gender relations (Pembroke, 1992). In all these areas of formal 'diagnosis', survivors have made it possible for people to re-examine themselves and their difficulties in the light of shared experience, without stigma or negative stereotyping.

They have also provided a practical basis for the development of collective action, mutual aid, support and self-help (for example, the National Self-Harm Network). In the case of self-harm, for instance, this has led to service users developing practical tools for limiting the damage done, while not invalidating those who experience it. As well as developing support and information for service users, survivors' efforts have also been linked with the development of user-led training for professionals and highlighted the need for better training, understanding and advocacy in accident and emergency departments.

Thus in a sense it can be argued that explicit and detailed service user/survivor models for understanding and reconceiving madness and distress, may significantly be growing out of practical activities, rather than have provided the clear basis or inspiration for them.

The potential for change

In contrast, the disabled people's movement has developed its own alternative ways of interpreting the situation and experience of disabled people, which provide a changed basis for responding to both. The social model of disability, developed by the disabled people's movement, has had a major impact on public policy and understanding in countries such as the UK, leading to major new legislation, new support roles and new approaches to service provision. The social model of disability draws a distinction between the (perceived) physical, sensory or intellectual impairment of the individual and the *disabling* social response to people seen as impaired. It highlights the oppressive nature of the dominant social response to impairment, which excludes, segregates and stigmatises disabled people, creates barriers to their equality and participation and discriminates against them, restricting their human and civil rights. This approach to understanding has encouraged disabled people to highlight the problems they face as primarily a civil rights (rather than welfare) issue, although there is a keen and ongoing debate about the social model of disability (Barnes, Oliver and Barton, 2002; Corker and Shakespeare, 2002). There is no doubt that the social model of disability has influenced public understanding of disability, as well as many disabled people's own perceptions of themselves.

While mental health service users/survivors may not have developed their own explicit philosophy or theory, they have nonetheless over the years identified a range of key principles and core values underpinning their views, aims and activities. These have constantly been highlighted by service users and their organisations. These include:

- service users speaking for themselves
- recognition that mental health service users/survivors are (valid) people too
- service users doing things together
- service users having a right to their own say and views
- service users are not defective or pathological
- service users should have a right to regain and take control of their own lives.

The large and growing body of mental health service user literature also highlights an approach to 'mental health' issues which is holistic and both crosses and goes beyond policy divisions. Service user/survivor discourses address both material and spiritual issues: the personal as well as the political. Service user/survivor organisations have frequently been characterised by their twin emphasis on mutual aid/personal support and campaigning and action for broader (social and political) change. While, as has been said, their activities have frequently had to focus on the (mental health) service system – because this is where they have been able to access resources – their concern has been much broader.

In addition, there can be little doubt that most, if not all, mental health service users/survivors, are well aware of the discrimination and oppression which they face, for example, as parents, in relation to financial services like banking and insurance, and in terms of stigma, negative stereotyping and their exclusion from employment.

There have been attempts over a decade or more to develop closer links and understanding between the disabled people's and mental health service users'/survivors' movements (Beresford, Gifford and Harrison, 1996; Beresford, Harrison and Wilson, 2002; Morris, 1996). These have often been obstructed by the fears of each group of being additionally marginalised by the stigma associated with the other. However, in the last few years, interest among survivors and their organisations in advancing common concerns with the disabled people's movement has accelerated. A number of reasons for this can be identified. These include the pioneering work of some individuals and organisations, including, for example, the Common Agenda project of Greater London Action on Disability, which has sought to bring together both groups and their concerns as a basis for greater understanding and further action (GLAD, 2002). It can also be traced to the impact of proposals for extending compulsory 'treatment' in mental health legislation, leading to increasing awareness of their situation in rights terms among survivors and an expansion in direct action and campaigning. Mental health service users/ survivors have also been made increasingly aware of their (constructive) identity as disabled people through their entitlements and rights through the Disability Discrimination Act, Human Rights Act and Disability Rights Commission, as well as their increasing access to disability benefits and to the highly valued 'direct payments' system pioneered by the disabled people's movement.

Towards an alternative social approach

This is an important time to be developing an alternative to traditional medicalised individual interpretations of madness and distress. This is signified by:

- the intellectual weaknesses and internal contradictions of the dominant 'mental illness' framework, which are increasingly exposed and highlighted by current unmanageable tensions between control and empowerment in proposals for policy and practice
- the renewal of interest in 'social approaches' among key stakeholders, reflected in the development of the Social Perspectives Network
- the successful development of the social model of disability, challenging traditional medicalised understandings in the closely related field of disability
- the development of a large and rapidly growing body of individual and collective knowledge based on mental health service users'/survivors' direct experience
- mental health service users'/survivors' growing interest in exploring a related 'social model of madness and distress'.

If the aim is to develop an alternative framework for understanding, then it is important to recognise that the mere fact of it being a 'social' approach may not be sufficient, if it is to overcome the limitations of its individualised predecessor. It is not sufficient to develop a social approach which still rests on the over-arching framework of 'mental illness'. What is needed is a framework for understanding that goes beyond acceptance of the existing 'mental illness' model, but which instead is based on a systematic critiquing of it – in the same way that the social model of disability has done with traditional individual models of disability.

If this project is to be taken forward in an equal and inclusive way, then it will require the full and equal inclusion of both mental health service users/survivors and their knowledge in its process. It will mean including service users':

- perspectives
- knowledges
- analyses – including their interpretations, meanings, hypotheses and theories.

It will not be enough to include service users' knowledge and for the process of analysing and interpreting it to remain with traditional professional stakeholders, as this will almost inevitably have an unequal and tokenising effect.

If the process of framework building and theoretical development in mental health is to involve service users/survivors fully and equally, then a comprehensive strategy will need to be developed. This will need to take account of the diversity of mental health service users/survivors and make it possible for all who wish to contribute. This will include:

- addressing the support needs of survivors who may also have physical, intellectual and sensory impairments, be Black and from minority ethnic communities, have different linguistic or cultural backgrounds and who may communicate, for example, through signing and other forms of non-verbal communication
- challenging the categorisation of individuals and groups included in social care categories in terms of 'deserving' and 'undeserving' and conventional reluctance to include the latter
- questioning the dismissal of service users and their organisations as 'unrepresentative', particularly when their views conflict with the status quo (Beresford and Campbell, 1994).

To develop inclusive processes of knowledge and theory development will mean working towards equality between service users and other actors in discussion and action in three main areas. These are:

- *Equality of respect.* The same respect should be attached to users of services as to other participants, without any imposition of stigma or assumption of their deficit or inferiority, challenging rather than reinforcing dominant discriminations.

- *Equality of validity of contributions.* Contributions to theory building from people who use services should be accorded the same validity as others. Assumptions about objective, neutral and value-free social science cannot be sustained. Recognition should be given to the validity of the subjective knowledges, analyses and perspectives of people included in mental health categories.

- *Equality of ownership and control of the debate and of knowledge.* Users, not just a few token users, must be included in the process and they need to have equal ownership of it. This requires a shift in power, in the control of knowledge and what counts as knowledge, with service users having more say in both.

Key requirements for working for inclusive debate include:

- Support for people to take part in discussion about models and theories of madness and distress. This includes information, practical support, support for people to increase their confidence and self-esteem, development costs, personal assistance, etc. (Croft and Beresford, 1993).

- Support for equal opportunities, to ensure that everyone can take part on equal terms regardless of age, 'race', gender, sexuality, culture, disability, distress, or class.

- Open debate which includes service users on equal terms.

Involving mental health service users/survivors in mainstream debates to develop new frameworks for both understanding and responding to madness and distress, however, should not be seen as an alternative to supporting them to develop *their own* independent discussions and analyses. Part of the problem for service users/survivors collectively has been that pressures to work in 'partnership' with the service system and the failure to gain adequate independent funding, have frequently resulted in survivors having to adopt a reactive rather than proactive stance in their activities. The increasingly contradictory nature of mental health policy, with its twin commitments to social control and empowerment has resulted in more independent and campaigning activity by survivors. It is to be hoped that this growing impetus will enable and encourage service users and their organisations to take forward the process of developing independent frameworks for understanding madness and distress (building on the social model of disability) which in turn can provide a basis for consistent and supportive policy and practice for the future.

References

Arnold, L. and Magill, A. (1996) *Working With Self Injury: A Practical Guide.* Bristol: Basement Project.

Barnes, C., Mercer, G. and Shakespeare, T. (1999) *Exploring Disability: A Sociological Introduction.* Cambridge: Polity Press.

Barnes, C., Oliver, M. and Barton, L. (eds) (2002) *Disability Studies Today.* Cambridge: Polity Press.

Barnes, M., Harrison, S., Mort, M. and Shardlow, P. (1999) *Unequal Partners: User Groups and Community Care.* Bristol: The Policy Press.

Beresford, P. (1999) 'Making participation possible: movements of disabled people and psychiatric system survivors.' In T. Jordan and A. Lent (eds) *Storming The Millennium: The New Politics of Change.* London: Lawrence and Wishart.

Beresford, P. (2002) 'User involvement in research and evaluation: liberation or regulation?' *Social Policy And Society 1,* 2, 93–103.

Beresford, P. (2003) 'Madness, distress, research and a social model.' In C. Barnes (ed.) *The Social Model Of Disability And Research.* Leeds: Disability Press.

Beresford, P. and Campbell, J. (1994) 'Disabled people, service users, user involvement and representation.' *Disability And Society 9,* 3, 315–325.

Beresford, P. and Croft, S. (1993) *Citizen Involvement: A Practical Guide for Change.* Basingstoke: Macmillan.

Beresford, P., Gifford, G. and Harrison, C. (1996) 'What has disability got to do with psychiatric survivors?' In J. Reynolds and J. Read (eds) *Speaking Our Minds: Personal Experience of Mental Distress and its Consequences.* Open University Reader for new Open University course, 'Mental Health: Issues, Skills and Perspectives'. Basingstoke: Palgrave.

Beresford, P., Green, D., Lister, R. and Woodard, K. (1999) *Poverty First Hand.* London: Child Poverty Action Group.

Beresford, P., Harrison, C. and Wilson, A. (2002) 'Mental health service users and disability: implications for future strategies.' *Policy And Politics 30,* 3, July, 387–396.

Beresford, P., Stalker, K. and Wilson, A. (1997) *Speaking For Ourselves: A Bibliography.* London: Open Services Project in association with the Social Work Research Centre, University of Stirling.

Beresford, P. and Wallcraft, J. (1997) 'Psychiatric system survivors and emancipatory research: issues, overlaps and differences.' In C. Barnes and G. Mercer (eds) *Doing Disability Research.* Leeds: The Disability Press, University of Leeds.

Campbell, J. and Oliver, M. (1996) *Disability Politics: Understanding our Past, Changing our Future.* Basingstoke: Macmillan.

Campbell, P. (1996) 'The history of the user movement in the United Kingdom.' In T. Heller, J. Reynolds, R. Gomm, R. Muston and S. Pattison (eds) *Mental Health Matters: A Reader.* Basingstoke: Macmillan in association with the Open University.

Chamberlin, J. (1988) *On Our Own.* London: Mind Publications.

Coleman, R. (1999) 'Hearing voices and the politics of oppression.' In C. Newnes, G. Holmes and C. Dunn (eds) *This Is Madness: A Critical Look at Psychiatry and the Future of Mental Health Services.* Ross-on-Wye: PCCS Books.

Coleman, R. and Smith, M. (1997) *Working With Voices! Victim to Victor.* Runcorn: Handsell Publications.

Coppick, V. and Hopton, J. (2000) *Critical Perspectives On Mental Health.* London: Routledge.

Corker, M. and Shakespeare, T. (eds) (2002) *Disability/Postmodernity: Embodying Disability Theory.* London and New York: Continuum.

Craine, S. (1998) 'Shrink resistant: the survivor movement and the survivor perspective.' US Network Working Papers 3, unpublished paper.

Croft, S. and Beresford, P. (1993) *Getting Involved: A Practical Manual.* London: Open Services Project.

Croft, S. and Beresford, P. (1996) 'The politics of participation.' In D. Taylor (ed.) *Critical Social Policy: A Reader.* London: Sage.

Department of Health (1999) *A National Service Framework For Mental Health: Modern Standards and Service Models.* London: Department of Health.

Department of Health (2002) *Mental Health Bill.* London: The Stationery Office.

Duggan, M. with Cooper, A. and Foster, J. (2002) *Modernising the Social Model In Mental Health: A Discussion Paper.* London: Social Perspectives Network.

Evans, C. and Fisher, M. (1999) 'Collaborative evaluation with service users: moving towards user controlled research.' In I. Shaw and J. Lishman (eds) *Evaluation And Social Work Practice.* London: Sage.

Faulkner, A. (2003) 'The Emperor's New Clothes.' *Mental Health Today,* October, 23–26.

Faulkner, A. and Layzell, S. (2000) *Strategies For Living: A Report of User-led Research into People's Strategies for Living with Mental Distress.* London: The Mental Health Foundation.

Faulkner, A. and Nicholls, V. (1999) *The DIY Guide To Survivor Research.* London: The Mental Health Foundation.

Giddens, A. (1998) *The Third Way: The Renewal of Social Democracy.* Cambridge: Polity Press.

GLAD (2002) *Common Agenda Newsletter.* London, Greater London Action on Disability, October.

Holden, W. (1998) *Shell Shock: The Psychological Impact of War.* London: Channel Four Books.

James, A. (2001) *Raising Our Voices: An Account of the Hearing Voices Movement.* Gloucester: Handsell Publications.

Laing, R.D. (1965) *The Divided Self.* Harmondsworth: Pelican.

Lindow, V. (2001) 'Survivor research.' In C. Newnes, G. Holmes and C. Dunn (eds) *This Is Madness Too: Critical Perspectives on Mental Health Services.* Ross-on-Wye: PCCS Books.

Mental Health Alliance (2002) *Rights Not Compulsion, Mental Health Alliance Lobby of Parliament 23 October.* Leaflet. London: Mental Health Alliance.

Mental Health Media (2000) *Testimony: Telling the Stories of Those who Survived the Old Victorian Asylums.* London: Mental Health Foundation.

Morris, J. (ed.) (1996) *Encounters With Strangers: Feminism and Disability.* London: Women's Press.

National Self-Harm Network (1998) *The Hurt Yourself Less Workbook.* London: National Self-Harm Network.

Oliver, M. and Barnes, C. (1998) *Disabled People And Society: From Exclusion to Inclusion.* London: Longman.

Pacitti, R. (1998) 'Damage limitation.' *Nursing Times 94,* 36–39.

Pembroke, L. (1992) *Eating Distress, Perspectives from Personal Experience.* Chesham: Survivors Speak Out.

Pembroke, L. (ed.) (1994) *Self-Harm: Perspectives from Personal Experience.* London: Survivors Speak Out.

Plumb, A. (1994) *Distress Or Disability? A Discussion Document.* Manchester: Greater Manchester Coalition of Disabled People.

Read, J. and Reynolds, J. (eds) (1996) *Speaking Our Minds: An Anthology.* Basingstoke: Macmillan.

Rogers, A. and Pilgrim, D. (2001) *Mental Health Policy In Britain (Second Edition).* Basingstoke: Palgrave.

Romme, M. and Escher, S. (eds) (1993) *Accepting Voices.* London: Mind.

Sayce, L. (2000) *From Psychiatric Patient To Citizen: Overcoming Discrimination and Social Exclusion.* Basingstoke: Macmillan.

Shakespeare, T. (ed.) (1998) *The Disability Reader: Social Science Perspectives.* London: Cassell.

Shaughnessy, P. (2002) 'On community treatment orders (CTOs) and injustice.' Quoted in *S.U.N. Newsletter,* December, Manchester, Survivors' United Network, 2.

SPN (2002) *New Network To Promote 'Social Model' Of Mental Health.* News Release, 14 February, Leeds, Social Perspectives Network/Topss (England).

Survivors Speak Out (1987) *Charter Of Needs And Demands (Edale Conference Charter).* London: Survivors Speak Out.

Taylor, P. and Gunn, J. (1999) 'Homicides by people with mental illness: myth and reality.' *British Journal of Psychiatry 174,* 9–14.

Trump, A. (2001) 'Making Meaning From Tragedy.' www.psychminded.co.uk

Wallcraft, J. with Read, J. and Sweeney, A. (2003) *On Our Own Terms: Users and Survivors of Mental Health Services Working Together for Support and Change.* London: Mental Health Foundation.

CHAPTER 3

Beyond Biomedical Models

A Perspective from Critical Psychiatry

Duncan Double

The Critical Psychiatry Network

The Critical Psychiatry Network (CPN) first met as the 'Bradford Group' in January 1999. It is a group of psychiatrists that forms a network to develop a critique of the contemporary psychiatric system.

The first meetings of the group coincided with publication of the UK government's intention to undertake a root and branch review of the Mental Health Act 1983. The initial phase of this review involved a scoping exercise, undertaken by a small expert group chaired by Professor Genevra Richardson, to which CPN submitted evidence. CPN has also responded at each stage of the subsequent consultation process leading to the draft Mental Health Bill 2002.

CPN's position statement in October 1999 made clear its opposition to compulsory treatment in the community, and preventive detention for people who are considered to have 'personality disorders'. A new response to the conflict between care and coercion was proposed that recognised the way values inform medical decisions. This ethical perspective resists attempts to make psychiatry more coercive.

CPN was an original member of the Mental Health Alliance, a coalition of organisations that share common concerns about the government's proposals to reform the Mental Health Act. The core members have subsequently been joined by the Royal College of Psychiatrists, but initially CPN was the only group of psychiatrists that was part of the alliance.

Critical psychiatry is partly academic and partly practical (Thomas and Moncrieff, 2000). Theoretically it is influenced by critical philosophical and political theories. Three main elements have been identified: (1) a challenge to the dominance of clinical neuroscience in psychiatry (although this is not excluded); (2) a strong ethical perspective on psychiatric knowledge and practice; and (3) the politicisation of mental health issues.

Over recent years, it has become popular to regard critical thinking as something that can be taught (Fisher, 2001). Critical thinking is seen as the art of taking charge of one's mind. If we can take charge of our own minds, the theory is that we can take charge of our lives; we can improve them, bringing them under our command and direction. Critical thinking involves getting into the habit of reflecting on our inherent and accustomed ways of thinking and leads to action in every dimension of our lives. Similarly, critical psychiatry wants to promote critical reflection on practice and research in psychiatry.

More generally, critical psychiatry is supported by critical theory, which is a term that can be used quite loosely to refer to a range of theories which take a critical view of society (Macey, 2000). In particular, critical theory seeks to understand how systems of collective beliefs legitimate various power structures. In relation to psychiatry, this can be applied to appreciating why people are so ready to adopt the biomedical model in psychiatry. Critical theory has also distinguished itself through its critique of science as positivism. In other words, there is a tendency to believe that natural science is the only valid mode of knowledge and that progress continues to be made in uncovering facts through science. Psychiatry, for example, is said to have advanced over recent years in its understanding of the mind and mental illness. It suits people's expectations to think that psychiatry has found the solution to mental illness on the basis of natural scientific facts.

The Critical Psychiatry Network makes various statements in its March 2002 mission statement about its objectives. These include that CPN:

- is sceptical about the validity of the medical model of mental illness
- is opposed to the over-emphasis on biological research and treatments in psychiatry
- does not believe that psychiatric practice needs to be justified by postulating brain pathology as the basis for mental illness
- believes that the practice of psychiatry must recognise the primacy of social, cultural, economic and political contexts
- minimises the use of compulsory detention and treatment

- recognises the importance of working in alliance with service users to explore approaches that give them control over their lives

- believes that a combination of two types of expertise, expertise by experience and by profession, is a pre-requisite for the highest quality mental health services

- recognises the value of user-led research, independent peer advocacy, and the employment of service users in mental health services

- attempts to find alternatives to drug treatment whenever possible.

The sceptical attitude to the use of psychotropic medication has influenced contributions as a stakeholder to various guidelines produced by the National Institute for Clinical Excellence (NICE). The scientific limits of the possibilities of randomised controlled trials are acknowledged, as is the general bias in the interpretation of the data.

CPN's campaigning on the reform of the Mental Health Act has emphasised the importance of rights to advocacy and advance statements. It is also currently campaigning against pharmaceutical company sponsorship of psychiatric conferences and educational activities. CPN has also organised and participated in various conferences, where papers have been presented which develop the notions on which critical psychiatry is based. Some of these papers have been published on the CPN website (www. criticalpsychiatry.co.uk), as have the other documents prepared by the group.

Critical psychiatry and 'anti-psychiatry'

The Critical Psychiatry Network has never hidden its historical link with so-called 'anti-psychiatry'. However, the label 'anti-psychiatry' needs to be understood for what it is. The terminology was disowned by both R.D. Laing and Thomas Szasz, two people who are probably most closely and consistently identified with the anti-psychiatry movement. The general view is that anti-psychiatry was a passing phase in the history of psychiatry and that it is no longer of any influence (Tantam, 1991).

In a way, the spectre of 'anti-psychiatry' has functioned as a means of identifying and thereby marginalising psychiatry's critics. Anti-psychiatry is seen as disreputable, and part of this chapter's aim is to attempt to change that perception. There is an orthodoxy about current psychiatric practice which feels threatened by any challenge to its foundation (Double, 2001). Identifying psychiatry's critics as its opponents, therefore, allows them to be confronted and undermined.

Not all psychiatrists have seen the issue of anti-psychiatry in this way. For example, Kees Trimbos, one of the founders of Dutch social psychiatry, in his book *Antipsychiatrie* warned against supposing that it was just a fad: 'After all, anti-psychiatry is also psychiatry!' (quoted in Ingleby, 1998). The Critical Psychiatry Network also wishes to avoid the polarisation created by the antagonism between psychiatry and anti-psychiatry. Being open to the uncertainties of psychiatric practice needs to be encouraged (Double, 2002).

So what is the 'anti' element in anti-psychiatry? Essentially, the biomedical model of mental illness regards mental illness as a brain disease. Therefore it creates the tendency to reduce people to their biological base. Objectification of the mentally ill can make psychiatry part of the problem rather than necessarily the solution to mental health problems (Jones, 1998).

Anti-psychiatry had a popular, even romantic, appeal as an attack on psychiatrists' use of psychiatric diagnosis, drug and ECT treatment and involuntary hospitalisation. The apparently anti-authoritarian nature of anti-psychiatry obscures how much the ideas that amounted to anti-psychiatry predated its emergence.

This is the issue I wish to examine in this chapter. In particular, I wish to highlight the extent to which a biopsychological model of mental illness has been promulgated within mainstream psychiatry. Although the somatic hypothesis has always been the dominant model of mental illness, the view that mental illnesses have primarily psychological and social causes is not new. The essential importance of context for the understanding of mental health problems has been previously recognised. In particular, I submit that the most complete of such perspectives is linked with the name of Adolf Meyer.

The psychobiology of Adolf Meyer

Adolf Meyer (1866–1950) was an immigrant to the US from Switzerland. He had an important role in American psychiatry and was arguably the foremost American psychiatrist in the first half of the twentieth century. His ideas came to Britain via psychiatrists such as David Henderson and Aubrey Lewis (Gelder, 1991).

His theoretical approach, which was called Psychobiology, has not always been well articulated. Although he lived in the US for many years, Meyer had a rather convoluted style of communication in English. His ideas never really took hold as a systematic theory of psychiatry (O'Neill, 1980). Few references are now made to his writings in the literature. His collected works have been published, but are little read (Winters, 1951–2).

Essentially Meyer saw his views as an advance over the mechanistic notions of mental illness of the nineteenth century. He regarded the person as the focus for theory and practice in psychiatry. Psychiatric assessment should concentrate on understanding the patient as a person.

The assumptions of the biopsychological model are listed by Wilson (1993). Anyone can become mentally ill if exposed to sufficient trauma. The boundary between normality and insanity is therefore fluid. The cause of mental illness is postulated to be an untoward mixture of harmful environment and psychic conflict. Mental illness is conceived along a continuum of severity from neurosis through borderline conditions to psychosis. The mechanisms by which mental illness emerges in an individual are psychologically mediated.

Such a biopsychological perspective can be contrasted with the biomedical approach of Emil Kraepelin. For example, Kraepelin (1921) viewed the origins of schizophrenia (or dementia praecox, as it was then called) very differently to Meyer (1906). For Kraepelin (1921), dementia praecox, like manic-depressive illness, was a single morbid process. Meyer questioned the biological basis of Kraepelin's concept of dementia praecox. Meyer had a psychogenic understanding of dementia praecox, and believed that such psychological understanding should apply to dementia praecox as much as for any other psychiatric disorder. The reasons why people become psychotic are not understood by suggesting that such a process happens because of a condition behind the symptoms called dementia praecox.

Typically, Meyer called speculation about the biological basis of mental illness 'neurologising tautology'. Thomas Szasz (1972) has been criticised for suggesting that mental illness is a 'myth'. Although Meyer would not have agreed with Szasz that the notion of mental illness is meaningless, he did concur with Szasz's contention that belief in mental illness as a disease of the brain is a negation of the distinction between persons as social beings and bodies as physical objects. To quote from Meyer, 'Very often the supposed disease at the back of it all is a myth and merely a self-protective term for an insufficient knowledge of the conditions of reaction' (quoted in Winter 1951–2 vol 2, p.585).

Meyer's views are important because of the increasing hegemony of the biomedical model over the last 40 or more years. In fact, the drive to create a systematic biological perspective over recent years was at least partially driven by the wish to replace the perceived vagueness about psychiatric diagnosis blamed on the Meyerian perspective. Other factors were of course also important in encouraging the biomedical somatic hypothesis, such as the increasing development and marketing of psychotropic medication, related to biochemical theories of mental disorder.

I do not want to over-estimate the differences in psychiatry 40 years ago compared with the present. The dominant model of mental illness has always been biomedical. The natural assumption has been to presuppose that mental illness is a physical disease and that the 'answer' will be found in biological discoveries. However, I do want to highlight the relative pluralism of psychiatry of the past. Modern psychiatry has become so governed by biological psychiatry that we need to be reminded that biopsychological and social perspectives are not new.

Pluralism in psychiatry

In the mid twentieth century, there was little in the way of psychotropic medication. Although there was a certain enthusiasm for physical treatments such as electroconvulsive therapy (ECT) and insulin coma therapy, there was much interest in psychoanalysis and psychotherapy. A disparity existed between the relatively pessimistic situation regarding therapeutic options for serious psychiatric illness and increasing investment in out-patient work with people with neurotic and personality disorders. In the US in particular, the highest calling was to go into psychoanalytic training. At the Maudsley hospital, the centre of postgraduate psychiatry in Britain in the early 1950s, and one of the best in the world, half of the trainees were in analysis (Clark, 2000). There were Freudian, Kleinian and Jungian trainees, all vociferously defending their schools.

Meyer ultimately rejected psychoanalysis but still encouraged a psychological understanding in terms of the patient's life history. More generally, psychoanalytic theories were re-evaluated by focusing on environmental factors and the critical nature of disturbances in human relationships.

For example, few people now recognise the name of William Alanson White. During the first third of the twentieth century, he was one of America's leading psychiatrists. White played a major role in the introduction of psychoanalysis in the US after 1910, advancing its role as a theory and treatment method. He was also mentor to Harry Stack Sullivan. The interpersonal approach of Sullivan focused on relationships and the effects of the individual's social and cultural environment on inner life (Barton Evans, 1996).

In the immediate post-war years, Karl Menninger's (1963) *The Vital Balance* represented a broadly conceived psychosocial theory of psychopathology (Wilson, 1993). As Menninger himself says, 'As a result of Meyer's efforts and those of William Alanson White, American psychiatrists began to ask, not "What is the name of this affliction?" but rather, "How is this man reacting and to what?"'. American psychiatry came to have a distinctively pragmatic, instrumental and pluralistic approach (Lidz, 1966).

The foundation of the William Alanson White Institute can be seen as representative of this view. In the early 1940s Clara Thompson supported Karen Horney's departure from the New York Psychoanalytic Society. Not long after Erich Fromm joined Thompson, as did subsequently Harry Stack Sullivan, Freida Fromm-Reichmann and Janet and David Rioch at the William Alanson White Institute. They formed an unusual alliance, based more on respect for freedom of thought than unanimity of perspective (Lionells, 2000). What they did agree on was the importance of interactions between individuals and their interpersonal environment.

Contrast this pluralism with the current dominant emphasis on natural scientific causation, rather than psychologically meaningful experiences. This trend has been reinforced by factors like the therapeutic advances in psychopharmacology since the introduction of chlorpromazine and the development of brain imaging. These biological perspectives tend to lack the whole-person viewpoint of a biopsychological approach.

The attempt to make psychiatric diagnosis more reliable, combined with a return to a biomedical model of mental illness, has been called the 'neo-Kraepelinian' approach (Klerman, 1978). I want to concentrate on the neo-Kraepelinian perspective as the modern representation of the biomedical model in psychiatry. I then want to move on to compare the neo-Kraepelinian position with the views of Adolf Meyer.

The neo-Kraepelinian approach in psychiatry

The modern explicit and intentional concern with psychiatric diagnosis contrasts with earlier views, such as Meyer's, de-emphasising diagnosis in favour of understanding the life story of the individual patient. Psychiatric diagnosis became increasingly codified following the original paper by Feighner *et al.* (1972) and the introduction of the Research Diagnostic Criteria (Spitzer, Endicott and Robins, 1975), through editions of the latter revisions of the *Diagnostic and Statistical Manual* of the American Psychiatric Association (DSM-III, DSM-IIIR and DSM-IV) (American Psychiatric Association, 1994). Symptom checklists and formal decision-making rules for psychiatric diagnoses were produced. This operationalisation of diagnostic criteria was developed specifically to respond to criticisms of the basis of psychiatric classification.

This development promotes many of the ideas associated with the views of Emil Kraepelin, often considered to be the founder of modern psychiatry. Psychiatry is regarded as a scientific, medical speciality that qualitatively differentiates mentally ill patients, who require treatment, from normal people. Scientific psychiatry's task is to investigate the causes, diagnosis and treatment of different mental illnesses, which are seen as discrete from each other. Biological aspects of mental illness are regarded as psychiatry's central concern. Diagnosis and classification are intentionally viewed as important. Belittling of the value of psychiatric diagnosis is discouraged. Mental illness should not be seen as a myth. Instead diagnostic criteria should be codified and research should attempt to validate these criteria, using statistical techniques to improve reliability and validity.

The most visible product of the neo-Kraepelinian movement was the third edition of the *Diagnostic and Statistical Manual* of the American Psychiatric Association (DSM-III). The change in diagnostic classificatory systems between DSM-II and DSM-III was dramatic (Blashfield, 1984). This can be seen if only from the size of the manual. The chapter related to psychiatric disorders in DSM-II is a thin pamphlet. In contrast, in DSM-III it is a large textbook.

Robert Spitzer chaired the task force that produced DSM-III. Spitzer was particularly concerned about the reliability of psychiatric diagnosis (Spitzer and Fleiss, 1974). What especially perturbed him was a study by Rosenhan (1973), called 'On being sane in insane places'. Rosenhan was a sociologist who was interested in the labelling effect of psychiatric diagnoses. In a classic study, he arranged for normal accomplices to be admitted to psychiatric hospital, by presenting themselves saying they were hearing a voice, saying a single word. There were three variations in the trial: the pseudopatient said they were hearing the voice say either 'thud', 'hollow' or 'empty'. This was the only symptom they had. There were no other indications of mental illness such as delusions or thought disorder. The only complaint was of a simple hallucination, and even then just one word, which is not in itself particularly characteristic of mental illness.

All of the pseudopatients were admitted to hospital. After admission they stopped feigning their symptom of hearing a voice. Some of the real patients detected that they were pseudopatients, because they saw them writing notes about their experience.

All of the pseudopatients apart from one received a diagnosis of schizo-phrenia; the other was diagnosed as manic-depressive. There is some qualification to this process because although the pseudopatients had acquired a psychiatric diagnosis they were noted to be in remission, improved or asymptomatic. Specific reference to this designation in psychiatric hospital discharge summaries is generally unusual.

The response of the psychiatric establishment to this study was disbelief. Rosenhan therefore informed the staff of a research and teaching hospital to which at some time during the following three months, one or more pseudopatients would attempt to be admitted. No such attempt was actually made. Yet approximately 10 per cent of real patients were apparently sus-pected by two or more staff members to be pseudopatients.

Rosenhan concluded from his work that psychiatric diagnosis is subjec-tive and does not reflect inherent patient characteristics. Spitzer (1976) was one of the main critics in the literature of his study and its conclusion.

Spitzer was so panicked that psychiatric diagnoses may be unreliable that he made every effort to ensure that they were clearly defined. The inherent vagueness in category definitions, which could be linked to Meyerian views and other pragmatic perspectives, was blamed. Although careful analysis of the evidence presented in reliability studies of psychiatric diagnosis may not be as negative as is commonly assumed, the commitment to increase diagnos-tic reliability became a goal in itself (Blashfield, 1984). Transparent rules were laid down for making each psychiatric diagnosis in DSM-III.

In retrospect, what could be seen to have happened is that the response to the attack on psychiatric diagnosis, for example by the labelling theorists such as Rosenhan, also served to undermine the Meyerian perspective. The neo-Kraepelinian approach provided an argument for mainstream psychiatry to re-establish the reality of mental illness, seen as under threat from anti-psychiatry (Roth and Kroll, 1986).

Meyerian ideas, if they are restated, now may appear tainted with the unorthodoxy of anti-psychiatry. It is almost as though they are held respon-sible for allowing the threat of anti-psychiatry to be taken so seriously. The underlying assumption seems to be that if psychiatry had not allowed itself to become so imbued with the vague and woolly ideas of Meyer about diagnosis, anti-psychiatry would not have been able to take such hold and to have had such credence. The biomedical model, reinforced in its neo-Kraepelinian form by the operationalisation of diagnostic criteria, has again become dominant in current psychiatric practice.

Comparison of Meyerian and neo-Kraepelinian approaches

I have previously compared Meyer's perspective and the neo-Kraepelinian approach and concluded that Meyer would have been profoundly critical of the emphasis and assumptions of the neo-Kraepelinian approach (Double, 1990). I argued for a neo-Meyerian revival. Klerman (1978), who originally stated the neo-Kraepelinian principles, had expected such a reaction, but it seems slow to have been formulated.

Spitzer (2001) maintains that DSM-III takes a neutral approach to causation and that it is not covertly committed to a biological approach to explaining mental illness. There is truth in this observation. The link between DSM-III and biological aetiology is merely associative, not logical causal. A classificatory system in itself is not necessarily biomedical. This is illustrated by the fact that DSM-I was influenced by the reaction types proposed by Adolf Meyer, despite Meyer's concern about the general over-emphasis on psychiatric diagnosis.

However, the biopsychological model of mental illness is undermined by a specific focus on diagnosis, as in DSM-III. For Meyer, the first aim of the psychiatrist should be to get at the facts of the case rather than to make a diagnosis. Indeed if the facts do not constitute a diagnosis, the patient still needs to be managed without a clear-cut diagnosis being made. Meyer understood the craving for certainty in classification but thought that there were dangers in one-word diagnoses, which gave a false impression that matters are known and understood better than they really are.

Spitzer (2001) concedes that biologically orientated clinicians, who generally regard psychiatric diagnosis as crucial to their work, are positive about the development of DSM-III. For example, Samuel Guze (1989), a central member of the neo-Kraepelinian movement, has suggested that there can be no psychiatry that is not biological. For Guze, it is inescapable that psychopathology is the manifestation of disordered brain processes.

Meyer also, of course, did not fail to recognise the neurobiological substrate of mental states and behaviour. His emphasis on the person, however, meant that mental illness was understood as a maladaptation in terms of the patient's life experiences. Although he maintained an interest in neuropathology, biological considerations hardly ever arose in dealing with everyday psychiatric problems. In contrast, modern psychiatric practice tends to focus on the biomedical hypothesis.

It is not unusual in current practice for patients to be told that they have a 'biochemical imbalance' in the brain. To give the pharmaceutical industry its due, statements that it makes about the biochemical hypothesis are generally couched in appropriately cautious terminology. The stance taken tends to be that research has shown that mental disorders *could be* linked to a chemical imbalance in the brain. The hypothesis is not necessarily taken as proven. The clinical error is introduced by doctors and other mental health practitioners acting as though the conjecture is true. Meyer recognised this fallacy and modern biological psychiatric practice needs to be repeatedly reminded of it.

Much psychiatric research has had the aim of looking for a physical lesion. Yet if the premise is wrong, is it surprising the work has ended in so many blind alleys? This statement may be thought to show my prejudice about psychiatric research. The general impression has been created that there have been many research discoveries that have produced great advances in psychiatric knowledge over recent years.

In practice, initial enthusiasms have commonly been shown for the speculations that they are. To give an example: investigators have periodically claimed that they have found the location of genetic markers for mental illness. There were highly publicised announcements that chromosome 5 is linked to schizophrenia (Sherrington *et al.*, 1988) and that chromosome 11 is linked to bi-polar disorder (Egeland *et al.*, 1987). Although not confirmed to be the case, it is widely believed that such markers for schizophrenia and bi-polar disorder have been proven. Despite the hype, accurate prediction may never be possible because of the complexity of the genetics of common disorders (Holtzman and Marteau, 2000).

Let me give another example of current research into biomedical hypotheses, just picking a study arbitrarily from the literature. Over recent years, carbamazepine and valproic acid have been added to the pharmacological armamentarium in bi-polar disorder (manic-depressive illness), even though they were originally introduced into the pharmaceutical market for their anti-epileptic activity. Their mechanism of action in bi-polar disorder remains unknown. Rapoport and Bosetti (2002) have recently proposed that lithium and antimanic anti-convulsants, like carbamazepine and valproic acid, act by targeting parts of the 'arachidonic acid cascade', which may be functionally hyperactive in mania.

Let's see how long this speculation lasts! I doubt it will. It has been published in a prestigious psychiatric journal, but it is as likely to languish for lack of evidence or disconfirmation as have many other short-lived biomedical speculations. As these words are in print, people will be able to look back to see if my prediction proves to be correct or whether Rapoport and Bosetti's hypothesis that the over-activity of the arachidonic acid cascade is implicated

in the aetiology of mania is confirmed. I very much doubt whether their conjecture will be of any lasting value, either scientifically or clinically, but its
promotion in a prestigious psychiatric journal adds to the impression that
great progress is being made in scientific psychiatry.

Meyer would have shared my concerns about a positivistic view of science, in the sense that he did not believe that what we need is simply more
scientific 'findings'. For example, at the time he was practising, he regarded
the advent of insulin shock therapy as a resurgence of medical emphasis where
humane psychological interest should have prevailed. Biological psychiatry
has continually perpetuated the illusion that just round the corner lies some
vital new discovery that will settle the arguments once and for all. For Meyer,
there is already a wide range of facts, usually left to untrained common sense.
The job of the psychiatrist is to organise this information as a body of 'facts'
and methods of study and therapeutic procedures. For biomedical psychiatry,
such a view is too unscientific. To quote from Roth and Kroll (1986): 'Such a
closure of the model at the level of vague statements that all factors are important and must be taken into account threatens to interfere seriously with the
continued progress of medicine' (p.64).

Psychiatry is a form of hermeneutical science in that it recognises the
importance of interpretation in establishing objective facts. It is part of the
human sciences, not natural sciences. Biomedical psychiatrists to buttress their
case should not abrogate the authority of science. There is a perceived certainty about the biological viewpoint, which is highly valued and gives an
apparent justification to the biomedical hypothesis. As there are difficulties in
deciding *a priori* between the legitimacy of the biomedical and biospsycho-
logical models of mental illness, factors like this do sway heavily.

In summary, Meyer and the neo-Kraepelinian approach find different
ways of accommodating to two main conceptual issues: (1) the mind-body
problem; and (2) the application of scientific method to the study of human
nature. Meyer sought an integration of mind and body, whereas biomedical
psychiatry postulates an underlying physical lesion as the cause of mental
illness. The neo-Kraepelinian approach encourages a positivistic view of mental science, whereas Meyer recognised the interpretative nature of human
knowledge.

Post-psychiatry and critical psychiatry

Bracken and Thomas (2001) have recently outlined a new direction for
mental health, which they call 'post-psychiatry'. This approach emphasises

the significance of social, political and cultural contexts for the understanding of mental illness. While recognising the importance of empirical knowledge, it gives priority to interpretation and to meaningful experiences. It argues that mental health practice does not need to be based on an individualistic framework centred on medical diagnosis and treatment.

Post-psychiatry is about creating a space in which a new debate can take place. There is a need for an open, genuine and democratic debate about mental health.

Bracken and Thomas (2001) suggest that post-psychiatry is the post-modern deconstruction of modernist psychiatry. Following the Enlightenment, or the Age of Reason as it is called, the concept of psychiatry developed as a separate area of medical endeavour. Foucault (1967) views the associated emergence of institutions in which mad people were housed as the 'The Great Confinement'.

According to Bracken (2001), modernist psychiatry is made up of three elements:

1. technical reasoning and a belief in science

2. exploration of the individual self; and

3. coercion and control of madness.

Post-psychiatry sees this agenda as no longer tenable because of various post-modern challenges to its basis. These include questioning simple notions of progress and scientific expertise. The rise of the user movement, with its challenging of the biomedical model of mental illness, is seen as being of particular importance. Recent government policy emphases on social exclusion and partnership in health are viewed as an opportunity for a new deal between professionals and service users.

Post-psychiatry is, therefore, context-centred and takes its philosophical foundations from 'hermeneutical' philosophers such as Wittgenstein and Heidegger and the Russian psychologist Vygotsky (Bracken, 2002). Such approaches give priority to meaning and interpretation rather than causal explanation.

Post-psychiatry also emphasises the importance of values rather than causes in research and practice. This theme chimes with the so-called 'new philosophy of psychiatry' (Fulford *et al.*, 2003).

Post-psychiatry proposes a new relationship between society and madness and challenges doctors to rethink their role and responsibilities. For example, in relation to the proposals for reform of the Mental Health Act, decontextualising the biomedical model weakens the argument for relative medical control of the detention process.

Post-psychiatry, therefore, is probably the best articulated form of critical psychiatry. However, critical psychiatry covers a broad span of approaches. Those interested may wish to consult the Critical Psychiatry website (www.anti-psychiatry.co.uk). The internet has tended to provide a forum for more marginalised views, such as critical psychiatry. Some of the best articles explaining the basis of the approach are only available on the internet. Links to four articles by David Kaiser are at www.critpsynet.freeuk.com/ Kiser.htm. They were originally published by Mental Health Infosource, an internet-based continuing medical education resource. Those interested in reading books on the theory behind critical psychiatry may wish to consult Lucy Johnstone's (2000) *Users and Abusers of Psychiatry*.

For the purpose of this chapter, what I want to look at again is the more general link to what I have been calling the pluralistic emphasis in psychiatry of the past. In many ways, post-psychiatry is not a new direction. In my view, critical psychiatry does not need to be tied to post-modernism. In this way, critical psychiatry avoids philosophical critiques of post-modernism, such as that it tends to retreat into the irrational.

What is crucial is that psychiatric practice is not taken for granted. It needs to be self-conscious, self-critical and non-objectifying. Its world view, collective beliefs and attitudes need to be examined. This is why I prefer the term 'critical psychiatry'.

On the other hand, I do have some reservation that the term 'critical' may be open to misinterpretation. It tends to have a negative connotation and imply antagonism. This meaning may be the first one that you will find in dictionaries. In this sense, critical means 'inclined to find fault, or to judge with severity'. However, critical also has other meanings, such as being 'characterised by careful, exact evaluation and judgement'. Also, it may have something to do with a crucial turning point, in this sense meaning 'of the greatest importance to the way things might happen'. It is in these later senses that I am using the word 'critical' in relation to psychiatry.

Critical psychiatry could be accused of caricaturing psychiatry as a reductionist, biomedical behemoth, crushing all dissent and interested only in drug treatment. In fact, modern American psychiatry studied by participant observation appears to be 'of two minds', in that there is a divided consciousness created between the practices of drug therapy and psychotherapy (Luhrmann, 2000). Psychopharmacology may be the dominant force in contemporary psychiatry, and psychiatrists may tend to act as though psychiatric illness picks out real disease processes in the body, but there is a general recognition that this model impoverishes the sense of human possibility. The professional split between biological psychiatry and psychotherapy represents this dilemma. Not that psychotherapy monopolises the benefits of attempting to understand a person's problems. It too can degrade and cause harm.

Critical psychiatry is clearly not saying that all that is required is a combination of drug treatment and psychotherapy, as tends to be the position of those that criticise critical psychiatry for its apparent over-statement. The disadvantage of such an eclectic solution is that it suggests that to explain mental illness all one needs to do is to select the approach from the various alternatives of biological, psychological or social that seem most reasonable at the time. A fusion is created without necessarily resolving conflicts. Critical psychiatry is seeking a new synthesis. This synthesis is a continuation of the pluralism of the past. In terms of theory, it could be seen as a restatement of the position of Adolf Meyer in a post-antipsychiatric age.

The critical issue in modern psychiatry is the apparent benefit of psycho-pharmacology, which has grown since Meyer's time, following the introduction of chlorpromazine in the 1950s. How much is this advantage due to the placebo effect? People have always sought to bolster and restore their health by taking medications. They have not always taken a rational approach to this key problem of life. Quackery was profitable because sufferers believed in the cures for their ailments. The difference now is that large international pharmaceutical companies make the profits rather than the travelling vendor. The safety and effectiveness of modern medicines is regulated, but there are biases towards the interests of industry and trade against the interests of patients and public health.

We may want a placebo solution to our problems, because it seems easy and quick, but more long-lasting benefits may emerge from the difficult task of dealing more thoroughly with our problems. The way we conceive of mental illness as a society does matter.

Conclusion

What I have tried to do in this chapter is to describe how critical psychiatry wishes to change the dominant paradigm in mental health practice from a biomedical to a biopsychological model. This interpretative model recognises the centrality of social perspectives. What is not always clear is that mainstream psychiatry has always had elements that have acknowledged these perspectives. I have attempted to elucidate the relationships with so-called anti-psychiatry, and its history in the pluralism of mid-twentieth-century psychiatry before the development of psychopharmacology.

What I hope I have demonstrated is that critical psychiatry cannot easily be dismissed and its strength should not be under-estimated in the current mental health debate. Objectification of the mentally ill in the biomedical model can make psychiatry part of the problem rather than necessarily the solution to the problem of mental illness. For this reason, the Critical Psychiatry Network has supported and seen itself as an essential member of the Social Perspectives Network.

References

American Psychiatric Association (1994) *Diagnostic and Statistical Manual of Mental Disorders (Fourth Edition)*. Washington: American Psychiatric Association.

Barton Evans III, F. (1996) *Harry Stack Sullivan. Interpersonal Theory and Psychotherapy*. London: Routledge.

Blashfield, R.K. (1984) *The Classification of Psychopathology. Neo-Kraepelinian and Quantitative Approaches*. New York: Plenum.

Bracken, P. (2001) 'Democacy and mental health: the idea of post-psychiatry.' www.critpsynet.freeuk.com/PatBracken.htm

Bracken, P. (2002) *Trauma. Culture and Philosphy in the Post-modern Age*. London: Whurr.

Bracken, P. and Thomas, P. (2001) 'Post-psychiatry: a new direction for mental health.' *British Medical Journal 322*, 7288, 724–727.

Clark, D.H. (2000) *How I Learned my Trade*. www.pettarchiv.org.uk/survey-dhclark-learningtrade.htm

Double, D.B. (1990) 'What would Adolf Meyer have thought of the neo-Kraepelinian approach?' *Psychiatric Bulletin 14*, 472–474.

Double, D.B. (2001) 'Integrating critical psychiatry into psychiatric training.' In C. Newnes, G. Holmes and C. Dunn (eds) *This is Madness Too*. Ross-on-Wye: PCCS Books.

Double, D.B. (2002) 'The limits of psychiatry.' *British Medical Journal 324*, 7342, 900–904.

Egeland, J.A., Gerhard, D.S., Pauls, D.L., Sussex, J.N. and Kidd, K.K. (1987) 'Bipolar affective disorders linked to DNA markers on chromosome 11.' *Nature 325*, 783–787.

Feighner, J.P., Robins, E., Guze, S.B., Woodruff, R.A., Winokur, G. and Munoz, R. (1972) 'Diagnostic criteria for use in psychiatric research.' *Archives of General Psychiatry 26*, 57–63.

Fisher, A. (2001) *Critical Thinking: An Introduction*. Cambridge: Cambridge University Press.

Foucault, M. (1967) *Madness and Civilization: A History of Insanity in the Age of Reason*. London: Tavistock.

Fulford, B., Morris, K., Sadler, J. and Stanghellini, G. (eds) (2003) *Nature and Narrative: An Introduction to the New Philosophy of Psychiatry*. Oxford: Oxford University Press.

Gelder, M. (1991) 'Adolf Meyer and his influence on British psychiatry.' In G.E. Berrios and H. Freeman (eds) *150 Years of British Psychiatry, 1841–1991*. London: Gaskell.

Guze, S. (1989) 'Biological psychiatry: is there any other kind?' *Psychological Medicine 19*, 315–323.

Holtzman, N.A. and Marteau, T.M. (2000) 'Will genetics revolutionize medicine?' *New England Journal of Medicine 342*, 141–144.

Ingleby, D. (1998) 'A view from the North Sea.' In M. Gijswijt-Hofstra and R. Porter (eds) *Cultures of Psychiatry*. Amsterdam: Rodopi.

Johnstone, L. (2000) *Users and Abusers of Psychiatry: A Critical Look at Psychiatric Practice (Second Edition)*. London: Routledge.

Jones, C. (1998) 'Raising the anti: Jan Foudraine, Ronald Laing and anti-psychiatry.' In M. Gijswijt-Hofstra and R. Porter (eds) *Cultures of Psychiatry*. Amsterdam: Rodopi.

Klerman, G.L. (1978) 'The evolution of a scientific nosology.' In J.C. Shershow (ed.) *Schizophrenia: Science and Practice*. Cambridge, Mass: Harvard University Press.

Kraepelin, E. (1921) *Manic-depressive Insanity and Paranoia*. Edinburgh: Livingstone.

Lidz, T. (1966) 'Adolf Meyer and the development of American psychiatry.' *American Journal of Psychiatry 123*, 320–332.

Lionells, M. (2000) 'The William Alanson White Institute yesterday, today and tomorrow.' *American Psychoanalyst 34*. Also available at www.wawhite.org/history/brief_history_WAWI.htm

Luhrmann, T.M. (2000) *Of Two Minds. The Growing Disorder in American Psychiatry*. New York: Knopf.

Macey, D. (2000) *The Penguin Dictionary of Critical Theory*. London: Penguin.

Menninger, K. with Mayman, M. and Pruyser, P. (1963) *The Vital Balance*. New York: The Viking Press.

Meyer, A. (1906) 'Fundamental concepts of dementia praecox.' *British Medical Journal 2*, 757–759.

O'Neill, J.R. (1980) 'Adolf Meyer and American psychiatry today.' *American Journal of Psychiatry 137*, 460–464.

Rapoport, S.I. and Bosetti, F. (2002) 'Do lithium and anticonvulsants target the brain arachidonic acid cascade in bipolar disorder?' *Archives of General Psychiatry 59*, 592–596.

Rosenhan, D.L. (1973) 'On being sane in insane places.' *Science 179*, 250–258.

Roth, M. and Kroll, J. (1986) *The Reality of Mental Illness*. Cambridge: Cambridge University Press.

Sherrington, R., Brynjolfsson, J., Petursson, H., Potter, M., Duddleston, K., Barraclough, B., Wasmuth, J., Dobbs, M. and Gurling, H. (1988) 'Localisation of a susceptibility locus for schizophrenia on chromosome 5.' *Nature 336*, 164–167.

Spitzer, R.L. (1976) 'More on pseudoscience in science and the case for psychiatric diagnosis.' *Archives of General Psychiatry 33*, 459– 470.

Spitzer, R.L. (2001) 'Values and assumptions in the development of DSM-III and DSM-IIIR: an insider's perspective and a belated response to Sadler, Hulgus, and Agich's "On values in recent American psychiatric classification".' *Journal of Nervous and Mental Disease 189*, 351–359.

Spitzer, R.L., Endicott, J. and Robins, E. (1975) *Research Diagnostic Criteria (RDC) for a Selected Group of Functional Disorders*. New York: New York State Psychiatric Institute.

Spitzer, R.L. and Fleiss, J.L. (1974) 'A reanalysis of the reliability of psychiatric diagnosis.' *British Journal of Psychiatry 125*, 341–347.

Szasz, T.S. (1972) *The Myth of Mental Illness*. London: Paladin.

Tantam, D. (1991) 'The anti-psychiatry movement.' In G.E. Berrios and H. Freeman (eds) *150 Years of British Psychiatry, 1841–1991*. London: Gaskell.

Thomas, P. and Moncrieff, J. (2000) 'Joined up thinking.' *Health Matters 39*, 15 www.healthmatters.org.uk/stories/pthomas.html

Trimbos, K. (1978) Antipsychiatine. Een Overzicht. Deventer: Loghum Slaterus.

Wilson, M. (1993) 'DSM-III and the transformation of American psychiatry: a history.' *American Journal of Psychiatry 150*, 399–410.

Winters, E. (1951–2) (ed.) *The Collected Papers of Adolf Meyer. Vols 1–4*. Baltimore: Johns Hopkins Press.

CHAPTER 4

Power Relations, Social Order and Mental Distress

Jerry Tew

Although the connections may not always be straightforward, mental distress may often link to experiences of power and powerlessness. It is a theme which underpins many of the topics covered in this book – for example, understanding the impact of trauma and abuse (Chapter 6), and making sense of the different experiences of mental distress (and levels of incidence) encountered by subordinated social groups, such as women, Black people, or lesbian and gay people (Chapters 7–9).

Factors such as oppression, injustice, social exclusion or abuse at the hands of powerful others may be implicated in the sequences of events that lead up to many people's experiences of mental or emotional breakdown. Power issues may also shape the reactions that people receive from professionals and the wider community – for example, evidence suggests that African-Caribbean people may be more likely than many 'white' groups to be dealt with more coercively (Browne, 1997; see also Chapter 7).

Indeed, the very form taken by experiences of distress may reflect issues of power. For example, many psychotic experiences would appear to have a somewhat metaphoric quality and may be characterised by images of power and powerlessness – such as believing that one's mind or body is being controlled by strange external forces, or that one possesses special forms of influence and is able to determine external events in unusual ways. People with eating disorders have talked of being stuck within a paradoxical power struggle: that they have come to feel that their only remaining area of control by which to assert their existence is through the refusal of food; but this desperate assertion of power may threaten to end their biological existence

(Lawrence, 1984). Depression and anxiety may be seen, in different ways, as extreme internalisations of powerlessness – although they may, in turn, exert a paralysing power both over those who may experience such forms of distress, and those who share their lives.

The process of recovery from mental distress also connects with issues of power. Recovery may involve reclaiming a place in social, cultural, family or economic systems from which one has been excluded (Warner, 1994; see also Chapter 11). It may involve a much more personal sense of empowerment, feeling more in control of one's life and able to set a more positive and less self-destructive direction. It can involve a shift in power relationships with professionals – claiming the position of being an 'expert by experience' in relation to one's mental health and taking an active and responsible role in negotiating one's needs for therapy and support. It may also involve a shift in the terms of personal relationships, from a 'one-down' position of needing care, to establishing connections with others that feel more mutual – having something to give as well as to receive.

Despite this, power issues have tended to be sidelined within the domi-nant ways in which mental distress has been understood within modern society. They can be largely absent from the biomedical discourse of 'mental illness' that seeks to describe mental distress primarily in terms of some inter-nal pathology. They can be absent from many psychological accounts, including both psychoanalytic and cognitive behavioural approaches, which can ascribe dysfunction to internal difficulties relating to people's irrational drives or belief systems. However, some have sought to link these difficulties with the power-laden contexts in which people may have come to internalise potentially destructive or self-limiting drives and beliefs – and I will explore how this may provide a crucial dimension in understanding mental distress.

Power does not operate in a vacuum – its possibilities, its influences and its effects depend on the specific construction of the social order. As societies have changed from traditional to modern forms, madness and mental distress have come to be viewed in very different ways. Within modern societies, ratio-nality has come to be prized as the arbiter of economic efficiency and effective social functioning – and so irrationality has been seen as a potential threat to social stability. This may be seen as having a particular impact on how people defined as mentally distressed may be situated within social power relations.

What is power and how does it operate?

For something that seems so familiar within our everyday experience, there is remarkably little consensus as to what power actually is or how it operates in the ways that it does. Within modernist thought, power has usually been construed as some form of an individual attribute or status – as a 'thing' to be possessed (Westwood, 2002 p.1). Max Weber defined it as 'the capacity of an individual to realise his will', potentially 'even against the opposition of others' (1968, p.1111). While such definitions of *power to* may echo the world view and aspirations of, say, 'white', upper-middle-class men, they may fail to engage with many less privileged people's lived experiences of injustice and oppression.

Instead of conceptualising power as a 'thing', more critical approaches have sought to examine power as a social relation between people, one that 'may potentially open up or close off opportunities for individuals or social groups' (Tew, 2002 p.165). This may involve accessing, or being denied access to, particular forms of social relationships and specific 'allocative and authoritative resources' (Giddens, 1994).

Within societies that are organised on the basis of unequal relations of power between individuals and social groups, being seen as 'different' from dominant cultural, social or economic norms may often turn out to be disadvantageous or injurious to one's well-being. Those in dominant positions may set up 'them–us' divisions which 'label "others" as inferior and legitimate the exercise of *power over* them' (Dominelli, 2002 p.18). Such *power over* can take the form of systematic oppression, exploitation or exclusion from dominant modes of social participation.

Nevertheless, it would be wrong to see those who may be subject to forms of oppression as lacking any possibility of exercising power for themselves. On the contrary, people may develop strategies for survival and influence that involve the creative deployment of a variety of forms of power. For many, everyday survival may depend on operating networks of mutual support and co-operation, whether involving the distribution and sharing of scarce material resources, offering mutual forms of understanding and emotional support, or establishing formal or informal organisations of solidarity by which to resist the oppressive or exclusionary actions of dominant groups. Such strategies of *power together* may come as 'second nature' to many women, working-class people and members of Black or ethnic minority groups (Jordan *et al.*, 1991). People who lack power may become adept at resisting or subverting the expectations that may be made of them, or the identities that they may be expected to perform – often in subtle and even unconscious ways. Such manoeuvres, sometimes construed as being 'difficult' or 'manipulative' by those in positions of relative dominance, may nevertheless represent some people's most realistic strategies for having any influence over their situation.

As a first step in making sense of the complexities of power, it may be helpful to construct a framework by which to understand some of the different ways in which power may operate. Following Foucault, it may be seen that, although power can be damaging or restrictive, it may also underpin possibilities for change and achievement, having the potential of 'adding to the capacities and abilities of individuals' (Helliwell and Hindess, 1999 p.90). This suggests one criterion by which to distinguish how power may be operating: is it *limiting* of opportunity or is it *productive* of new possibilities? A second criterion is to differentiate between the 'vertical' operation of *power over*, in which certain groups or individuals are situated in a position of dominance over, or are placed in charge of others, and the more lateral operation of *power together* that may emerge through the ways in which people interact with one another on the same level.

Using these as two key dimensions by which to analyse power, the matrix shown in Figure 4.1 may help to clarify the potentially complex and contradictory operation of power within a given situation (Tew, 2002 p.166). Each cell of the matrix may be seen to define a specific mode of power relations.

	POWER OVER	**POWER TOGETHER**
PRODUCTIVE MODES OF POWER	*PROTECTIVE POWER* Deploying power in order to safeguard vulnerable people and their possibilities for advancement	*CO-OPERATIVE POWER* Collective action, sharing, mutual support and challenge – through valuing commonality *and* difference
LIMITING MODES OF POWER	*OPPRESSIVE POWER* Exploiting differences to enhance own position and resources at the expense of others	*COLLUSIVE POWER* Banding together to exclude or suppress 'otherness' whether internal or external

Figure 4.1 Matrix of power relations

Each of these modes of power may potentially operate at a range of different scales, from the systematic division of societies into social groupings of 'us' and 'them', to localised and everyday interactions between individuals. Furthermore, as will be explored later, power relations may not just operate 'out there', but may also become internalised within how we are constructed as individuals.

Limiting modes of power and the negative construction of social difference

In modern societies, where diversity exists within a context of oppressive forms of *power over*, certain social differences may become constructed by those in dominant positions as the 'markers' of superiority and inferiority. This may lead to systematic patterns of inequality on the basis of characteristics such as gender, race or culture, class, age, disability and sexual orientation – with particular sections of society having secured positions of relative dominance by a range of economic, physical, ideological and other means (see, for example, Bradley, 1996; Crompton, 1993; Payne, 2000; Thompson, 1998). Such *oppressive power* may then be used to construct a lifestyle of privileged opportunity at the expense of those constructed as 'other', who may then face systematic forms of exploitation, abuse or social exclusion. The French sociologist, Pierre Bourdieu, moved beyond more conventional Marxist analyses of social class and economic capital, to identify a more complex array of social, cultural and symbolic 'capitals' to which different people may or may not have access (1987, 1989; see also Chapter 5). Life chances may be seen to depend, not just on membership of wider socio-economic groupings, but on more localised processes of relationship, culture, geography and social network, as well as the acquisition and performance of particular valued forms of identity or 'disposition'.

Although correlations are not entirely straightforward, people living with systematic experiences of oppression are more likely to suffer forms of mental distress or breakdown:

> In terms of the three main dimensions of power in the western capitalist nations – class, race and gender – there is considerable evidence to indicate that those at the powerless ends – the working class, black people and women – tend to be more prone to psychological problems. The precise extent to which this distribution is a product of these power relations is difficult to determine. That the relationship exists, however, seems clear. (Goodwin, 1997 p.76; see also Pilgrim and Rogers, 1999)

These themes are explored more fully in Chapters 7 to 9. In addition, once their distress has passed beyond some socially defined threshold, people may find themselves constructed within a stigmatised social category (the 'mentally ill') that is itself systematically oppressed and excluded by mainstream social groupings (Miles, 1987).

An understanding of the pervasiveness of processes of social oppression provides a useful context in which to locate both sociological ideas of deviance (Becker, 1963) and psychological concepts of stereotyping and prejudice (Billig, 1985; Pickering, 2001). Underlying inequalities of power may give force to, and may in turn be reinforced by, everyday processes of labelling and stigmatising those who are seen as 'different'. This may be seen as one of the core mechanisms through which oppressive *power over* is enforced in modern societies. Thus, for example, within a social context in which 'mental illness' comes to mark a category of social exclusion, harmless but different behaviour, such as talking to one's voices, may come to be labelled in extremely negative terms. Where the perspective of deviance theory may be particularly helpful is to show how quickly the imposition of a label (of 'nutter', 'mentally ill', 'schizophrenic', etc.) can come to define the whole person within lay or professional discourses, so that all their behaviour, beliefs and thoughts come to be seen as symptomatic of, and further evidence for, their label (Goffman, 1991).

Faced with such powerful forms of external definition, it becomes very hard not to internalise this. For example, the experience of the Hearing Voices movement in the UK has been that new members coming to a meeting may typically introduce themselves as 'I'm John. I'm a schizophrenic', and only later, after much support from other group members, start to reclaim a range of more positive identities, such as 'I'm John. I'm a Manchester City supporter. I am a father...' Hearing voices then becomes something that they do, from time to time – but no longer constitutes the basis of their defining their identity as belonging to a category of 'otherness'.

In order to protect their shared position of relative advantage, those in privileged positions may operate among themselves in ways that are *collusive*, constructing specific forms of *power together* through shared practices, social and cultural codes and common understandings that bind people together and secure their positions of dominance. These may involve processes whereby those who are seen as 'other' are discriminated against and are denied the opportunity to join their exclusive 'club'. While these may be made explicit, they may often be more covert, using social codes or markers to define who is, and is not, 'one of us' – and this may take place at any scale from the school playground to wider social groupings in society.

The existence of such exclusionary processes may be denied, or they may be rationalised and justified through constructing collusive ways of seeing which shift responsibility onto those who are victimised – defining inequalities as somehow natural or inevitable, resulting from the inherent inadequacies or wayward natures of those defined as 'other'. These dominant perspectives may be policed through disallowing the possibility of alternative viewpoints that might undermine the construction of oppressors' superiority, or suggest a continuity of common experiences and characteristics between 'us' and 'them'. While being up against any wall of collusion or discrimination may be hurtful and distressing, dealing with covert processes of collusion may have a particularly pernicious effect in undermining one's hold on reality (and therefore one's mental health), particularly if one is continually fed the line that whatever feels amiss is actually one's own fault – as is, for example, often the case for victims of childhood sexual abuse (see Chapter 6).

For those in dominant positions, such processes of banding together will tend to lack any true spirit of co-operativeness. They may be seen as alliances of strategic convenience which may be somewhat at odds with an underlying culture of competitiveness, in which people may be continually jostling with one another to attain higher positions within 'pecking orders' of hierarchical *power over*. Such a construction of identities would tend to militate against any exposure of feelings of vulnerability or the formation of deeper bonds of affection. In turn, this may have certain adverse consequences on the mental health of people occupying relatively privileged positions in society – and this is discussed in more detail later in this chapter.

While there has sometimes been a tendency to view power as 'monolithic, unidirectional and oppressive' (Proctor, 2002 p.40), and to construct those who may be subject to forms of oppression or exclusion as social 'victims', historical analysis reveals that power relations are continually shifting as oppression is contested or subverted, both on a macro-societal scale and, just as importantly, as identities and relationships are renegotiated between individuals and small-scale social groups (Weedon, 1997). Power may be seen as something that is always present in the everyday discourses and interactions that take place between people. These may, often outside awareness, be 'colonised...by more general mechanisms' that set one party in a position of *power over* the other (Foucault, 1980b p.99). In turn, such controlling tendencies may be met with, or provoke, particular localised responses – and the outcomes of such micro-conflicts may potentially adhere together and provide the impetus for larger-scale social change, as it can be 'the strategic codification of these points of resistance that makes a revolution possible' (Foucault, 1981 p.96).

What is crucial in Foucault's account, and is taken up and developed by Judith Butler (1993, 1997), is the insight that such resistances may not be straightforward and intentional acts of will, but may be more complex refusals to play out exactly the (gender, cultural, 'sane'…) identities that are expected of us – and so our resistances may often take place outside our conscious awareness. However, every time we get our performance 'wrong', ever so slightly, we may start to blur the boundaries of the social categories by which we are identified – and thereby challenge some of the certainties which are crucial in maintaining oppressive aspects of the current social order.

Productive modes of power

Exploring ideas of alliance and solidarity, authors such as Hannah Arendt (1963) and Janet Surrey (1991) have suggested that *power together* with others may be a more effective strategy for mobilising energies, strengths and resources than unco-ordinated instances of people asserting their individualised *power to*. It is this that may be seen to underpin the success of social movements from trade unionism and feminism, through to more recent examples such as eco-warriors and Mad Pride. However, conventional notions of group solidarity have tended to be founded on somewhat limiting assumptions of common identities, with rather narrow and unidimensional definitions of the 'struggle' in which people are engaged. For example, many women and gay people have felt excluded from a trade unionism that was founded on the somewhat macho image of the working man. Similarly, working-class and Black women did not always find a place for the diversity of their identities within the feminist struggles of the 1970s and 1980s. Thus, while such solidarities were successful in furthering certain aspects of social emancipation, their long-term effectiveness was compromised by their tendencies to fall into certain *collusive* patterns of 'us' and 'them' identities that were unable to embrace internal or external diversity. Thus, paradoxically, 'solidarity constructed around some shared characteristics may have the effect of reproducing existing inequalities' (Crow, 2002 p.6; see also Llewelyn-Davies, 1978).

Perhaps the greatest potential of *co-operative power* lies in its ability to view difference as an opportunity rather than a threat. Instead of difference being an excuse for playing out a politics of superiority and inferiority, it may be embraced as a resource for change and movement. Indeed the very dynamism and energy of *co-operative power* may be seen to stem as much from mutual challenge as from mutual support, so that difference within social relationships may be seen as enhancing of possibilities. In practice, achieving such forms of *co-operative power* within a society dominated by oppressions and inequalities is no easy task. There is a need to build social movements that can draw their dynamism from dialogues around '*both* points of commonality and difference' (Barton, 1996 pp.185–186).

An interesting example of the development of *co-operative power* and dialogue across difference may be seen in the recent struggles by people with mental distress to contest their social and political construction as a category of intrinsically dangerous 'others' who require ever more pervasive forms of compulsion in order to police and control them. The formation of the Mental Health Alliance provided a collective voice of resistance which, at least temporarily, caused the government to rethink its plans for a more coercive Mental Health Act. Through establishing a dialogue with professional groups, including those who had traditionally taken on parts of this policing role, mental health user groups and voluntary organisations started to transcend, and establish *co-operative power* across, certain previously entrenched 'us' and 'them' divisions. The consequent blurring of 'mentally ill' and professional identities may be seen, in turn, to have provided a context for the current President of the Royal College of Psychiatrists to be 'out' about his own experience of service use – a small but significant turning point in contesting the 'othering' of people with mental distress.

Protective power may also be seen to approach questions of difference in a non-abusive way. Instead of utilising others' (perhaps temporary) disability or vulnerability in order to further one's own advantage, *protective power* may be deployed to shield them from potential abuse, exploitation or exclusion. Effective protection is not based on repeated acts of rescue or a mindless crusade to eliminate 'risk' – which may generate increasing dependence by undermining people's already diminished resources and abilities to control their lives – but must aim to reflect the wishes and preferences of those who are vulnerable, and to maximise their capabilities through, among other strategies, supporting controlled risk taking (see Chapter 10). *Protective power* involves giving people space in which to develop their capacities to take power for themselves, not wrapping them up in cotton wool.

The complex issue of how it feels to be (supposedly) protected for one's own safety is a very real issue for those subject to compulsion under the Mental Health Act. Research indicates that it may only be a minority who, reflecting on their experience, would see it as something that *felt* protective (Barnes, Davis and Tew, 2000). For many, any protective aspects may become overwhelmed by an oppressive sense of violation and infantilisation, and of forcible dislocation of already strained networks of *co-operative power* with family, friends and professional networks. A clearer understanding of how to operate *protective power* may be helpful in re-orienting legislation and practice in this area, with an increasing emphasis being given to offering a wider range of treatment options (and settings) that may be experienced as less disabling or invasive, and to supporting people in drawing up directives or care plans in advance, detailing what forms of protective interventions may be most (or least) helpful on the basis of past experience, and who they may wish to be involved in overseeing their care.

The internalisation of power relations: resilience, vulnerability and crisis

Psychological research has suggested that personal resilience, and the ability to take part in social networks characterised by relationships of mutual recognition and support, may depend on having had 'good' earlier attachments with parents and others in protective roles (Bowlby, 1988; Rutter, 1990; Taylor, 1997). Locating this within a context of power relations, it may be seen that people's experiences of *protective* and *co-operative power* may become internalised within the construction of their personalities or identities.

It would seem likely that those who may have been in receipt of effective and enabling deployments of *protective power* may internalise capacities and strategies for self-nurturing in situations of oppression or collusion. Similarly, those familiar with contexts of *co-operative power* may internalise an openness to giving and receiving support, and a tendency not to feel threatened by difference. In such ways, experiences of productive forms of power may be re-enacted as forms of self-organisation that are relatively empowering – resulting in an enhanced capacity to resist victimisation and an in-built orientation towards mobilising *co-operative* or *protective* modes of power.

By contrast, a person who has faced prolonged exposure at the receiving end of oppressive or collusive forms of power may internalise, as part of their self-image, the attributions of 'otherness' and inferiority to which they may be subjected, lacking sufficient support or social resources with which to contest these. They may learn to lower their aspirations accordingly, leading to 'learned helplessness', low self-esteem and depression (Proctor, 2002;

Seligman, 1974). Beyond this, evidence suggests that those who are already in situations of relative powerlessness may then be more likely to suffer more extreme forms of victimisation, such as sexual abuse, and these are implicated as contributory factors leading to many forms of mental distress and 'personality disorder' (see Chapter 6).

People in subordinated power positions may not only have to suffer instances of injustice or abuse, but may also be denied any opportunity to express their hurt and anger about what has happened to them (Baker Miller, 1983). It may not only be the *collusive* practices of those in positions of superior power which may punish, ignore or disbelieve such expressions of emotional pain; there may also be *collusive* patterns of expectation within the culture of oppressed groups that construct such events as inevitable, as things that have to be endured without protest (Lipsky, 1987). Linking this to a psychodynamic perspective, it may be seen how, if experiences of trauma and oppression cannot be expressed and acknowledged within relations of *protective* or *co-operative power*, they may become suppressed and embedded internally as a knot of unresolved feelings of anger, shame and self-blame (Tew, 2002 p.189). Holding down such a 'hot potato', while simultaneously trying to live up to the expectations of daily life, may be at some personal cost, and this may be reflected in the form of a 'distress pattern' which may comprise some combination of rigid, destructive or ineffective feelings, thoughts and behaviours (Lipsky, 1987). Distress patterns may best be understood as being, at one and the same time, our best available survival strategy and a somewhat oblique signalling of the fact that all is not well within (see Chapter 1).

Living with internalised oppressive or collusive relations of power may impede us in the performance of the tasks of everyday life, and may intrude into our interpersonal relationships. For some of us, culturally available opportunities for *co-operative power* may equip us with sufficient resources by which to cope with, and even resolve, some of what may be held inside – and also to withstand continuing experiences of oppression and social exclusion. For others of us, our ongoing distress patterns may tend to be reinforced by the very actions and interactions that we may undertake in order to live with our internal conflicts and survive in the external world as best we can (see Chapter 6). We may then, perhaps precipitated by some 'last straw' experience, reach a point of crisis or breakdown in which both the suppressed 'hot potato', and the distress pattern that may surround it, start to take over, apparently with an energy of their own (Tew, 2002).

Those who are inducted into positions of relative privilege may be invited to take on identities that take dominance for granted. As was suggested earlier, living out dominant roles may require an exclusion of any feelings of neediness, vulnerability or tenderness from one's identity. If they cannot be tolerated in oneself, characteristics such as vulnerability, irrationality, stupidity or immorality may be 'relegated and projected onto all subordinate groups' (Baker Miller, 1988 p.47; see also Lucey and Reay, 2000). Using such a psychodynamic perspective, it may be seen how, for example, women and Black people have been forced into being the repositories for disowned feelings of 'soul' and emotional sensitivity, while at the same time being treated as inferior because they were in the position of 'holding' such characteristics. In the same way, people experiencing mental distress may have little choice but to become repositories for the irrationalities and terrors that supposedly 'well' people cannot tolerate in themselves – and thereby they are landed with a 'double whammy' of hostility and revulsion from 'well' people who are trying to project their own emotional 'hot potatoes' as far away from themselves as possible.

However, maintaining such dominance may exert a price in terms of people's mental health. Insertion within the competitive relations of power hierarchies can induct people into individualised, self-seeking identities which would tend to rule out possibilities for trust, intimacy or *co-operative power*. Systems of *collusive power* may become transposed into internalised patterns of prejudice towards, and stereotyping of, those defined as 'other' – thereby imposing a rigidity of belief and perception (Pickering, 2001). Any significant deviation from the rules of conduct that are required may lead to being perceived as weak, or as a threat to the established order – thereby legitimating the predatory advances of others. The underlying fear of such a downfall, and increasingly desperate efforts to live up to expectations, may exacerbate distortions of identities and relationships to the point where some form of breakdown may occur.

Citizenship, rationality and the demonisation of mental distress

With the emergence of modern forms of social relations after the Enlightenment, discourses of reason and citizenship may be seen to have taken the place of traditional forms of authority (such as allegiance to God and King) as the guarantor of social morality and cohesion. Enfranchising more of the population in participatory citizenship, and a belief in rational debate and the power of argument, may be seen to have underpinned emancipatory tendencies within modernity, such as representative democracy. However, ideas of citizenship and rationality have also been deployed in a more covert fashion, both to regulate potential dissidence, and to legitimate forms of discrimination and injustice (Venn, 1997).

In order to be recognised as a citizen, and thereby have the freedom to participate fully in modern societies, one has had to demonstrate a particular capacity for self-regulation. One has not only to appear rational, but also to act, in the main, as a unitary, consistent socio-economic subject – apparently free and self-directing, but actually behaving in a relatively predictable manner, sticking to commitments and taking responsibility for one's actions. In this way, one may be inducted into taking a very active, although largely unconscious, role in imposing particular ways of thinking and acting upon oneself. Social and economic opportunities may come with the price of particular forms of conformity and self-disciplining. It is through such paradoxes that individuals may be led to believe that they are the authors of their own *power to*, when they are in fact 'one of its prime effects' as they actively 'choose' to play out the requisite role of the 'docile subject' (Foucault, 1980a p.98).

Not only may modernist citizenship impose particular forms of self-oppression, it may also constitute categories of social inclusion and exclusion. Prejudicial assumptions as to who did and did not possess the necessary capacity for reason have been used to define who could legitimately occupy positions of power and authority, or even participate in meaningful citizenship at all within modern societies (Pateman, 1988; Venn, 1997). Members of dominant groups have been able to construct superior identities as 'rational' and 'responsible' by playing these off against subordinate identities onto which opposite characteristics may be projected (Rattansi, 1997). Thus, in the early modern period, it was constructed as 'common sense' that women, working-class people and Black people would be so dominated by 'base' emotions or animal instincts that it would be dangerous to allow them full social, political or economic emancipation. Only slowly have these ideological positions been modified, allowing some limited opportunity for certain members of excluded groups to access positions of citizenship, although not always on an equal basis (see Lister, 1997). But to enter such roles, they too would have to demonstrate their commitment to construct themselves in the mould of the 'modern subject': living out the pretence of being at all times consistent, responsible, accountable and, above all, rational.

Whereas expressions of intuition, spontaneity or passion could be seen as part of everyday life in traditional societies, or even valued as sources of spiritual truth and inspiration, they came to be seen as threatening to a modern social order that required rational and coherent subjects. If such expressions were not suppressed or marginalised, the legal and ethical basis for civil society could be undermined, and the ideological basis for dominant groups to carry on occupying positions of power and authority might be brought into question. It is in this context that mental distress may be seen to have posed particular problems for modernity. Conducting oneself on the basis of apparently irrational insights, overwhelming or volatile emotions and 'abnormal' behaviour could be 'deemed inimical to society or the state – indeed could be regarded as a menace to the proper workings of an orderly, efficient, progressive, rational society' (Porter, 1987 p.15).

In response to situations where processes of self-regulation may be seen to be fragile or breaking down, modernity has required strategies for 'correcting' deviance and rehabilitating people as rational and docile subjects. This has typically been achieved through devolving power to a burgeoning army of professionals, whose role it is to induce and coerce people into conformity within an array of medical, educational, legal, psychological and social care discourses – ideally in a way that avoids the naked threat of force as far as possible and within a social construction in which professionals are seen as acting in people's best interests (Foucault, 1967, 1977).

Professional discourses have sought to neutralise the power implications of mental distress and of societal responses to it. Distress becomes cast as an infirmity or illness – an individual misfortune without social causation, which might arise simply by bad luck, or as a result of a person's genetic weakness or moral laxity. The power of rational or scientific discourses has been deployed to specify, and define as the symptoms of 'mental illness', forms of apparent irrationality that might otherwise disturb the veneer of social order that was vital to the project of modernity (Foucault, 1972 p.32). In this way, angry discordant outbursts, or refusals of expected social roles could simply be read as 'symptoms' of illness or as reflecting dysfunctional belief systems – which could best be treated or managed by psychiatric or psychological interventions.

While apparently removing questions of power from the treatment of the 'mentally ill', modernist practice has established a new power-laden dichotomy between 'us' and 'them': it is professionals who are seen as having knowledge and expertise, while the insights and understandings of those experiencing mental distress are to be systematically ignored or devalued (see Chapter 2). However, in recent years there has been an interesting shift in the terms of the dominant discourse (not just in relation to mental health, but also affecting criminal justice and child protection). While maintaining an ethos of 'doing unto' rather than 'doing with', there is less emphasis on interventions defined in terms of treatment or care and a new focus of professional expertise and activity around risk assessment and risk management (Parton, 1991; see also Chapter 10).

Thus, instead of the political and ideological threat posed by mental distress being neutralised in apparently benign professional discourses as an 'illness to be treated', it has become increasingly transposed into an embodied form as physical dangerousness. 'Them' and 'us' distinctions are recreated as people experiencing mental distress are now to be seen primarily as a 'risk' rather than an 'illness' – as an alien menace lurking in the shadows and waiting to harm 'normal' citizens (Laurance, 2003). It is important to recognise that this discursive shift has taken place at a time when, in reality, there has been no increase in the proportion of homicides committed by people experiencing mental distress, and research has shown that it is social factors, such as substance misuse or unstable family circumstances, rather than any categories of medical diagnosis, that correlate most closely with the risk of violence (Monahan, 1993; Taylor and Gunn, 1999).

Empowerment and recovery

Just as power relations may be seen to be implicated in the construction of mental distress and in societal responses to it, so restructuring power may be seen to be an integral part of processes of recovery. If recovery is to be defined holistically, rather than just in terms of remission of symptoms, then it may be seen to involve aspects of personal and social empowerment (see Chapter 11). Using the matrix of power outlined earlier, this may be understood in terms of shifts from being caught up within limiting forms of *oppressive* or *collusive power* – both internalised and within current patterns of social and professional relationships – to receiving nurturing and facilitative forms of *protective power*, and discovering opportunities for constructing relations of *co-operative power* with others.

Such shifts may need to be gradual and incremental, given the reality of people's likely starting points in terms of depleted social and personal resources. Sources of oppression are not usually overcome at a stroke, nor are exclusionary barriers broken through in one concerted act of confrontation. Instead of challenging patterns of oppression or collusive social attitudes 'head on', more lateral (and gentler) strategies for developing possibilities for *protective* or *co-operative power* may be more likely to succeed (see Tew, 2002). Part of the change process may need to be internal – identifying self-destructive or self-limiting distress patterns, accepting them as strategies that may have been crucial for survival at one time, but recognising that they may now be creating more problems than they are solving. Recovery may also involve taking the risk of emerging from the paradoxical safety of colluding with (and even exaggerating) one's own powerlessness (see Coleman, 1999). Some of the change process may be external – starting to deploy more effective forms of *protective* and *co-operative power* through renegotiating the terms of key personal, social and economic relationships, perhaps with support from particular friends, allies and professionals.

Bourdieu's notions of social and cultural capital, which broaden out Marxist notions of economic capital, may be useful here in identifying key resources and mapping out strategies for the journey from powerlessness and isolation to participation in valued social roles (1987, 1989; see also Chapter 5). However, it is important not to accept the existing social, cultural and symbolic order as given – as with the somewhat naïve assimilationist dream of 'normalisation' or social role valorisation (Wolfensberger, 1983) – and thereby inadvertently collude with some of the oppressive processes that may have contributed to people's distress in the first place.

Instead there may be a need to challenge (gently but persistently) the dominant identities and power relations of the mainstream. Recovery may need to entail an uncomfortable compromise between 'playing the game' to some extent in order to secure participation in key social discourses, while at the same time refusing to erase all the challenges, creative excitements and rejections of the current social order that may belong within the 'madder' parts of our identities. In doing so, we thereby challenge those playing out 'normal' identities to reconsider whether they may need to hold onto such rigid (and potentially self-limiting) constructions of how one is supposed to be.

Conclusion

From this discussion, it may be seen that power acts, often 'behind the scenes', in defining many aspects of our identities and social relationships. In its more negative forms (*oppressive* or *collusive power*), it may be seen to play a role in constructing social situations which may contribute to distress or breakdown – and, through its internalisation, it may become bound up in the form taken by people's distress. In its more positive forms (*protective* or *co-operative power*), it starts to define the territory for effective partnership working, anti-oppressive practice and the enabling of recovery and social inclusion. This discussion in relation to the use of professional authority is taken further in Chapter 7.

An analysis of power relations can add a crucial dimension to sociological and psychological concepts such as stigma, resilience, trauma and social capital – providing them with a context in which they can become more effective tools for bringing about change, rather than simply serving as descriptors of the status quo. Awareness and clarity in relation to issues of power and powerlessness form the cornerstone of emancipatory mental health practice.

References

Arendt, H. (1963) *On Revolution.* London: Penguin.

Baker Miller, J. (1983) *The Construction of Anger in Women and Men.* Wellesley College MA: Work in Progress.

Baker Miller, J. (1988) *Towards a New Psychology of Women (Second Edition).* Harmondsworth: Pelican.

Barnes, M., Davis, A. and Tew, J. (2000) 'Valuing experience: users' experiences of compulsion under the 1983 Mental Health Act.' *Mental Health Review 5,* 3, 11–14.

Barton, L. (1996) 'Citizenship and disabled people: a cause for concern?' In J. Demaine and H. Entwistle (eds) *Beyond Communitarianism: Citizenship, Politics and Education.* Basingstoke: Macmillan.

Becker, H. (1963) *Outsiders: Studies in the Sociology of Deviance.* Basingstoke: Macmillan.

Billig, M. (1985) 'Prejudice, categorisation and particularisation.' *European Journal of Social Psychology 15,* 79–103.

Bourdieu, P. (1987) 'What makes a social class? On the theoretical and practical existence of groups.' *Berkeley Journal of Sociology 22,* 1–18.

Bourdieu, P. (1989) 'Social space and symbolic power.' *Sociological Theory 7,* 14–25.

Bowlby, J. (1988) *A Secure Base: Clinical Applications of Attachment Theory.* London: Routledge.

Bradley, H. (1996) *Fractured Identities: Changing Patterns of Inequality.* Cambridge: Polity.

Browne, D. (1997) *Black People and 'Sectioning'.* London: Little Rock Publishing.

Butler, J. (1993) *Bodies that Matter.* New York: Routledge.

Butler, J. (1997) *Excitable Speech.* New York: Routledge.

Coleman, R. (1999) *Recovery: An Alien Concept.* Gloucester: Handsell.

Crompton, R. (1993) *Class and Stratification.* Cambridge: Polity.

Crow, G. (2002) *Social Solidarities.* Buckingham: Open University Press.

Dominelli, L. (2002) *Anti-oppressive Social Work Theory and Practice.* Basingstoke: Palgrave.

Foucault, M. (1967) *Madness and Civilisation.* London: Tavistock.

Foucault, M. (1972) *The Archaeology of Knowledge.* London: Tavistock.

Foucault, M. (1977) *Discipline and Punish: The Birth of the Prison.* London: Allen Lane.

Foucault, M. (1980a) *Power/Knowledge: Selected Interviews and Other Writings.* Brighton: Harvester.

Foucault, M. (1980b) *Herculin Barbin: Being the Recently Discovered Memoirs of a Nineteenth Century French Hermaphrodite.* New York: Pantheon.

Foucault, M. (1981) *The History of Sexuality, Vol. 1.* Harmondsworth: Penguin.

Giddens, A. (1994) *Beyond Left and Right: The Future of Radical Politics.* Stanford CA: Stanford University Press.

Goffman, E. (1991) *Asylums.* London: Penguin.

Goodwin, S. (1997) *Comparative Mental Health Policy.* London: Sage.

Helliwell, C. and Hindess, B. (1999) 'Power.' In S. Taylor (ed.) *Sociology: Issues and Debates.* Basingstoke: Palgrave.

Jordan, J., Kaplan, A., Baker Miller, J., Stiver, I. and Surrey, J. (1991) *Women's Growth in Connection.* New York: Guilford.

Laurance, J. (2003) *Pure Madness: How Fear Drives the Mental Health System.* London: Routledge.

Lawrence, M. (1984) *The Anorexic Experience.* London: Women's Press.

Lipsky, S. (1987) *Internalised Racism.* Seattle: Rational Island Publishers.

Lister, R. (1997) *Citizenship: Feminist Perspectives.* Basingstoke: Macmillan.

Llewelyn-Davies, M. (1978) 'Two contexts of solidarity among pastoral Maasai women.' In P. Caplan and J. Bujra (eds) *Women United, Women Divided: Cross-Cultural Perspectives on Female Solidarity.* London: Tavistock.

Lucey, H. and Reay, D. (2000) 'Social class and the psyche.' *Soundings 15,* 139–154.

Miles, A. (1987) *The Mentally Ill in Contemporary Society.* Oxford: Blackwell.

Monahan, J. (1993) 'Dangerousness: an American perspective.' In J. Gunn and P. Taylor (eds) *Forensic Psychiatry.* London: Butterworth-Heinemann.

Parton, N. (1991) *Governing the Family: Child Care, Child Protection and the State.* Basingstoke: Macmillan.

Pateman, C. (1988) *The Sexual Contract.* Cambridge: Polity.

Payne, G. (2000) *Social Divisions.* Basingstoke: Macmillan.

Pickering, M. (2001) *Stereotyping: The Politics of Representation.* Basingstoke: Palgrave.

Pilgrim, D. and Rogers, A. (1999) *A Sociology of Mental Health and Illness.* Buckingham: Open University Press.

Porter, R. (1987) *A Social History of Madness: Stories of the Insane.* London: Weidenfield and Nicholson.

Proctor, G. (2002) *The Dynamics of Power in Counselling and Psychotherapy.* Ross on Wye: PCCS Books.

Rattansi, A. (1997) 'Postcolonialism and its discontents.' *Economy and Society 26,* 4, 480–500.

Rutter, M. (1990) 'Psychosocial resilience and protective mechanisms.' In J. Rolf, A. Masten, D. Cicchetti, K. Neuchterlein and S. Weintraub (eds) *Risk and Protective Factors in the Development of Psychopathology.* New York: Cambridge University Press.

Seligman, M. (1974) 'Depression and learned helplessness.' In R. Friedman and M. Katz (eds) *The Psychology of Depression: Contemporary Theory and Research.* Washington DC: Winston.

Surrey, J. (1991) 'Relationship and empowerment.' In J. Jordan, A. Kaplan, J. Baker Miller, I. Stiver and J. Surrey *Women's Growth in Connection.* New York: Guildford.

Taylor, P. and Gunn, J. (1999) 'Homicides by people with mental illness: myth and reality.' *British Journal of Psychiatry 174,* 9–14.

Taylor, S. (1997) 'Social integration, social support and health.' In S. Taylor and D. Field (eds) *Sociology of Health and Health Care (Second Edition).* Oxford: Blackwell.

Tew, J. (2002) *Social Theory, Power and Practice.* Basingstoke: Palgrave.

Thompson, N. (1998) *Promoting Equality.* Basingstoke: Macmillan.

Venn, C. (1997) 'Beyond enlightenment? After the subject of Foucault, who comes?' *Theory, Culture and Society 14*, 3, 1–26.

Warner, R. (1994) *Recovery from Schizophrenia: Psychiatry and Political Economy.* New York: Routledge.

Weber, M. (1968) *Economy and Society Vol. 1.* New York: Bedminster Press.

Weedon, C. (1997) *Feminist Practice and Poststructuralist Theory (Second Edition).* Oxford: Blackwell.

Westwood, S. (2002) *Power and the Social.* London: Routledge.

Wolfensberger, W. (1983) 'Social role valorisation.' *Mental Retardation 21*, 6, 234–239.

CHAPTER 5

Social Capital and Mental Health

Martin Webber

Introduction

Social scientists and policy makers have seized upon the concept of social capital as a panacea for the post-modern disintegration of grand social theory. It has consequently been applied to fields as diverse as international development (World Bank, 2003), democracy and governance (Putnam, 1993) and population health profiles (Kawachi *et al.*, 1997). However, the concept has multiple definitions and dimensions, creating a conceptual minefield that is almost too treacherous to explore.

This chapter will survey this territory to uncover the origins of the concept and the key dimensions of social life to which it refers. It will explore its relevance to mental health and contribute to the emerging debates in the empirical literature, which are still in their infancy. Some tentative conclusions will be reached about its potential use for mental health practitioners and service users.

Conceptual origins

Social capital refers to the social context of people's lives. The key dimensions it encompasses include trust (Coleman, 1988), social norms and reciprocity (Putnam, 2000), features of social structures and networks (Burt, 1992; Lin, 2001b) and the resources embedded within them (Bourdieu, 1997). Its contemporary origins can be traced to two sociologists, Pierre Bourdieu and James Coleman, and the American political scientist Robert Putnam. Although there is not space for a full conceptual review here (see Baron, Field and Schuller, 2000, for a good critical introduction), it is important to understand the contribution made by these key figures.

Pierre Bourdieu

The influence of Bourdieu in the development of the concept of social capital is often under-stated. This is likely to be because his work is steeped in heavy abstraction, a characteristic of French social theory, undoubtedly a deterrent to more empirically minded British and American intellectuals (Fine, 2001).

The first English translation of Bourdieu's treatment of the concept was contained in a text on the sociology of education. In this, he defined social capital as 'the aggregate of the actual or potential resources which are linked to possession of a durable network of more or less institutionalised relationships of mutual acquaintance or recognition' (Bourdieu, 1986 p.248). His treatment of the concept is instrumental, focusing on the benefits accruing to individuals by virtue of participation in groups.

Portes (1998) identified two essential elements of his definition. First, there is the social relationship itself, which allows individuals to claim access to resources possessed by their associates. Second, there is the amount and quality of those resources (Portes, 1998). These resources are characterised by the notion of 'capital', which refers to the capacity to exercise control over one's own future and that of others. As such, it is a form of power. For example, through social capital individuals can gain access to economic capital (e.g. cheap loans), and they can increase their cultural capital through contacts with experts (e.g. academics) or by affiliating to institutions which confer valued credentials (e.g. political parties). In short, the powerful remain powerful by virtue of their contacts with other powerful people.

James Coleman

Coleman developed his ideas about social capital through empirical work on the relationship between educational achievement and social inequality. For him, 'social capital constitutes a particular kind of resource available to an actor' (Coleman, 1988 p.98). Conceptualised and refined within an educational framework, 'social capital is the set of resources that inhere in family relations and in community social organisation and that are useful for the cognitive or social development of a child or young person' (Coleman, 1994 p.300).

In contrast to Bourdieu, Coleman extended the scope of the concept to encompass the social relationships of non-elite groups. He argued that social relations constituted useful capital resources for actors through processes such as establishing obligations, expectations and trustworthiness, creating channels for information, and setting norms backed by efficient sanctions

(Coleman, 1988). For example, 'if A does something for B and trusts B to reciprocate in the future, this establishes an expectation in A and an obligation on the part of B to keep the trust. This obligation can be conceived of as a "credit slip" held by A to be redeemed by some performance by B' (Coleman, 1994 p.310).

Coleman focused largely on kinship and neighbourhood, as his primary interest was schooling. He has been criticised for over-emphasising close ties, to the neglect of weaker ties which might prove more effective in providing access to new knowledge and resources (Portes, 1998). However, his work was a central source for Putnam, who has since popularised the concept.

Robert Putnam

Putnam's seminal study on social capital was on the rather unlikely topic of regional government in Italy (Putnam, 1993). In this he argued that civic traditions in the north of Italy promoted the growth of voluntary organisations, norms and trust which made possible good governance, legitimate democratic government, as well as economic growth, in contrast to the south of the country.

Transferring his attention to his native US, Putnam investigated the perceived decline in civic engagement. In an evocative paper entitled 'Bowling Alone' (Putnam, 1995), he used the example of the decline in the number of bowling clubs. He argued that these served not just as recreational channels but as sustainers of the wider social fabric. Together with analyses of attitudes and behaviour, he identified a general secular decline in levels of social capital and put the blame on television for distracting people from opportunities for social engagement.

Putnam subsequently conceptualised social capital as 'features of social life – networks, norms, and trust – that enable participants to act together more effectively to pursue shared objectives' (Putnam, 1996 p.34). Social capital became characterised as the 'glue' which holds societies together by collective efficacy, social trust/reciprocity, participation in voluntary organisations and social integration for mutual benefit (Lochner, Kawachi and Kennedy, 1999). Putnam's definition viewed social capital as a contextual property of communities rather than an individual trait. Its benefits are hypothesised to affect everyone equally within that community, regardless of differences in individual behaviour or values.

Social capital and public health

A number of mental health researchers (e.g. McKenzie, Whitley and Weich, 2002, Sartorius, 2003) accept Putnam's work almost uncritically and argue that social capital benefits all members of a community equally. They suggest that it is a 'public good' arising from participation in civic activities, mutually beneficial norms of reciprocity and the trust people place in other members of the community. This conception of social capital has two essential elements – structural and cognitive components. The former refers to regulated networks that foster mutually beneficial relationships, whereas the latter is the value system that is shared by members of a community and fosters participation in social relationships.

The cognitive component of social capital is best explained by looking at its horizontal and vertical links. First, a distinction is often made between 'bonding' and 'bridging' forms of horizontal social capital. Bonding social capital relies on strong ties between people. It is inward-focused and characterised by homogeneity, loyalty and exclusivity. An example is London's Chinatown, which is characterised by a dense concentration of Chinese firms employing a significant proportion of their co-ethnic labour force.

Bonding social capital can be good for mental health through its close relationships and a mutual responsibility for caring for vulnerable members of the community. The well-developed norms of trust and reciprocity in such communities may affect help-seeking behaviour to the extent that a high proportion of people seek help when unwell. In a US study, for example, Hendryx and Ahern (2001) found that people living in areas high in social capital accessed mental health services more than those with low social capital. These areas may also provide better mental health services. In another US study, for example, communities with high social capital provided better housing for homeless people with mental health problems, although this did not necessarily lead to significant improvements in their health (Rosenheck *et al.*, 2001).

Bonding social capital has a significant downside as a tightly knit homogeneous community might be one intolerant of individual diversity (Baum, 1999). This could possibly explain why the incidence of schizophrenia among people from non-White ethnic minorities is greater in neighbourhoods where they constitute a smaller proportion of the total population (Boydell *et al.*, 2001). A pilot study has found that people who live in areas with high perceived community safety have higher hospital readmission rates (McKenzie, 2000). This could be due to the local community viewing people with mental health problems as potentially dangerous and being less tolerant of them. The most extremely bonded communities or groups, such as religious cults or mafia families, further exemplify how bonding social capital is not necessarily a public good.

Bridging social capital, in contrast, links diverse groups and people. It is characterised by weak ties and has an outward focus. Examples are business associates, friends of friends or internet virtual encounters. It is likely to foster social inclusion and is generally viewed as positive.

Bridging social capital is the process whereby people with mental health problems can develop social connections with diverse groups and people. It is commonly recognised that this form of social capital is useful for finding employment (Stone, Gray and Hughes, 2003). For example, people involved in groups or volunteering are likely to interact with people they do not know, who in turn may have links with a range of work environments. As employment is key to many conceptions of social inclusion (Stewart, 2000), it can often mean the difference between 'inclusion' and 'exclusion' for some people. This is particularly true for people with mental health problems who face discrimination both at work and in the welfare benefits system (Cullen *et al.*, 2004; Office of the Deputy Prime Minister, 2004). Implicit in the UK government's Social Exclusion Unit focus on mental health is the development of bridging forms of social capital to foster the inclusion of people with mental health problems (Social Exclusion Unit, 2003).

'Vertical' social capital is often distinguished from 'horizontal' social capital by virtue of the connections being made within a hierarchical structure to government and other institutions, rather than within and between communities. Vertical social capital provides a community's institutional integration and, together with bridging forms of social capital, equates to an inclusive and cohesive society (Colletta and Cullen, 2000).

The effect of vertical social capital on mental health is under-researched, but it is possible that it is associated with a community's aggregated socioeconomic status. For example, some relatively deprived inner-London council estates with high rates of mental health problems have high horizontal and low vertical social capital (Cornwell, 1984; Whitley, 2003). Or, in other words, these communities have a multitude of social relations but few to people in positions of power. A contrasting group, for example, are the freemasons who are generally of higher socio-economic status and are very well connected to people in positions of power (high vertical social capital). However, little is known about their mental health.

The cognitive component of social capital appears to relate to Putnam's ideas about altruism and civic responsibility (Putnam, 1996, 2000). It is commonly measured in surveys by aggregating responses to questions about trust, reciprocity and perceptions of civic engagement and seems to have a complex relationship with structural social capital.

Structural social capital provides the context for the development of mutually beneficial relationships. These are often networks governed by rules and procedures. The most frequently used measure of structural social capital is voluntary group membership, closely following Putnam's ideas. For example, in Italy he found a good correlation between the number of choral societies and the efficiency of the local health management system (Putnam, 1993). The precise relationship between cognitive and structural social capital is not known. However, it seems that both forms of social capital can erode fast and be destroyed fairly quickly, compared to the building up of such capital, which takes time (Uphoff, 2000).

What is the evidence?

Social capital is considered to be important for health. On the one hand, it is thought that communities rich in social capital may promote health-enhancing behaviours (Campbell, Wood and Kelly, 1999). On the other, people living in communities with high levels of social capital are more likely to have high levels of perceived control over their lives. People who feel more in control of their lives are more likely to take control of their health and access health services (Wilkinson, 1996).

US social epidemiologists have used the area-based conception of social capital to explore these regional variations in health (Berkman and Kawachi, 2000). In the tradition of Durkheim (1951), they hypothesised that social context has an effect on the health of the whole community or area studied. Their work has taken a variety of proxy measures of social capital with a geographical area as the locus (Lochner *et al.*, 1999). For example, applying Putnam's (1995) indicators of social capital to the US General Social Survey, Kawachi and colleagues (1997) found that lower levels of trust (a cognitive component) and group membership (a structural component) were associated with higher death rates.

A similar result has been found at a neighbourhood level in Chicago. Here, high levels of social capital, as measured by reciprocity, trust and civic participation, correlated with lower death rates (Lochner *et al.*, 2003). A positive relationship between state-level social capital and self-rated health has also been discovered in the US (Kawachi, Kennedy and Glass, 1999; Subramanian, Kawachi and Kennedy, 2001).

The same researchers found a similar correlation of social capital and health in Russia. Here, social capital – as measured by trust in local government, political participation, crime and divorce rates, and conflicts in the work place – accounted for a large proportion of the variation in mortality and life expectancy across the regions of the country (Kennedy, Kawachi and Brainerd, 1998).

There have been similar studies conducted in the UK. For example, Cooper *et al.* (1999) analysed data from the Health and Lifestyle Survey 1992 and the General Household Survey for 1994, taking six questions about local neighbourhoods as an index of social capital. They found a small association between social capital and health, with a more positive influence for men than for women. However, individual material living conditions and socio-economic status were much stronger predictors of ill health than social capital or social support.

Kawachi and Kennedy argue that the relationship between income inequality and mortality seems to be 'mediated through the withering of social capital' (Kawachi and Kennedy, 1997b p.1039). Or, in other words, social capital studies provide evidence to support the 'Wilkinson Hypothesis' of health inequalities. This suggests that the major determinant of differing levels of health status between areas lies in their degree of income inequality (Wilkinson, 1996). They argue that higher income inequality produces lowered social cohesion and trust, which in turn causes health problems (Kawachi and Kennedy, 1997a).

However, the model connecting health inequalities, social cohesion and health ignores class relations, a factor that might help explain how income inequalities are generated and account for both relative and absolute deprivation (Muntaner and Lynch, 1999). Lynch and colleagues (2001, 2000) argue that the interpretation of links between income inequality and health must begin with the structural causes of inequalities, and not just focus on perceptions of that inequality. Further, the importance of neo-liberalism in producing *both* higher income inequality and lower social cohesion is often ignored (Coburn, 2000).

Empirical work examining the association between social capital and mental health is less well developed and somewhat contradictory. The strongest evidence of an association is found in a UK study (McCulloch, 2001). This found that social capital, as measured by perceptions of the neighbourhood in which you live, appears to be related to common mental disorders such as depression or anxiety. McCulloch's analysis of data from the British Household Survey found that people with low social capital had an increased risk of suffering from mental health problems. It is not possible to infer causation due to the cross-sectional nature of this data. However, he highlights the contextual role of neighbourhoods, independent of the socio-economic status of its residents, in this pattern (McCulloch, 2003).

Other studies have found positive associations. For example, the Health Survey for England 2000 (Boreham, Stafford and Taylor, 2002) found an association between low levels of trust in people in general and common mental disorders such as depression or anxiety. In Russia, Rose (2000) found that social capital and measures of social integration had a substantial impact on self-rated emotional health. Further, a US survey indicated that perceptions of community problems are inversely correlated with psychological health (Hendryx and Ahern, 1997).

There has been some similar work looking at social capital as a risk factor for schizophrenia. Boydell *et al.* (2002) found an association between low levels of perceived social cohesion and high levels of social hostility, and higher rates of schizophrenia in a pilot study. It could be possible that social hostility and lack of social cohesion are risk factors for schizophrenia. Alternatively, they may be associated with other variables such as urbanicity, which is already believed to be a causative factor (e.g. Marcelis, Takei and van Os, 1999; van Os *et al.*, 2002, Pedersen and Mortensen, 2001).

In contrast, a number of studies have found no association between social capital and mental health. In Colombia, for example, a poor education or lack of employment explains more of the variation in the mental health of young people than cognitive social capital (Harpham, Grant and Rodriguez, 2004). Further, a study of Gospel Oak in north London, which has a particularly high prevalence of depression among older people in comparison with a number of areas in Europe (Copeland *et al.*, 1999), found that it had high levels of social capital (Whitley, 2003). Informal networks of friends, neighbours and relatives were a major source of social capital in Gospel Oak, similar to findings in Luton (Campbell *et al.*, 1999). This pattern has also been observed in communities that suffer socio-economic deprivation and high rates of mental disorder in east London (Cattell, 2001; Cornwell, 1984).

Although these are only relatively small studies of local communities, they do suggest that social capital, as a property of an area, is not a protective factor for mental health problems. It is more likely that the high prevalence of depression is caused by 'compositional' factors. Examples of these are local authority housing policies that place people with mental health problems within a specified geographical area, or other reasons that attract people who are vulnerable to mental health problems to the area, such as employment or affordable housing.

Conceptual and empirical limitations

The ecological concept of social capital has often been used without careful consideration of its meaning or definition. Woolcock (1998) has notably stated that it has been adopted indiscriminately, adapted uncritically and applied imprecisely. In particular, Putnam's conception of social capital has come under fierce criticism. Fine (2001, 2002) argues that it is definitionally imprecise, it ignores the reproduction and exercise of power as initially conceived by Bourdieu, and is built upon shaky empirical foundations. He disputes the casual bringing together of the complex notions of 'social' and 'capital', arguing that the concept is essentially meaningless.

Putnam's reliance on formal group membership as an indicator of social capital does not take into account informal groups or networks, important sources of social capital for many people (Schudson, 1996). This introduces a class bias to the conception, as people are more likely to report membership of a golf club than a street gang, for example (Forbes and Wainwright, 2001). For example, he excluded groups formed after 1967 such as those around civil rights, the environment and consumerism (Jackman and Miller, 1998). Further, Putnam's ideas about the nature of community do not stand up well to empirical scrutiny. For example, a study of social capital in Luton concluded that:

> Putnam's essentialist conceptualisation of a cohesive civic community bore a greater resemblance to people's romanticised reconstructions of an idealised past than to people's accounts of the complex, fragmented and rapidly changing face of contemporary community life – characterised by relatively high levels of mobility, instability and plurality. (Campbell *et al.*, 1999 p.156)

Social capital is often accepted uncritically as a public good, but it can be a mixed blessing (Portes and Landolt, 1996). It is perhaps ironic that Timothy McVeigh, convicted of the Oklahoma bombing in 1995, was a member of a bowling league with his co-conspirators (Levi, 1996). Also, homogeneous communities with strong ties and members obedient to social norms can be asphyxiating places to live in and exclusionary to outsiders (Baum, 1999). Such places are likely to be hostile to the development of community mental health facilities in their area, for example (Mind, 1997). Alternatively, industries with strong social ties, or characterised by 'old boy' networks, are likely to be unwelcoming of newcomers who do not know the 'right' people or are discriminatory towards people who are perceived as being 'different'. Further, working-class communities could be pathologised as having dysfunctional levels of social capital and either written off or subjected to centrally imposed government initiatives (e.g. Social Exclusion Unit, 1998).

There are empirical complications with this research that has implications for understanding the relationship between the ecological conceptualisation of social capital and mental health. First, the proxy measures of social capital are problematic and side-step the complexities of the concept (Portes, 1998). It is not possible to be certain that they are actually measuring social capital as they are giving, at best, a superficial view of the concept (Muntaner, Oates and Lynch, 1999). For example, the studies referred to above all use different proxy measures of social capital, including perceptions of local community (McCulloch, 2001), social cohesion and social hostility (Boydell *et al.*, 2002) and local surveys and voting records (Rosenheck *et al.*, 2001). It is not possible to conclude with certainty that they are measuring the same social phenomena.

Second, the use of cross-sectional survey data to measure social capital has been criticised as being methodologically and theoretically flawed (Forbes and Wainwright, 2001). As there are no true ecological measures of social capital, many studies (e.g. Veenstra, 2000) have relied upon aggregated individual outcomes to measure collective social capital. The upward extrapolation from aggregated individual level data to group level characteristics, known as the atomistic fallacy, is scientifically invalid (Diez Roux, 1998). For example, bringing together a number of brilliant football players into a team does not necessarily mean that the team will perform well together. Aggregated survey data often erroneously makes such assumptions. Survey data also tends to under-represent rural, working-class or marginalised communities (Graham, 1995).

Third, the multi-level statistical models used in a number of these studies do not account for 'selection effects' (Oakes, 2004). This refers to the effect of people's options about where they live being conditioned by social class or socio-economic status. For example, wealthy people will often choose to purchase expensive houses and middle-class people will often choose to live in middle-class neighbourhoods. Poorer people will have less choice about where to live, but will be excluded from wealthy neighbourhoods. It follows that an individual's socio-economic background, which is known to be associated with mental health, clouds the effect of a neighbourhood on their mental health as they are not there by chance alone.

Finally, a common problem with cross-sectional studies that measure eco-logical social capital is the difficulty in making inferences about causation. It is not possible to say whether low social capital causes mental health problems or whether low social capital results from aggregated mental distress. It is questionable, therefore, what conclusions can be reached from using survey data to examine the relationship between social capital and health. This is unfortunate, as most research about social capital and mental health has been in this tradition.

The social capital of individuals

A prevalent view in psychiatric epidemiology is that social capital can only be measured at the area level (McKenzie et al., 2002). However, a number of researchers dispute this claim (e.g. Pevalin, 2003; Webber and Huxley, 2004) and call for a move away from Putnam's broad conception of social capital to a more rigorously defined one that builds on Bourdieu's (1986) ideas about the acquisition and use of resources within social networks.

This approach shifts the focus from geographical areas to individuals. It takes a dynamic view of the concept and adopts a quasi-Marxist view of capital. Here, social capital is the 'investment in social relations by individuals through which they gain access to embedded resources to enhance expected returns of instrumental or expressive actions' (Lin, 2001a pp.17–19). For example, just as someone can invest money (financial capital) in a bank or the stock market and expect to get a return on their investment, people can invest in social relationships to gain access to the resources of other people (Hean et al., 2003).

This approach to social capital can be illustrated in terms of family struc-ture. In families where both parents work, each partner promotes the career and income of the other, leading to an accumulation of advantages (Bernasco, de Graaf and Ultee, 1997). However, the loss of social capital in one-parent families through divorce has a detrimental effect on the educational and occu-pational achievements of the children and of the divorced couple themselves (McLanahan, 1984). Further, research in Taiwan has shown that wives are more reliant on their husbands for access to social resources than visa versa (Fu, Lin and Chen, 2004). It is possible that the loss of these resources on divorce or separation may be more detrimental for women than men. An emerging research programme seeks to answer these questions (Flap, 2004).

Little is known about the association between social capital and the onset of, and recovery from, mental health problems. In fact, it has been noted that the embeddedness of individual social ties within the broader social structure as a function of obtaining access to material goods, resources and services has not yet been researched within mental health services (Lynch, 2000; Berkman and Glass, 2000). However, this appears to be a promising field of enquiry.

Social ties, or connections between people, are central to this conception and much is known already about their impact on mental health (Kawachi and Berkman, 2001). In general, your life chances are literally enhanced by five to nine years if you are socially well integrated (Berkman and Syme, 1979). In particular, social support has a buffering effect against depression (Brown *et al.*, 1986) and a perceived lack of support increases the likelihood of neurotic symptoms (Berkman and Glass, 2000; Boreham *et al.*, 2002; Henderson, 1981). This is particularly true for women (Cooper *et al.*, 1999). However, paradoxically, social connections may make women with low resources more vulnerable to mental health problems, especially if such connections oblige them to provide social support to others (Belle, 1987; Kawachi and Berkman, 2001).

The nature of social ties can determine what resources are available to individuals within social networks. For example, it has long been established that weak ties between people – such as acquaintances – may lack intimacy, but facilitate the distribution of influence and information (Granovetter, 1973). In terms of employment, informal social networks are influential in helping unemployed people find work (Perri 6, 1997). It has been estimated that more than a third of the workforce do so by this method (Flap, 1999). Further, occupational status attainment is largely attributed to the employment of social resources within one's own network (Lin, Vaughn and Ensel, 1981). Thus, people with mental health problems, for example, can improve their employment or promotion prospects by extending their informal social networks. This can be compared to the bridging form of social capital referred to above.

Strong ties, or close relationships to friends or family members, can be of great importance to people suffering from mental health problems. If these ties are instrumental in providing support, they can protect people's mental health (Cassel, 1974; Brown *et al.*, 1986). It is also known that positive social support has been found to precede recovery from depression (Brown, Adler and Bifulco, 1988; Leenstra, Ormel and Giel, 1995). However, strong ties may also inhibit free choice (Cattell, 2001; Cooper *et al.*, 1999). This may lead to stress or high expressed emotion within families, known triggers for depression (Cohen and Wills, 1985) or relapse in schizophrenia (Leff and Vaughn, 1981), for example.

It is important to note here the distinctions between social capital, social support and social networks. Social capital represents the resources of other people within an individual's social network. These may be accessed to meet a number of goals such as finding a job, obtaining help with DIY or finding new accommodation, for example. Social support is best perceived from the perspective of the person receiving it and can include both emotional and practical support. In short, an individual can gain social support from the supply of social capital they hold within their social network.

Let us consider how social capital may assist an individual in his or her recovery from a mental health problem. A study of religious attendees from a series of surveys conducted in Alameda County in the US between 1965 and 1994 showed that weekly religious attendance was associated with improving mental health, particularly for women (Strawbridge *et al.*, 2001). It may be possible that the resources within the network of the local religious community helped to alleviate symptoms of mental illness. These resources may be emotional support such as 'a shoulder to cry on', practical resources such as financial support or advice and information leading to a successful job application, for example. Alternatively, the social relationships maintained through regular religious attendance may have had a direct beneficial effect on mental health by producing a sense of purpose, belonging, security and recognition of self-worth (Cohen, Underwood and Gottlieb, 2000). There is some evidence to suggest that the availability of resources (broadly defined) appears to reduce stress and the onset of depression for older adults (Norris and Murrell, 1984). However, research tends to indicate that stronger relationships exist between health and resources such as health-specific support than more general support (Tijhuis *et al.*, 1995).

In the context of substance misuse, it appears that social capital is important in the process of natural recovery. Overcoming addictive behaviours strongly correlates to the social context and the resources that adhere to a person's social position (Tucker, 1999; Tucker, Vuchinich and Gladsjo, 1990–1). From a series of in-depth interviews with 46 people who resolved their drug or alcohol dependency without treatment, Granfield and Cloud (2001) suggested that these people may have possessed more social capital than those who were involved in treatment. The participants in the study emphasised the crucial role of social capital, as resources embedded within their social networks, in their recovery.

Implications for mental health services

Emerging evidence about the role of social capital in the mental health of individuals raises a number of questions for mental health services. For example, do people with more social capital recover more quickly from mental health problems? Are they less likely to access support or treatment from mental health services as they have more resources at their disposal within their social network? Do long periods of hospitalisation diminish the value of an individual's social capital that may be important in their long-term recovery? More work needs to be conducted with mental health service users to investigate these and other questions in this emerging research programme.

It is possible that mental health problems, or the interventions of mental health services, can damage reciprocal relationships that are crucial to the transmission of resources or the paying back of social debts. It follows that interventions focusing on strengthening relationships and networks containing useful resources can be beneficial to people with mental health problems. This could possibly explain why supported employment is more effective than pre-vocational training in helping people with severe mental health problems to obtain competitive employment (Crowther *et al.*, 2001), for example. People placed in competitive jobs with support from 'job coaches' or employment specialists are more likely to be exposed to more diverse social networks than those who receive pre-vocational training in sheltered workshops or on training courses. It is possible that resources embedded within these networks are important to help people to sustain or find new employment.

If there is an association between social capital and recovery from mental health problems, either with or without the assistance of mental health services, it could result in a paradigm shift from a focus on individual pathology to supporting the development of resourceful networks and strengthening interactions within them. This could highlight an important role for social networks beyond the traditional boundaries of the mental health resource centre or psychiatric ward.

Social capital and social inclusion

People with mental health problems face oppression on the street, at work and even at home, perhaps more than any group in society. This results in social exclusion, of which unemployment is perhaps its most visible element (Warr, 1987). For example, the employment rate of people receiving treatment and support from the mental health services rarely reaches more than 10 per cent and, when working, they work fewer hours and earn only two thirds of the national average hourly rate (Meltzer *et al.*, 1995; Office for National Statistics, 2002).

Tackling social exclusion has underpinned much of the 'Third Way' policy agenda of the UK government (Giddens, 1998). Reducing exclusion from social capital has been one of the aims of this policy thrust. This approach has been criticised as downplaying the material roots of inequity (Muntaner, Lynch and Davey Smith, 2000). However, there is evidence that access to social capital may vary according to a range of characteristics including socio-economic status (Ziersch, 2002), ethnicity (Boisjoly, Duncan and Hofferth, 1995) and gender (Campbell *et al.*, 1999). This may be relevant in terms of the way that differential access to social capital may link to the broader processes of social exclusion. For example, poorer people often have less access to resourceful people than wealthier people (Lin, 2000). This difference in access to social capital may reinforce existing mental health inequalities.

Sayce (2001) challenges psychiatrists to embrace social inclusion as a treatment goal in line with Standard One of the National Service Framework (Department of Health, 1999). In support of this objective, Huxley and Thornicroft (2003) argue that mental health professionals are able to exert influence on 'ethnos' sources of social exclusion. 'Ethnos' refers to the shared values, identification and sense of cohesion that are engendered by membership of social groups and communities (Berman and Phillips, 2000). Fostering the growth of social relationships and resourceful networks within the community or, in other words, building the infrastructure for social capital, is a key component of this.

In practice, this requires mental health services to be outward-looking and use resources within the local community rather than provide them internally (Leff, 1996). For example, people referred to community mental health teams need to be encouraged to attend social, leisure and educational activities provided by local services rather than specific mental health day services. This is not to denigrate the latter, which do some valuable work and are valued by their users (e.g. Catty and Burns, 2001). Instead, engaging with community resources will provide opportunities for people to develop social networks that may provide potentially important resources for recovery from mental health problems. Such resources may be contacts for employment opportunities, a tradesman to do a domestic job cheaply or a reliable mechanic who could mend your car in exchange for some babysitting, for example. Even the smallest of favours could relieve a stressful situation.

The oppression and discrimination people with mental health problems face in society poses a huge challenge to this approach. The association between mental illness and violence in the eyes of the public remains strong, although it is empirically weak (Shaw *et al.*, 2004; Taylor and Gunn, 1999). This heightens the stigma surrounding these diagnoses and makes it more difficult for those labelled with the disorder to access networks outside of the mental health services. An anti-oppressive approach by mental health professionals is required to redress power imbalances and to combat this stigma (Thompson, 2001). With the support of organisations such as Rethink Mental Illness, Mentality and Mental Health Media, this approach can facilitate the generation of social capital and alleviate mental distress.

Conclusion

Social capital is a burgeoning field of enquiry for academics and policy makers. However, its connections with mental health are not yet firmly established and any conclusions to be reached about it must be tentative. The majority of work has focused on social capital as an attribute of a community or geographical area. This has encountered measurement problems and has tended to look at a number of different indicators of social capital. The results are mixed and sometimes contradictory.

A focus on the individual may provide a promising way forward for our understanding of social capital and mental health. Bridging forms of social capital can provide employment opportunities and bonding forms can provide support to people with mental health problems, though they are not without their downsides. Resources within social networks may assist recovery, although more work is needed to establish this connection. Emancipatory and anti-oppressive approaches to mental health practice are called for to provide the foundations for the building of social capital.

References

Baron, S., Field, J. and Schuller, T. (eds) (2000) *Social Capital: Critical Perspectives.* Oxford: Oxford University Press.

Baum, F. (1999) 'Social capital: is it good for your health? Issues for a public health agenda.' *Journal of Epidemiology and Community Health 53*, 4, 195–196.

Belle, D. (1987) 'Gender differences in the social moderators of stress.' In R.C. Barnett, L. Biener and G.K. Baruch (eds) *Gender and Stress.* New York: The Free Press.

Berkman, L. F. and Glass, T. (2000) 'Social integration, social networks, social support, and health.' In L.F. Berkman and I. Kawachi (eds) *Social Epidemiology.* Oxford: Oxford University Press.

Berkman, L. F. and Kawachi, I. (eds) (2000) *Social Epidemiology.* Oxford: Oxford University Press.

Berkman, L. F. and Syme, S. L. (1979) 'Social networks, host resistance, and mortality: a nine-year follow-up study of Alameda County residents.' *American Journal of Epidemiology 109,* 2, 186–204.

Berman, Y. and Phillips, D. (2000) 'Indicators of social quality and social exclusion at national and community level.' *Social Indicators Research 50,* 3, 329–350.

Bernasco, W., de Graaf, P. and Ultee, W. (1997) 'Coupled careers.' *European Sociological Review 14,* 15–31.

Boisjoly, J., Duncan, G. J. and Hofferth, S. (1995) 'Access to social capital.' *Journal of Family Issues 16,* 5, 609–631.

Boreham, R., Stafford, M. and Taylor, R. (2002) *Health Survey for England 2000: Social Capital and Health.* London: The Stationery Office.

Bourdieu, P. (1986) 'The forms of capital.' In J. Richardson (ed.) *Handbook of Theory and Research for the Sociology of Education.* New York: Greenwood Press.

Bourdieu, P. (1997) 'The forms of capital.' In A.H. Halsey, H. Lauder, P. Brown and A. Stuart Wells (eds) *Education, Culture, Economy, Society.* Oxford: Oxford University Press.

Boydell, J., McKenzie, K., van Os, J. and Murray, R. (2002) 'The social causes of schizophrenia: an investigation into the influence of social cohesion and social hostility. Report of a pilot study.' *Schizophrenia Research 53,* 3, Supplement 1, 264.

Boydell, J., van Os, J., McKenzie, K., Allardyce, J., Goel, R., McCreadie, R. G. and Murray, R. M. (2001) 'Incidence of schizophrenia in ethnic minorities in London: ecological study into interactions with environment.' *British Medical Journal 323,* 7325, 1336–1338.

Brown, G., Adler, Z. and Bifulco, A. (1988) 'Life events, difficulties and recovery from chronic depression.' *British Journal of Psychiatry 152,* 4, 487–498.

Brown, G. W., Andrews, B. A., Harris, T. O., Adler, Z. and Bridge, L. (1986) 'Social support, self-esteem and depression.' *Psychological Medicine 16,* 4, 813–831.

Burt, R. S. (1992) *Structural Holes. The Social Structure of Competition.* Cambridge, MA: Harvard University Press.

Campbell, C., Wood, R. and Kelly, M. (1999) *Social Capital and Health.* London: Health Education Authority.

Cassel, J. (1974) 'Psychosocial processes and "stress": theoretical formulations.' *International Journal of Health Services 4,* 471–482.

Cattell, V. (2001) 'Poor people, poor places, and poor health. The mediating role of social networks and social capital.' *Social Science and Medicine 52,* 10, 1501–1516.

Catty, J. and Burns, T. (2001) 'Mental health day centres: their clients and role.' *Psychiatric Bulletin 25,* 2, 61–66.

Coburn, D. (2000) 'Income inequality, social cohesion and the health status of populations: the role of neo-liberalism.' *Social Science and Medicine 51,* 1, 135–146.

Cohen, S., Underwood, L. G. and Gottlieb, B. H. (eds) (2000) *Social Support Measurement and Intervention. A Guide for Health and Social Scientists.* New York: Oxford University Press.

Cohen, S. and Wills, T. A. (1985) 'Stress, social support, and the buffering hypothesis.' *Psychological Bulletin 98,* 2, 310–357.

Coleman, J. (1988) 'Social capital in the creation of human capital.' *American Journal of Sociology 94* (Supplement), S95–S120.

Coleman, J. (1994) *Foundations of Social Theory.* Cambridge, MA: Belknap Press.

Colletta, J. J. and Cullen, M. L. (2000) *Violent Conflict and the Transformation of Social Capital.* Washington DC: International Bank for Reconstruction and Development/World Bank.

Cooper, H., Arber, S., Fee, L. and Ginn, J. (1999) *The Influence of Social Support and Social Capital on Health.* London: Health Education Authority.

Copeland, J. R., Beekman, A. T., Dewey, M. E., Hooijer, C., Jordan, A., Lawlor, B. A., Lobo, A., Magnusson, H., Mann, A. H., Meller, I., Prince, M. J., Reischies, F., Turrina, C., deVries, M. W. and Wilson, K. C. (1999) 'Depression in Europe. Geographical distribution among older people.' *British Journal of Psychiatry 174,* 312–321.

Cornwell, J. (1984) *Hard Earned Lives: Account of Health and Illness from East London.* London: Tavistock.

Crowther, R. E., Marshall, M., Bond, G. R. and Huxley, P. (2001) 'Helping people with severe mental illness to obtain work: systematic review.' *British Medical Journal 322,* 7280, 204–208.

Cullen, L., Edwards, S., Marks, S., Phelps, L. and Sandbach, J. (2004) *CAB Evidence on Mental Health and Social Exclusion.* London: Citizens Advice.

Department of Health (1999) *National Service Framework for Mental Health. Modern Standards and Service Models.* London: Department of Health.

Diez Roux, A. V. (1998) 'Bringing context back into epidemiology: variables and fallacies in multilevel analysis.' *American Journal of Public Health 88,* 2, 216–222.

Durkheim, E. (1951) *Suicide.* New York: Free Press.

Fine, B. (2001) *Social Capital versus Social Theory. Political Economy and Social Science at the Turn of the Millennium.* London: Routledge.

Fine, B. (2002) 'It ain't social, it ain't capital and it ain't Africa.' *Studia Africana 13,* 18–33.

Flap, H. (1999) 'Creation and returns of social capital. A new research program.' *La Revue Tocqueville XX,* 1, 5–26.

Flap, H. D. (2004) 'Creation and returns of social capital. A new research program.' In H.D. Flap and B. Völker (eds) *Creation and Returns of Social Capital. A New Research Program.* London: Routledge.

Forbes, A. and Wainwright, S. P. (2001) 'On the methodological, theoretical and philosophical context of health inequalities research: a critique.' *Social Science and Medicine 53,* 6, 801–816.

Fu, Y.-c., Lin, N. and Chen, J. C.-j. (2004) 'Marital networks as social capital: data from the newly weds.' Paper presented at the Sunbelt XXIV International Social Network Conference, Portoroz, Slovenia.

Giddens, A. (1998) *The Third Way. The Renewal of Social Democracy.* Cambridge: Polity Press.

Graham, H. (1995) 'Diversity, inequality and official data: some problems of method and measurement in Britain.' *Health and Social Care in the Community 3,* 1, 9–13.

Granfield, R. and Cloud, W. (2001) 'Social context and "natural recovery": the role of social capital in the resolution of drug-associated problems.' *Substance Use and Misuse 36,* 11, 1543–1570.

Granovetter, M. S. (1973) 'The strength of weak ties.' *American Journal of Sociology 78,* 6, 1360–1380.

Harpham, T., Grant, E. and Rodriguez, C. (2004) 'Mental health and social capital in Cali, Colombia.' *Social Science and Medicine 58*, 11, 2267–2277.

Hean, S., Cowley, S., Forbes, A., Griffiths, P. and Maben, J. (2003) 'The M-C-M cycle and social capital.' *Social Science and Medicine 56*, 5, 1061–1072.

Henderson, S. (1981) 'Social relationships, adversity and neurosis: an analysis of prospective observations.' *British Journal of Psychiatry 138*, 391–398.

Hendryx, M. S. and Ahern, M. M. (1997) 'Mental health functioning and community problems.' *Journal of Community Psychology 25*, 2, 147–157.

Hendryx, M. S. and Ahern, M. M. (2001) 'Access to mental health services and health sector social capital.' *Administration and Policy in Mental Health 28*, 3, 205–218.

Huxley, P. and Thornicroft, G. (2003) 'Social inclusion, social quality and mental illness.' *British Journal of Psychiatry 182*, 4, 289–290.

Jackman, R. and Miller, R. (1998) 'Social capital and politics.' *Annual Review of Political Science 1*, 47–73.

Kawachi, I. and Berkman, L. F. (2001) 'Social ties and mental health.' *Journal of Urban Health 78*, 3, 458–467.

Kawachi, I. and Kennedy, B. (1997a) 'Long live community: social capital as public health.' *The American Prospect 8*, 35, 56–59.

Kawachi, I. and Kennedy, B. P. (1997b) 'Socioeconomic determinants of health: health and social cohesion: why care about income inequality?' *British Medical Journal 314*, 7086, 1037–1040.

Kawachi, I., Kennedy, B. P. and Glass, R. (1999) 'Social capital and self-rated health: a contextual analysis.' *American Journal of Public Health 89*, 8, 1187–1193.

Kawachi, I., Kennedy, B. P., Lochner, K. and Prothrow-Stith, D. (1997) 'Social capital, income inequality, and mortality.' *American Journal of Public Health 87*, 9, 1491–1498.

Kennedy, B. P., Kawachi, I. and Brainerd, E. (1998) 'The role of social capital in the Russian mortality crisis.' *World Development 26*, 11, 2029–2043.

Leenstra, A., Ormel, J. and Giel, R. (1995) 'Positive life change and recovery from depression and anxiety. A three-stage longitudinal study of primary care attenders.' *British Journal of Psychiatry 166*, 3, 333–343.

Leff, J. (1996) 'Beyond the asylum.' In T. Heller, J. Reynolds, R. Gomm, R. Muston and S. Pattison (eds) *Mental Health Matters. A Reader.* Basingstoke: Macmillan.

Leff, J. and Vaughn, C. (1981) 'The role of maintenance therapy and relatives' expressed emotion in relapse of schizophrenia: a two-year follow-up.' *British Journal of Psychiatry 139*, 102–104.

Levi, M. (1996) 'Social and unsocial capital: a review essay of Robert Putnam's "Making Democracy Work".' *Politics and Society 24*, 1, 45–55.

Lin, N. (2000) 'Inequality in social capital.' *Contemporary Sociology 29*, 785–795.

Lin, N. (2001a) 'Building a network theory of social capital.' In N. Lin, K. Cook and R.S. Burt (eds) *Social Capital: Theory and Research.* New York: Aldine de Gruyter.

Lin, N. (2001b) *Social Capital. A Theory of Social Structure and Action. Structural Analysis in the Social Sciences.* Cambridge: Cambridge University Press.

Lin, N., Vaughn, J. C. and Ensel, W. M. (1981) 'Social resources and occupational status attainment.' *Social Forces 59*, 4, 1163–1181.

Lochner, K.A., Kawachi, I. and Kennedy, B. P. (1999) 'Social capital: a guide to its measurement.' *Health and Place 5*, 4, 259–270.

Lochner, K. A., Kawachi, I., Brennan, R. T. and Buka, S. L. (2003) 'Social capital and neighborhood mortality rates in Chicago.' *Social Science and Medicine 56*, 8, 1797–1805.

Lynch, J. (2000) 'Income inequality and health: expanding the debate.' *Social Science and Medicine 51*, 7, 1001–1005.

Lynch, J., Smith, G. D., Hillemeier, M., Shaw, M., Raghunathan, T. and Kaplan, G. (2001) 'Income inequality, the psychosocial environment, and health: comparisons of wealthy nations.' *The Lancet 358*, 9277, 194–200.

Lynch, J. W., Smith, G. D., Kaplan, G. A. and House, J. S. (2000) 'Income inequality and mortality: importance to health of individual income, psychosocial environment, or material conditions.' *British Medical Journal 320*, 7243, 1200–1204.

Marcelis, M., Takei, N. and van Os, J. (1999) 'Urbanization and risk for schizophrenia: does the effect operate before or around the time of illness onset?' *Psychological Medicine 29*, 5, 1197–1203.

McCulloch, A. (2001) 'Social environments and health: cross sectional national survey.' *British Medical Journal 323*, 7306, 208–209.

McCulloch, A. (2003) 'An examination of social capital and social disorganisation in neighbourhoods in the British household panel study.' *Social Science and Medicine 56*, 7, 1425–1438.

McKenzie, K. (2000) 'Neighbourhood safety and mental health outcomes.' www.worldbank.org/poverty/scaptial/sctalk/talk28.htm. Accessed in May 2004.

McKenzie, K., Whitley, R. and Weich, S. (2002) 'Social capital and mental health.' *British Journal of Psychiatry 181*, 280–283.

McLanahan, S. (1984) 'Family structure and the reproduction of poverty.' *American Journal of Sociology 90*, 873–901.

Meltzer, H., Gill, B., Petticrew, M. and Hinds, K. (1995) *OPCS Surveys of Psychiatric Morbidity in Great Britain: Report 2 – Economic Activity and Social Functioning of Adults with Psychiatric Disorders.* London: HMSO.

Mind (1997) *Respect: Tall Stories from the Back Yard.* London: Mind.

Muntaner, C. and Lynch, J. (1999) 'Income inequality, social cohesion, and class relations: a critique of Wilkinson's neo-Durkheimian research program.' *International Journal of Health Services 29*, 1, 59–81.

Muntaner, C., Lynch, J. and Davey Smith, G. (2000) 'Social capital and the third way in public health.' *Critical Public Health 10*, 2, 107–124.

Muntaner, C., Oates, G. and Lynch, J. (1999) 'Social class and social cohesion: a content validity analysis using a nonrecursive structural equation model.' *Annals of the New York Academy of Sciences 896*, 409–413.

Norris, F. H. and Murrell, S. A. (1984) 'Protective function of resources related to life events, global stress, and depression in older adults.' *Journal of Health and Social Behavior 25*, 4, 424–437.

Oakes, J. M. (2004) 'The (mis)estimation of neighborhood effects: causal inference for a practicable social epidemiology.' *Social Science and Medicine 58*, 10, 1929–1952.

Office of the Deputy Prime Minister (2004) *Mental Health and Social Exclusion: Social Exclusion Unit Report.* London: Office of the Deputy Prime Minister.

Office for National Statistics (2002) *Labour Force Survey 2002.* London: Stationery Office.

Pedersen, C. B. and Mortensen, P. B. (2001) 'Evidence of a dose-response relationship between urbanicity during upbringing and schizophrenia risk.' *Archives of General Psychiatry 58*, 11, 1039–1046.

Perri 6 (1997) *Escaping Poverty: From Safety Nets to Networks of Opportunity.* London: Demos.

Pevalin, D. (2003) More to social capital than Putnam (letter). *British Journal of Psychiatry 182*, 2, 172–173.

Portes, A. (1998) 'Social capital: its origins and applications in modern sociology.' *Annual Review of Sociology 24*, 1–24.

Portes, A. and Landolt, P. (1996) 'The downside of social capital.' *The American Prospect 7*, 26, 1–5.

Putnam, R. (1993) *Making Democracy Work: Civic Traditions in Modern Italy.* Princeton, NJ: Princeton University Press.

Putnam, R. (1995) 'Bowling alone: America's declining social capital.' *Journal of Democracy 6*, 1, 65–78.

Putnam, R. (1996) 'The strange disappearance of civic America.' *The American Prospect 7*, 24, 34–48.

Putnam, R. (2000) *Bowling Alone: The Collapse and Revival of American Community.* New York: Simon & Schuster.

Rose, R. (2000) 'How much does social capital add to individual health? A survey study of Russians.' *Social Science and Medicine 51*, 9, 1421–1435.

Rosenheck, R., Morrissey, J., Lam, J., Calloway, M., Stolar, M., Johnsen, M., Randolph, F., Blasinsky, M. and Goldman, H. (2001) 'Service delivery and community: social capital, service systems integration, and outcomes among homeless persons with severe mental illness.' *Health Services Research 36*, 4, 691–710.

Sartorius, N. (2003) 'Social capital and mental health.' *Current Opinion in Psychiatry 16* (Supplement 2), S101–S105.

Sayce, L. (2001) 'Social inclusion and mental health.' *Psychiatric Bulletin 25*, 4, 121–123.

Schudson, M. (1996) 'What if civic life didn't die?' *The American Prospect 7*, 25, 17–20.

Shaw, J., Amos, T., Hunt, I. M., Flynn, S., Turnbull, P., Kapur, N. and Appleby, L. (2004) 'Mental illness in people who kill strangers. Longitudinal study and national clinical survey.' *British Medical Journal 328*, 7442, 734–737.

Social Exclusion Unit (1998) *Bringing Britain Together: A National Strategy for Neighbourhood Renewal.* London: The Stationery Office.

Social Exclusion Unit (2003) *Mental Health and Social Exclusion. Scoping Note.* London: Social Exclusion Unit.

Stewart, A. (2000) 'Never ending story: inclusion and exclusion in late modernity.' In A. Stewart and P. Askonas (eds) *Social Inclusion. Possibilities and Tensions.* Basingstoke: Macmillan.

Stone, W., Gray, M. and Hughes, J. (2003) *Social Capital at Work. How Family, Friends and Civic Ties Relate to Labour Market Outcomes.* Melbourne: Australian Institute of Family Studies.

Strawbridge, W. J., Shema, S. J., Cohen, R. D. and Kaplan, G. A. (2001) 'Religious attendance increases survival by improving and maintaining good health behaviors, mental health, and social relationships.' *Annals of Behavioral Medicine 23*, 1, 68–74.

Subramanian, S. V., Kawachi, I. and Kennedy, B. P. (2001) 'Does the state you live in make a difference? Multilevel analysis of self-rated health in the US.' *Social Science and Medicine 53*, 1, 9–19.

Taylor, P. J. and Gunn, J. (1999) 'Homicides by people with mental illness: myth and reality.' *British Journal of Psychiatry 174*, 9–14.

Thompson, N. (2001) *Anti-Discriminatory Practice.* Basingstoke: Palgrave.

Tijhuis, M. A., Flap, H. D., Foets, M. and Groenewegen, P. P. (1995) 'Social support and stressful events in two dimensions: life events and illness as an event.' *Social Science and Medicine 40*, 11, 1513–1526.

Tucker, J. (1999) 'Recovery with and without treatment: a comparison of resolutions of alcohol and drug problems.' Paper presented at the International Conference on Natural History of Addiction: Recovery from Alcohol, Tobacco and other Drug Problems without Treatment, Les Diablerets, Switzerland, 7–12 March.

Tucker, J., Vuchinich, R. E. and Gladsjo, J. A. (1990–1) 'Environmental influences on relapse in substance use disorders.' *International Journal of the Addictions 25*, 1017–1050.

Uphoff, N. (2000) 'Understanding social capital: learning from the analysis and experience of participation.' In P. Dasgupta and I. Serageldin (eds) *Social Capital: A Multifaceted Perspective.* Washington, D.C.: World Bank.

van Os, J., Hanssen, M., de Graaf, R. and Vollebergh, W. (2002) 'Does the urban environment independently increase the risk for both negative and positive features of psychosis?' *Social Psychiatry and Psychiatric Epidemiology 37*, 10, 460–464.

Veenstra, G. (2000) 'Social capital, SES and health: an individual-level analysis.' *Social Science and Medicine 50*, 5, 619–629.

Warr, P. (1987) *Work, Unemployment and Mental Health.* Oxford: Oxford University Press.

Webber, M. and Huxley, P. (2004) Mental health and social capitals (letter). *British Journal of Psychiatry 184*, 2, 185–186.

Whitley, R. (2003) *Urban Living, Social Capital and Common Mental Disorder: A Qualitative Study of a North London Neighbourhood.* PhD thesis, Institute of Psychiatry, King's College London.

Wilkinson, R. G. (1996) *Unhealthy Societies. The Afflictions of Inequality.* London: Routledge.

Woolcock, M. (1998) 'Social capital and economic development: toward a theoretical synthesis and policy framework.' *Theory and Society 27*, 151–208.

World Bank (2003) *Social Capital for Development.* www.worldbank.org/poverty/scapital/index.htm. Accessed in May 2004.

Ziersch, A. M. (2002) *Access to Social Capital. The Implications for Health.* PhD thesis, Flinders University of South Australia.

CHAPTER 6

The Social/Trauma Model

Mapping the Mental Health Consequences of Childhood Sexual Abuse and Similar Experiences

Sally Plumb

The social/trauma model

This model is a perspective on the connections between experiences of abuse, trauma and oppression and adult emotional, cognitive and mental distress. These dynamics are summarised in a diagram and are then established and described. There follows a discussion of implications of the model for service users and helping services.

Although the diagram and text are designed specifically with reference to childhood experiences of sexual abuse they are generally applicable to a range of experiences and life events. These include adult sexual assault, abuse, rape, other forms of childhood abuse or neglect, disrupted childhood (e.g. being in care), trauma, bullying, domestic violence, sexual harassment and other experiences of being victimised. It may also apply to the experience of being oppressed on grounds of race, culture, religion, gender, age, ability and/or sexual orientation. All these experiences share certain features – that the person:

- is being treated in a way that is careless of, or deliberately harmful to, their well-being
- is being treated according to someone else's agenda

- is being treated this way for ostensible or actual reasons that may relate to certain elements of themselves as a person that they are unable to change (e.g. their gender, race or age)
- feels powerless to prevent whatever is happening.

This chapter will, however, focus on childhood sexual abuse experiences as these can be the most often ignored, denied, minimised and misunderstood.

Not all survivors of abuse and similar experiences face all of these difficulties or to the same degree. Responses to abuse experiences are as individual as the survivors and reflect a wide range of factors including their personal qualities, support structures, type and duration of abuse, relationship with the abuser, response to any disclosure, degree of threat used in coercion and the cultural, gender and class contexts which define the individual.

The connections that I will outline are derived from my experience as a mental health social worker and are therefore my opinion and not the result of research or experiment. However, I have shared them both with other people working in this field and with abuse survivors and they have generally felt that they reflect their experiences.

The diagram

The diagram (Figure 6.1) is a simplification of a complex set of interrelationships. It is not comprehensive. If it were, it would be impossible to decipher. Across the whole diagram could be written the word 'FEAR'.

Apart from the part called 'abuse' in the circle (used as a generic term as described above), what is demonstrated in the diagram is all logical, rational and necessary for the person to survive their experiences. Despite the presence in the diagram of a number of elements that can feature in psychiatric diagnoses and mental health problems, I would maintain that it is only the abuse that is not logical, rational and necessary, rather than the various responses to it.

About abusers

The social/trauma model is not about abusers but about the effects of their abuse. (I use the term 'abuser' rather than the more ubiquitous 'paedophile' because it is more accurate for my purposes – 'paedophile' means someone whose sexual orientation is towards children; they may or may not act on that orientation. Abusers abuse – I define them by their actions.) However, in order to understand the contexts and dynamics of being abused it is necessary to know something about the ways in which abusers go about abusing. In order to abuse 'successfully' (i.e. to abuse, get away with abusing and, ideally, be able to abuse again), abusers need to be able to identify potential victims, access them and prevent them stopping the abuse (by refusing, avoiding the abuse, fighting back or telling and being believed).

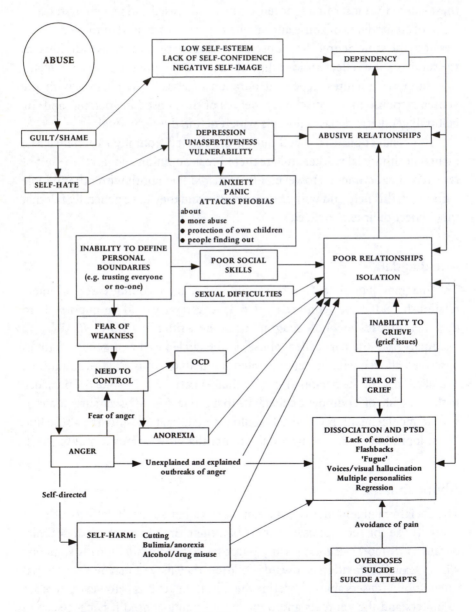

Figure 6.1 The social/trauma model (OCD = obsessive compulsive diorder; PTSD = post traumatic stress disorder)

Abuse is a function of power. One key dynamic in the abuse of power is the identification of someone less powerful (a child, someone disabled or learning disabled, someone in a less powerful life position) and ensuring that their power remains diminished. The opportunity to abuse is greatly enhanced by being in a position that combines access and power such as being a teacher, a religious leader, a doctor, a nurse or a celebrity. Befriending the carers and protectors of a potential victim can not only increase access but also undermine any disclosure. Intimidation (threats of violence, actual violence, threats against others) prevents both avoidance of abuse and its disclosure. Most powerful of all, making the victim take responsibility for the abuse can silence and disable them. This can be done cognitively by telling them it is happening because they are bad, dirty, sexy or special. Rewarding the victim (with sweets, money, attention) and/or making them abuse others can lock them into a guilty silence. Others' responses can compound these effects.

Guilt and shame, low self-esteem, lack of confidence and dependency

The way that abusers go about abusing, the way that children see the world, the responses of others to their abuse, and their sense of isolation, all come together to help ensure that people who are sexually abused in childhood are led to believe that they are responsible for what has happened to them. Feeling responsible for the abuse and guilty and ashamed of its sexual nature may lead survivors to hate themselves. They may have been more vulnerable to the abuse in the first place if they already felt that they were of little worth and value, having been treated by others in this way. Because they hate themselves, and have been treated as of no worth, they cannot value themselves. This produces low self-esteem: they lack self-confidence and believe themselves to be worthless. They may also believe they are neither able nor deserve to protect themselves, and this may well have been concretely demonstrated. This actual and learned powerlessness becomes ingrained. Indeed, powerlessness is one of the two key themes in the dynamics of the social/trauma model.

Abuse fundamentally changes victims' relationships with themselves and the world. Feeling they have neither the right to survive alone, nor the capabilities to do so, can create feelings of dependency. Self-hate causes self-directed anger, a cause of depression. Feeling worthless can cause feelings of hopelessness; feeling powerless can cause feelings of helplessness. Hopelessness and helplessness are key feelings in depression. Losses as a result of abusive experiences, believing one is worthless and dirty, poor relationships, isolation, panic attacks, flashbacks and nightmares are depressing experiences. It is no surprise that periods of depression are common among people who have had abusive experiences.

Vulnerability, unassertiveness and abusive relationships

If there is a belief that self-protection is not possible, feelings are created of vulnerability and powerlessness. Being abused once may make someone more vulnerable to being abused again. Not only does it confirm the powerlessness, it also confirms deserving to be abused. This further lowers self-esteem and can impact on the ability to care for oneself and/or accept caring from others. It will be almost impossible for people who have been abused to assert their own needs and wants if they believe that they have no worth or right to protect themselves. In turn, this may leave them vulnerable to abusive relationships in adult life as they may lack the will, or the ability, to protect themselves. If abusive relationships are what they grew up with, if they believe that they caused and deserved the abuse, then they may feel very anxious and confused in non-abusive relationships, expecting them to end up like all the others. Sometimes, it can even relieve their anxiety if they can push the other person into becoming abusive, because the rules of this form of relationship are familiar and fit with their view of themselves and the world. Being in an abusive relationship can further lower self-esteem and confirm powerlessness – making getting out of that relationship difficult if not impossible. The closed circle in the diagram that links these features describes what is known as 'battered women's syndrome'.

A learned need to please others, because of the potential dangers of upsetting someone who is more powerful and does not have one's best interests at heart, can create situations where people are unable to act on their own needs and interests. In order to be able to have their own wants, needs and interests taken into account, people have to have some concept that they have any, let alone have any techniques for making it happen (assertiveness).

Inability to trust – boundary difficulties

One of the main features of abuse by a trusted adult or close relative is that it is a fundamental betrayal of trust. It undermines any sense that other people, or oneself, can be trusted. This leaves feelings of anxiety and vulnerability.

Abuse and oppression are transgressions of personal boundaries. Abusers often 'groom' their victims by damaging or confusing other 'innocent' boundaries. People who have had their boundaries damaged often struggle with boundaries generally and experience anxiety and insecurity by not being able to identify and rely on boundaries. Personal boundaries are what give us a sense of who we are and where we stop and someone else starts. For all of us, when we are not sure where the boundary is for something, we can only feel secure if we go to an extreme end of any particular continuum. This can result in people whose boundaries have been damaged only feeling secure if they are at an extreme, with a consequent 'all or nothing' approach.

The quality and success of most interpersonal processes depend on being able to recognise and respect a whole range of boundaries. Thus boundaries are the second of the two key themes in the dynamics of the social/trauma model. Boundary difficulties can have a profound effect on the sorts of relationships that survivors of abuse and oppression can have with others, especially helpers. What people who have boundary difficulties most need, and often deeply resent, are good boundaries. Unfortunately, establishing and maintaining good boundaries can be received as rejection and abandonment. This is because the person's neediness can feel boundless, and combined with a need to please and a heightened fear of others' perception of their 'badness', it can make anything less than infinite attention, regard and caring feel like not enough. Attempts to elicit apparently boundless attention can be labelled 'attention seeking' or 'manipulative' – and potentially 'borderline personality disorder'.

Anger

Anger at abuse and the betrayal of trust is a valid and natural response. Anger can also be a positive energy for change. However, turned inwards it can be very damaging. It can cause digestive problems, ulcers and depression. Holding on to, or suppressing, anger takes up a lot of energy and can require muscle tension. This can lead to constant fatigue as well as musculo-sceletal problems. Behaviours such as cutting, bulimia (and to an extent anorexia), alcohol and substance misuse can all be ways of being angry with oneself. Outwardly directed anger can also be problematic when it is inappropriately directed or appears unexplained. High levels of apparently unexplained anger can attract psychiatric labels such as mania and personality disorder. It can also lead to legal difficulties and a criminal record.

There is a socially constructed, as well as culturally determined, difference in the way women and men can express anger without it being defined as deviant or unacceptable. Women's social identity is not construed to include being angry and so when it happens, women are seen as being deviant (or suffering pre-menstrual tension). Women are dealt with more harshly by the criminal justice system for violent offences and are more likely to be detained under the Mental Health Act if they attract an 'aggressive' label.

For the person who is being abused or oppressed, expressing their anger can be tantamount to telling or can elicit further abuse. Feeling angry can feel like being out of control. Feeling angry can be unacceptable.

Anxiety

Anxiety is our bodies' and minds' way of telling us that they feel under threat. The automatic physiological responses prepare us to deal with the perceived threat with explosive physical activity – the 'fight or flight' response. For the person who has experienced abuse, trauma and oppression, the world is a genuinely threatening place. Feeling powerless in an abusive and threatening world creates anxiety. We all rely on boundaries for a sense of safety and security and when our boundaries are damaged we lose that and become anxious.

Feeling vulnerable and unable to protect oneself, feeling there is no one who can be trusted, or being in a situation where physical or sexual abuse is still happening, are all valid causes of anxiety. Worry about being hurt or abused again, that your own children may be abused (or even that you may abuse them), and worrying about people finding out that you have been abused, all create a constantly heightened level of anxiety. Panic attacks and phobias are both results of high anxiety levels. Chronic anxiety is both exhausting and physically damaging. A permanently raised level of baseline arousal can result in poor sleep and an exaggerated startle response as well as producing digestive problems, ulcers and depression.

Sexual difficulties

It is not surprising that first experiencing sexual activity as frightening, coercive, confusing, shrouded in secrecy and often painful and physically harmful does not create a sense of sexuality and its expression being desirable, mutual, pleasurable or even safe.

Many survivors' sexual pleasure in adult life is also blocked by learned techniques of emotional and sensate withdrawal. Choosing not to experience sexuality either with self or others is one way of dealing with this. However, feelings of vulnerability and dependency can leave survivors feeling unable to remain outside romantic relationships and thus often unable to withdraw entirely from sexual activity.

Feeling a lack of free choice in expression of sexuality, either through a sense of duty or through overt coercion from a partner, can be an echo of the coercion and helplessness present in the first abusive experiences. Even with a sensitive and consciously non-coercive partner, the feelings, sights, smells, sounds, setting and fact of sexual activity can all recall the abusive experiences and result in withdrawal, distancing or 'flashbacks'.

Withdrawal from sexuality is one response. Confusion between sex and love, a sense of being already 'used goods', and unclear sexual boundaries, can all lead to unsatisfying sexual experiences that it may not be possible to limit. Many children who are sexually abused receive sex when what they really want is love and positive attention. If the abuse is accompanied by rewards in either money or kind, it can result in sexual activity being seen as both a tool and a weapon. In adult life, the search for a sense of worth and being loved, as well as a need to protect oneself or to survive economically can all lead to sexual activity which is not a mutual, pleasurable and chosen activity.

There is a belief that women who have been sexually abused by men may become lesbians, as they would wish to avoid sex with men. However, a lesbian survivor I know told me that she would hate to think that the most positive thing in her life (being lesbian) was anything to do with the most negative thing in her life. Men who have been sexually abused by other men (as adults or as children) may believe that they therefore must be homosexual. As survivors and practitioners agreed at a recent conference workshop, 'being sexually abused does not make you homosexual, it does not make you heterosexual, but it can make you confused'.

Fear of emotion, need to control

Being abused, traumatised and/or oppressed generates a whole range of feelings and emotions. These can feel overwhelming and out of control. Emotions can be socially constructed as signs of weakness (often being associated with female attributes) and feeling weak can feel the same as being vulnerable. As vulnerability is the factor that was exploited in the first place, feeling vulnerable makes one afraid of being or appearing weak, because that makes one feel vulnerable to being abused again. This leads to a need to maintain a strict control of everything in the environment, particularly feelings of anger and grief, both of which are logical and appropriate results of being abused. One of the causes of anorexia is a need to control food intake and body weight because of a feeling of not being able to control anything else. Cutting can be a way of converting out of control emotional pain into controlled physical pain, which is less distressing.

The rituals and obsessions described as obsessive compulsive disorder (OCD) can be a way of trying to take and hold control of one's environment. Rituals like counting to a certain number before acting, or having to do something a set number of times, can be ways of imposing control on apparently random or uncontrollable factors. Being obsessional about the way things are done, that everything has to be 'just so' (and getting distressed if it is not) has a dynamic of wanting the world to be knowable and in one's control. For people who feel dirty and ashamed as a result of how they have been treated, ensuring that they (and things around them) are supremely clean and neat, can be a way of hiding their dirt and shame from themselves and everyone else.

Avoidance of pain (dissociation)

The original abusive experiences were painful, both emotionally and usually physically. The feelings of guilt, anger, loss, self-hate and shame can still be painful.

At the time of the abuse, many survivors coped by withdrawing, or dissociating themselves from the pain. This is done by either believing that what is happening is happening to someone else, or that the person is actually not there at all. Survivors have been able not to experience pain to an extraordinary extent and, at the time, this can be a functional and very effective defence. One survivor has described to me how she had an imaginary friend who was the one who experienced the pain and fear, not her. Many abusers threaten their victims in case they tell someone about what is happening to them, or express their anger about their experiences. Thus anger or telling become unacceptable. The abuser may also tell the victim that they are bad, wicked or dirty. In order for the victim to survive, such self-destructive beliefs may have to be compartmentalised. Such habitual separation of feelings and urges from the 'self' as consciously experienced can mean that they are experienced as 'other', outside the self, and perceived as voices.

Repressed or extremely painful memories may be experienced as 'flashbacks', sometimes accompanied by the voice and behaviour regressing to the time of the memory. The survivor is, as far as they are concerned, actively reliving the event and the sounds and sights of that time seem really present and current. The dynamic behind this is that memories are not processed when there is a state of high arousal and so they are 'sent back' to be properly processed. To anyone observing this process the voices and sights are not real, that is, they are hallucinatory. Experiencing flashbacks and memories can intrude into a survivor's current attention – they 'tune out' and lose the ability to concentrate.

The separation, or fragmentation, can need to be so extensive that whole personality fragments can be separated out and experienced as 'multiple personalities', attracting the label of multiple personality or dissociative identity disorder (see American Psychiatric Association, 1994 World Health Organisation, 1994;). Another survivor has described to me how she can only feel and express anger when operating as a different self, with a different name, which dresses and behaves differently.

Habitual emotional withdrawal, as described in the section about sexual difficulties, can produce an inability to connect with emotions and feelings. This can be seen as an emotional flatness. Often, in order to tell others about their experiences, survivors have to disconnect from the emotional content, which can cause doubts about the authenticity of the disclosure.

The diagnostic criteria of post traumatic stress disorder (PTSD) can reflect many of the effects of dissociation, and indeed dissociation is the dynamic leading to much of this range of effects of trauma.

Avoidance of pain (self-harm and suicide)

Abuse survivors feel current pain. This is made up of memories of pain, pain of negative feelings and pain at the difficulties of living with all the consequences of the abuse. Many survival techniques that were useful and appropriate at the time of the abuse may now be destructive and dysfunctional and cause current pain.

Pain can be avoided in many ways, including blocking it by the use of alcohol and (prescribed and recreational) drugs or by substituting a more controlled and physical pain. Physical self-harm such as cutting, burning or other self-inflicted injury can bring genuine relief, albeit temporary, from emotional pain, because it is in the control of the survivor and the emotional pain is not. The bingeing, vomiting and laxative abuse behaviour in bulimia can bring the same relief. Unfortunately, all these pain-avoiding techniques have their own attendant difficulties. They add to feelings of self-hate and disgust. They also block the healing process of experiencing and resolving the feelings resulting from the abuse.

For many survivors the pain, helplessness and hopelessness are too much to bear and the ultimate pain avoidance is death. Urges to take overdoses or commit suicide are often very strong and can be ever-present.

Poor relationships and isolation

It is no coincidence that ultimately all the arrows seem to lead back to the box marked 'poor relationships/isolation'.

Feeling guilty and anxious about people finding out about the abuse makes it feel safer to avoid close friendships and relationships. Feeling unworthy, dirty and unlovable makes relationships seem inappropriate. Experiences of being abused, particularly when accompanied by learning that no one can be trusted, and feeling vulnerable, unassertive and unable to protect oneself, can make relationships seem dangerous. Sexual difficulties can lead to avoidance of sexual and romantic relationships, as can guilt about previous inappropriate sexual behaviour. Outbursts of anger (particularly if inappropriately directed), recourse to self-harming behaviours, and emotional flatness can all cause problems in relationships. Additionally, the stigma attached to mental illness can exacerbate these problems, if the consequences of the abuse have resulted in a psychiatric history.

It can seem that the safest option is not to be connected to any others, because other people are potentially or actively abusive, cannot be trusted, may find out about the abuse, and may judge or not believe. Thus to live as a 'lone rock' can feel like a good lifestyle choice. However, there may come a time when someone else is needed – for practical or emotional reasons. This then becomes fraught with anxieties and danger. Getting into a therapeutic relationship with a helper can feel like a very scary leap in the dark – a letting down of protective barriers, making the self vulnerable.

Parallels with psychiatric diagnostic categories

Particular clusters of responses to trauma and abuse can overlap with certain conventional psychiatric diagnostic criteria.

Features such as low self-esteem, lack of self-confidence, negative self-image, dependency, depression, unassertiveness, vulnerability, abusive relationships, anxiety, panic attacks, phobias, poor social skills and sexual difficulties may well attract a diagnostic label of neurotic disorder. This is a term with a particular meaning in psychiatry, but is popularly used in a dismissive way, particularly of women, and tends to put people outside the priority areas for mental health services.

When these features are combined with unexplained (and explained) outbreaks of anger, they may well attract a diagnosis of manic-depressive, or bi-polar, illness. This is especially so when someone can fluctuate between feeling low, depressed, unsure and at other times feeling angry, agitated and active. People who have compartmentalised their emotions into different parts of themselves can cycle swiftly between often contradictory mood states. Long-suppressed emotions can surface and 'burst out', followed later by guilt, shame and fear at losing control.

Poor social skills, poor relationships, isolation, lack of emotion, flashbacks, fugue, voices/visual hallucinations, multiple personalities and regression can easily be seen as the negative and positive symptoms of schizophrenia.

Low self-esteem, lack of self-confidence, negative self-image, dependency, depression, unassertiveness, vulnerability, abusive relationships, anxiety, panic attacks, phobias, poor social skills, poor relationships, isolation, inability to define personal boundaries, fear of weakness, inability to grieve, need to control, anger, self-harm, overdose, suicide and suicide attempts can attract a diagnosis of personality disorder, particularly borderline personality disorder.

Research is beginning to demonstrate that a high percentage of people with diagnoses of serious mental illness have histories of childhood sexual abuse – with a recent estimate being 43 per cent (Mueser *et al.*, 1998). The Department of Health (2003) suggests that at least 50 per cent of women within the mental health system may have had such experiences. It may be seen that many psychiatric symptoms can be understood as the logical, rational and necessary consequences of such abuse.

Abuse, trauma and oppression – links with multiple needs and homelessness

People who have experienced abuse, trauma and oppression are very likely to fit the description of 'multiple needs'. How these needs arise (and their relationship with adverse life events) are demonstrated by the social/trauma model. One of the ways that people cope with abuse and oppression is by escaping, often leading to homelessness due to a lack of alternative safe places. The difficulties that they experience as a result of their abuse can also lead to homelessness. Many of these difficulties can make them hard people to help and some services may exclude them because of self-harming, having a psychiatric diagnosis, suicidal feelings and/or difficulties in engaging with services. They may find it very hard to trust people and have poor social skills and boundaries.

Implications for helping services

The main effects of abuse and oppression are damaged boundaries and powerlessness. This has implications for how services are provided. Services need to be empowering and have good, appropriate boundaries. They also need to understand that people's difficulties are their most effective ways of coping with their experiences, given their circumstances, and these need to be respected, accepted and not judged nor punished. We cannot expect people to give up the ways that they cope unless they can find 'better' ways and/or a less abusive environment.

It is essential that services do not replicate the abuse. They need to be safe, accepting, empowering, nurturing, containing and appropriately structured. Negotiation rather than coercion is essential. They also need to offer unconditional acceptance, while retaining boundaries. People who have been abused and oppressed are often desperate to please, believing that it is their own unacceptability that has caused the abuse, and they need to be encouraged to make choices for their own benefit rather than to please others.

Abuse is (generally) an individual, isolated experience and many survivors have told me that they believed that it was only happening to them. This is one of the reasons why bringing survivors together in a situation of mutual help and support can be so extremely powerful – the isolation is demolished, the commonality of experience can suggest that the individual is perhaps, after all, not to blame, and survival strategies can be acknowledged and validated rather than being a further cause for shame. In such a situation it can be very hard to maintain a self-blaming position without holding other survivors responsible for their abuse, which is both instinctively wrong and intellectually untenable. Self-help and therapeutic groups can thus be very effective.

Because of the overlap with psychiatric diagnosis, it is essential to keep an open mind in the light of such diagnoses and not to view people through the lens that defines people by their diagnosis. A range of treatments needs to be available, not only medication.

Psychiatric medication can be effective in suppressing hallucinatory experiences that result from communication between dissociative elements, as it is actually a dissociator itself. As someone described it to me, 'it puts a nice layer of cardboard and cotton wool between me and my feelings'. However, although it can bring temporary relief from distressing intrusions of thoughts, feelings or separated material, it can work against the therapeutic aim of achieving integration of the dissociated parts. It can also prevent people from connecting with, and hopefully resolving, the feelings attached to their experiences.

If someone who has experienced abuse, particularly childhood sexual abuse, is given a diagnosis of psychotic illness, there is a risk that any disclosure of that abuse could be dismissed as delusional, especially if their experiences seem unbelievable. This will only compound their fear of not being believed. It may also lead to a professional reluctance to engage in discussions about the abuse in case it is felt to be 'colluding' with the 'delusion'.

Creating safety in helping services, particularly psychiatric in-patient services, is a key component to making those services helpful rather than abusive, traumatic or oppressive. People who are being given large doses of psychiatric medication are less able to protect themselves or assess threats. Their complaints of inappropriate behaviour by others may be less likely to be believed or responded to.

Many of these issues are well explored in the Department of Health's consultation and implementation documents on mental health services for women – although in many respects they are equally applicable to men (Department of Health, 2002, 2003).

Implications for disclosure

For most abuse survivors, disclosing is a very difficult and frightening process, no matter how desperate they are to do so. Some barriers are: difficulties in knowing whom they can trust; fear that their disclosure will be met with disbelief, blame and punishment; and any threats against disclosure made by their abusers. The gender, cultural background and status, and the position of the person they are considering disclosing to, may help or hinder this process. They can also fear the impact of their information on the hearer, wanting to protect them from the shocking, shameful, unbelievable and 'contaminating' contents. Feeling disempowered and with damaged boundaries, the survivor can only achieved sufficient safety to disclose if they are offered appropriate boundaries (including explicit boundaries on confidentiality) and are empowered by the interaction.

Disclosure of previous (or even current) abuse does not always come at the beginning of a helping relationship. The person may need to test out and assess the helper to see if they can be trusted with the information, can be trusted to believe, not to blame, not to abuse. They may not even be aware, at this stage, that their current difficulties have anything to do with their past experiences. If they have coped with those experiences by suppressing, minimising, separating or dissociating from their experiences and memories, they may not even be aware that there has been any past abuse to cause them any difficulties. Because of all this, timing becomes very important in disclosure. While helpers can do everything to facilitate disclosure, the information is the person's property and they retain the right, and the power, to decide when, and if, they are going to tell someone else. They also have the right to have their memories uncontaminated by helpers' own agendas or beliefs.

Telephone helplines can be ideal places for people to disclose and talk about their experiences. They can retain complete control over the interaction, by being able to choose what identity they give and always retaining the power to terminate the conversation by putting the phone down.

People are likely to choose to disclose when they feel they need to and/or feel safe enough to. Thus timing can be everything. However, there are certain things that can help facilitate disclosure. Clearly, creating a safe, empowering environment and demonstrating trustworthiness and good boundaries will contribute to this. One of the most helpful things people can do is to 'ask the question'. Research shows that many people are not asked about their past abuse experiences, but also that asking is most likely to elicit disclosure. By asking someone about any past abusive, traumatic or oppressive experiences, we are saying several things – that we can hear the answer, that we can believe the answer, that the answer can help us to help them. Many people may not have words to describe what has happened to them, so by asking the question we can provide a vocabulary.

Language is quite an important issue. Many children, particularly young children, may not have any actual words for what is happening to them. They may never develop cognitive concepts, only sense and feeling images. This can make it very difficult to put those experiences into words for someone else. It will be even harder to disclose if there is no shared language. If it is hard to tell someone about a shameful 'secret', it is even harder to do so through the intermediary of an interpreter. There may well be additional worries about confidentiality, especially if the person and interpreter are both members of a small, close-knit community. Some languages do not have words to describe abuse – this includes Makaton, which is a sign language for people who do not have verbal language.

Implications for helpers

Trying to help someone who has been abused and/or oppressed and who is cycling around in the dynamics of the social/trauma model can feel very much like being in that model oneself. The traumatic content of their experiences can traumatise those they talk to about them, their damaged boundaries can disrupt the helper's boundaries, coping through chaos can spread chaos, and their sense of hurt and helplessness can make the helper feel powerless and inadequate. Repeated crises, self-harm, suicidal feelings and actions, high levels of distress and despair can all stress and distress those around them who are trying to help them. As a result, helpers and supporters risk experiencing the effects of the social/trauma model and it is essential that they are given adequate support, boundaries and supervision as well as encouragement and permission to look after themselves.

Boundary issues can be the most difficult to deal with. Even if we have good, well-maintained boundaries ourselves, helping someone with (sometimes very) damaged boundaries can test and deform those boundaries. The person's neediness can elicit an urge to rescue and a reluctance to draw boundaries that can be received by the person as rejection and abandonment. It is very difficult to identify when boundaries are being distorted and sometimes it can be difficult to recognise that the frustration and anxiety (and even, on occasions, anger) that the person may generate in us are due to boundary issues. Formal and informal supervision, including peer group supervision, is essential in identifying and managing boundary issues.

Those helpers who have themselves experienced abuse, trauma and oppression in their own lives are very vulnerable to having those experiences reactivated. This does not mean that they should not do this work – indeed they often have rich resources and understandings to bring to it. However, they need to have achieved a level of understanding and resolution, and will require the best levels of support and supervision, as well as an ability to be honest with themselves and their supervisor about their experiences, so they can be appropriately supported.

The social/trauma model can be useful in devising helping strategies. The effects in and between the boxes are connected and rely on those connections to be created and maintained. Therefore, breaking those connections or diminishing the contents of boxes will begin to break down the dynamics. For example, assertiveness training, anger management or anxiety management can all be effective even without necessarily tackling the entirety of the abuse (particularly if someone has not disclosed). This opens up the possibility of

the creative use of a range of interventions, while not diminishing the usefulness of established therapeutic approaches.

Helping people who have been abused, traumatised or oppressed and
who are experiencing some of the dynamics of the social/trauma model can
be hard and painful work, but it can also be very rewarding. Walking alongside people as they reclaim themselves and their lives, as they move from
being victims to surviving and (hopefully) to thriving, seeing how resilient
the human spirit can be, how much strength and creativity people can bring to
surviving, can be exhilarating and enormously satisfying. And you do get to
meet the nicest people!

References

American Psychiatric Association (1994) *Diagnostic and Statistical Manual of Mental Disorders –
DSM IV*. Washington DC: American Psychiatric Association.

Department of Health (2002) *Women's Mental Health: Into the Mainstream*. London: Department of
Health.

Department of Health (2003) *Mainstreaming Gender and Women's Mental Health*. London:
Department of Health.

Mueser, K.T., Goodman, L.B.,Trumbetta, S.L., Rosenberg., S.D., Osher, C., Vidaver, R.,
Auciello, P. and Foy, D.W. (1998) 'Trauma and post-traumatic stress disorder in severe
mental illness.' *Journal of Consulting and Clinical Psychology 66*, 3, 493–499.

World Health Organisation (1994) *Pocket Guide to the ICD-10 Classification of Mental and
Behavioural Disorders*. London: Churchill Livingstone.

CHAPTER 7

Finding a Way Forward

A Black Perspective on Social Approaches to Mental Health

Peter Ferns

Black service users and practitioners welcome the current debate about the centrality of a social model in modern mental health services. However, there is a fear that once again the Black perspective will be an 'add on' feature to some other mainstream theory, as in many of the recent initiatives in the development of new approaches to coping with mental distress.

Equality and diversity are an inherent part of good practice in mental health services in our society. No new model of mental health service delivery, 'social' or otherwise, should be proposed without a thorough analysis of how it relates to issues of equality and diversity and how it actively promotes *both* of these outcomes. It is essential that that equality is not just replaced with the politically less contentious issue of 'cultural diversity' or worse still 'cultural awareness'. Awareness does not guarantee any change or action, and diversity does not guarantee structural change or any meaningful political analysis of the realities of institutional racism in mental health services. For example, there is currently concern that the new government strategy 'Delivering Race Equality' may have 'equality' in its title, but is really a narrower 'cultural diversity' and 'awareness' approach in disguise (Ferns, 2004).

This chapter seeks to raise some fundamental issues that need to be covered in the formulation of any social model of mental health, if it aims to address the specific issues for Black and ethnic minority people in need of services. At present, there is a valuable opportunity to move service development in a different direction, and this chapter aims to contribute to finding a way forward.

The term 'Black' is used here in its political sense where people who are visibly different in appearance from the White population then become vulnerable to White racism. The term recognises and acknowledges that White ethnic groups also face discrimination on the basis of culture, language, dialect and religion – which issues form part of an over-arching concept of racism. Although the experience of White racism is different for Black people, the discrimination faced by some White ethnic groups is no less important or serious. We need only look to the new 'demonisation' of asylum seekers and refugees, Black and White, in this and many other countries.

In this chapter, I will comment on the current context of Black people's experiences of mental health services and make some links to a common past for Black people that continue to inform and shape our experiences in this society. I will set out some key pre-requisites for any new social model of services if it is to incorporate a Black perspective of mental health. Finally, I will outline some key challenges for mental health services in the future if they are to address the concerns of Black service users.

Much of the thinking in this chapter has been shaped by recent research that others and I have undertaken with Black service users and survivors in Birmingham and London. They have crystallised many ideas through their constant questioning and challenging which I have found invaluable. I thank them for their generosity in giving their time, energy and honest views during the research. All of the service user quotes come from a recent Black service user-led audit conducted in Ealing as part of the LitTLE Project (Ferns, 2003), a local 'Letting Through Light' initiative using training materials commissioned by the Department of Health (Dutt and Ferns, 1998; Ferns *et al.*, in press).

Black people and the mental health system

A summary of research highlights the following key issues:

- an over-representation of Black people in the psychiatric system
- increased likelihood of Black people coming into the system through a compulsory route
- lack of preventative and after-care mental health services which are appropriate for Black and ethnic minority communities

- over-use of drugs and physical treatments with Black service users rather than talking therapies

- increased diagnosis of psychosis for Black people, particularly schizophrenia

- increased likelihood of being racially stereotyped by professionals in decisions about 'dangerousness'.

Prevalence of mental distress among African-Caribbean people

A number of studies over the last two decades have reported high rates of 'severe mental illness', in particular schizophrenia, among African-Caribbean people compared with White people. Research by McGovern and Cope (1987a) and Harrison *et al.* (1984) found that schizophrenia was diagnosed between 4 and 12 times more often among African-Caribbean immigrants, and between 7 and 18 times more often among British-born people of African-Caribbean descent.

The suggestion that this may be due to biological difference is not supported by the evidence from studies undertaken in the Caribbean which show no higher rate of diagnosed schizophrenia than for White Europeans (Nazroo, 1997). Similarly, explanations based on the migration experience itself do not fit with the evidence of higher incidence among British-born African-Caribbean people. We are therefore left with two possible hypotheses, each of which may be true to some extent. The experience of being Black in Britain may lead to a greater incidence of serious mental distress, and/or social attitudes and professional practice may lead to African-Caribbean people being selectively picked out and labelled as 'mentally ill' where this would not be the case if they were White British (Fernando, 1999; Nazroo and King, 2002; Sashidharan, 1989).

Prevalence of mental distress among Asian people

Evidence about the levels of mental illness experienced by Asian people is not consistent. While Cochrane (1977) suggests that the admission rate for Indian and Pakistani immigrants was lower than that for White English and Caribbean migrants, work carried out by Dean *et al.* (1981) showed higher admissions rates for Indian men than White English men, and that South Asian people may be around 1.5 times more likely to be admitted to hospital with schizophrenia than White British people. Among those who present to primary care, rates of anxiety and depression among South Asian service users appear the same or lower than in the general population (Balarjaran and Soni Raleigh, 1993).

This suggests either that levels of mental distress among people from Asian backgrounds are similar to (or lower than) those of White British people, or that they are higher, but Asian people tend not to access western forms of psychiatric help. Soni Raleigh (1995) suggests that mental illness in Asian people could be under-reported because of language and cultural difficulties which inhibit access to services, and because of the lack of culturally appropriate services (see also Furnham and Shiekh, 1993; Littlewood and Lipsedge, 1989). Despite the stereotypes that Asian people are better at 'looking after their own', research shows that family support does not necessarily protect against 'mental illness' (Butt and Mirza, 1996). For example, people within the Bangladeshi community, one of Britain's most disadvantaged ethnic communities, are reported to experience higher levels of psychological distress than their indigenous neighbours (MacCarthy and Craissati, 1989).

Use of compulsion and detention in secure settings

Not only are African-Caribbean people over-represented within the mental health system, but also they are found to be more likely to be admitted under a compulsory order, particularly so for young men who may be up to 17 times more likely to be detained in this way (McGovern and Cope, 1987b; see also Browne, 1997; Smaje, 1995). This has been shown to be the case where there is no significant difference in people's use of violent or threatening behaviour prior to admission (Harrison *et al.*, 1984).

The Mental Health Task Force Project reported that African-Caribbean males were over-represented among those formally detained in acute in-patient units and were more likely to be detained by the police under Section 136 of the Mental Health Act (quoted in Smaje, 1995). Within secure mental health provision, the rate of over-representation can become even greater, with studies showing that compulsorily detained African-Caribbean patients were four times more likely than White patients to be transferred to a high security unit (Bolton, 1984; Fernando, Ndegwa and Wilson, 1998).

Lack of appropriate community mental health services

Another theme running through the research is the relatively lower take-up of available services by Black people (Beliappa, 1991). The Mental Health Act Commission in its Fourth Biennial Report commented that many professionals seemed to lack basic knowledge about the different needs of minority ethnic communities and have little real understanding of institutional racism (Reed Report, 1990). There is also increasing evidence that points to the differential quality of after-care provision and follow-up for African-Caribbean people compared to their White counterparts (Cochrane and Sashidharan, 1996).

Lloyd and Moodley (1992) argue that a consequence of delay in getting psychiatric help is that individuals may be more disturbed by the time they receive services. This might lead to unwillingness to accept the need for treatment, resulting in their enforced detention – a point recently confirmed by the 'Breaking the Circles of Fear' study by the Sainsbury Centre (Keating *et al.*, 2002).

Over-use of drugs and physical treatments

There is substantial research evidence which suggests that both Asian and African-Caribbean people are consistently more likely to receive 'physical' treatments such as drugs and ECT rather than therapeutic 'talking' services (Fernando, 1995; Wilson and Francis, 1997). African-Caribbean people can be more likely to receive high peak doses of neuroleptic medication, and also to be given medication in the form of long-acting 'depot' injections (Chen, Harrison and Standen, 1991).

It is suggested that this mostly arises from professional stereotyping of Black patients as both being more 'dangerous' and also less likely to show appropriate 'insight' or be 'psychologically minded' (see, for example, Browne, 1997).

How services are experienced: common themes

> They look at Black people with mental health problems as the worst of the worst. (African-Caribbean man)

Control

Black experience of mental health services has been more one of 'control' rather than one of 'assistance' to overcome mental distress. The experience of social control has resulted in avoidance of mental health services especially by young Black people in mental distress. Avoidance then leads to crises which often leads to the involvement of the criminal justice system thereby increasing the sense of being controlled rather than being helped (Keating *et al.*, 2002).

Stereotyping

Decisions about dangerousness and risk assessments are still being based on stereotypical views of Black people. Broader stereotypes such as Asian families 'looking after their own', Black people being 'inarticulate', or Moslem communities not having alcohol or drug problems, can result in serious shortages of appropriate services for communities in need (Browne, 1997; Fernando, 2003; Sangster *et al.*, 2002).

Intellectual superiority

People who do not have English as their first language are often assumed to be unintelligent. If their culture is misunderstood or not valued, their cultural preferences may be seen as inferior to the norms of the dominant culture. It becomes more likely that practitioners with such assumptions will make decisions 'in the person's best interests' without involving them. The person on the receiving end of such decisions will inevitably experience them as being patronising.

Undermining autonomy

Lack of involvement in decision-making increases the dependency of people and reduces their autonomy. The lack of participation of Black service users in service delivery and development, even at times when they are not in distress, further emphasises a negative image of Black service users as being inarticulate, submissive or untrustworthy.

Divide and rule

Over-emphasis on diagnosis leads to false assumptions that people have very different needs and feeds fears arising from stereotypes about diagnostic labels. Black service users are not facilitated to create a sense of solidarity among themselves and build networks of mutual support. My personal experience of research has shown that, in some localities, differential levels of mental health services have developed for specific ethnic groups. This has led to tensions between various ethnic groups as they compete for scarce resources.

Cultural suppression

Black and ethnic minority service users are given subtle (and sometimes not so subtle) messages that their cultural identity is a problem for services. They are constantly being told that their needs require 'extra resources' and so cannot easily be met. For example, from my own experience, something as basic as food on a psychiatric ward can be designated as a 'special diet' for a person from a different culture. It is no wonder that many Black service users play down their cultural differences for fear of not getting a service at all.

Punishment

Services often set out clear rules for people to be able to use the service, which may seem perfectly logical to practitioners but may be mystifying or unnecessarily restrictive for Black service users. If rules are broken, service users often feel that they are 'punished' for stepping out of line, particularly in ward settings. For example, if service users are unhappy about their medication it is immediately framed as 'non-compliance'. Given that Black service users are more likely to receive higher dosages of drugs, they are more likely to be seen as being non-compliant and thus problematic for services. The perception of mental health services as being punitive towards Black people is reinforced by their over-representation at the 'heavy end' of psychiatric services (Fernando *et al.* 1998).

Demonisation

From the numerous surveys I have done with Black service users, it is evident that Black men in mental distress are acutely aware of media images of dangerousness and violence that are associated with them. Men who are big or tall particularly feel that they are feared rather than approached with genuine concern for their distress. Even within their own communities Black service users may experience rejection and distrust as these communities are also influenced by negative media images.

Slavery and colonialism revisited

> I was scared on the prison psychiatric wing. I couldn't speak English and someone tried to rape me there. (Male African refugee)

The Black experience of mental health services has a familiar feel to it, not least because it is a part of a legacy from the past. Deep in the psyche of Black people in this country there is a vaguely remembered experience of slavery and colonialism. It is, after all, what brought many of their families to this country. There are constant, almost imperceptible reminders of that past for many Black people here, even those born in this country. It may be argued that such old history has no relevance to young Black people born here, but there are some striking echoes of slavery and colonialism in the current experiences of Black people in mental health services.

Control was a key feature of colonialism and a great deal of effort was made to gain and maintain social, economic and political control of colonised countries. *Stereotyping* was used to justify a level of control and exploitation of certain countries with indigenous peoples being portrayed as 'primitive' or 'savage'.

One of the most damaging negative views of Black people was that they were intellectually inferior to White people. The assumption of *intellectual superiority* still emerges regularly in service delivery when professionals make decisions in relation to people from different cultural backgrounds. It was common for colonisers to actively *undermine* the *autonomy* of indigenous peoples – at first by military means and then by more subtle methods of political manoeuvring and economic dependence.

One of the most effective methods of control was the *divide and rule* approach. The cohesion of a country can be prevented through the exploitation of differences between people which makes it easier to dominate as no concerted opposition emerges. *Cultural suppression* was another means of total control by colonisers particularly in restricting usage of indigenous languages and artistic expression, while vigorously promoting a dominant White culture.

Any resistance to domination resulted in severe *punishment* for the ringleaders variously described as 'terrorists' or 'freedom fighters' according to the perspective taken. The final and most potent propaganda weapon by colonisers was the *demonisation* of certain individuals or groups as being 'evil', 'barbaric', unpredictable and 'out of control'. This approach enabled colonial authorities to do whatever they wanted to deal with such individuals or groups.

It should be no surprise that there are these links between Black experiences of mental health services, slavery and colonialism. The underlying mechanisms of oppression do not change over time if they continue to be effective. As these mechanisms become more embedded into the fabric of a society's institutions they become harder to detect and challenge, thereby increasing their effectiveness. Through mechanisms of professional intervention, social control may be disguised as concern for people's health and welfare.

The quick fix

A major problem for all service users is the addiction of many practitioners to the 'quick fix' in mental health service delivery. That is the tendency to focus only on the use of medication. Black service users are particularly prone to being subjected to the quick fix of physical or drug treatments where practitioners may feel 'out of their depth' with the complexities of transcultural work. Practitioners may not understand behaviour in its cultural and spiritual context and lack an effective theoretical framework by which to analyse what is really going on. The tendency to see 'problematic' or 'anti-social' behaviour as being inherent to the individual's 'illness' increases the likelihood of physical treatments being chosen.

The drawback about the quick fix is that it often leads to longer-term problems, as the social, economic and environmental causes of mental distress are ignored. In particular, a chemical solution takes away any wider responsibility from the mental health system or society at large: intervention becomes a technical problem to be solved by medical science. Furthermore, it takes away responsibility from the person in mental distress as well. Not surprisingly, the quick fix can be an attractive proposition. However, we have to cure our addiction to the quick fix and take a more holistic approach to tackling mental distress. It may be harder and more complex, but in the long run it is much more effective.

Pre-requisites for social models from a Black perspective

There are many possible social approaches to mental health, but if they are to incorporate a Black perspective they must address the following fundamental issues:

- oppression
- power and authority
- equality and diversity
- professionalism
- participation.

Oppression

Institutional racism is just one aspect of a wider problem of oppression for a variety of groups of people in our society. The abuse of power and authority is at the heart of oppression. People who are perceived as being different in society are vulnerable to stereotyping. Once stereotyping takes hold among people who hold power in society, negative values and norms become widely ascribed to certain groups, and embedded within many everyday discourses and practices.

The ascription of negative values and norms influences the culture of communities and organisations and shapes individual behaviours. The result of this process is discriminatory behaviour by individuals as well as institutional discrimination by organisations. An oppressive organisational culture begins to create systems and policies that are inherently and covertly discriminatory, which in turn drives even more discriminatory behaviour by individuals.

We can summarise the process with the following 'equation':

$$\text{Abuse of power and authority} + \text{Stereotyping} \Rightarrow \text{Negative values and norms} \Rightarrow \text{Oppression and discrimination}$$

Power and authority

I don't tell my social worker that I cut myself because she has threatened to take my children off me if I do it again. (Asian woman)

When I got caught by the police, the doctor told me that I'm not allowed to stay in this country. He phoned the Home Office saying that I had committed a crime and that I was mentally ill. (African male refugee)

All the people restraining me on the ward were men – I was really scared. (African-Caribbean woman)

The debate around the use of power and authority by mental health practitioners is a key one for Black service users but it rarely gets considered in depth, even in professional training.

Power is always present in any interaction between practitioner and service user. However, we need to go beyond individualised notions of power and see it as an important dimension of all human relationships between individuals, groups, communities, institutions and society at large. Jerry Tew suggests that power can best be defined as a social relation between people, one that 'opens up or closes off opportunities for individuals or social groups' (2002 p.165; see also Chapter 4). Power can be thought of as a 'potential force' to influence and shape people's:

- behaviours
- experiences
- life opportunities
- social relationships
- access to resources.

Power may be seen to operate regardless of any prescribed limits or authorisations that may be set within a specific social, political, legal and economic context. It is always present in any interaction between practitioner and service user – and in ways that may go far beyond (or even work against) the legal and organisational definition of their respective roles.

This definition of *power* allows us to differentiate it from a more circumscribed notion of *authority*:

> Authority is the direction of potential force to achieve an organisational, institutional or societal purpose within the prescribed limits of a wider social, political, legal and economic context.

Using the matrix of power relations that was explored in Chapter 4, authority may be compared to 'power over'. Just as any form of 'power over' may be analysed in terms of the degree to which it is productive or limiting, the use of authority may be differentiated in a similar way. It may represent a socially or legally sanctioned force that is *protective* of individuals or social groups who may be vulnerable or disadvantaged, which can be used to provide safety or resist exploitation in the short term and to promote their ability to take power for themselves in the longer term. However, if its purpose is (consciously or unconsciously) to create and maintain a discriminatory organisation or society, authority becomes corrupt and *oppressive*. In practice, many instances of authority may have both productive and limiting aspects.

Authority in mental health work may be seen as the capacity to influence the behaviours of others, but *within* the prescribed limits of a practitioner's role. The authority vested in such a role is defined by the policies and procedures of the service as well as the legal and ethical frameworks set out by government and professional bodies. The authority of a practitioner is further enhanced by their capability and the perceived status that people ascribe to the professional role.

Practitioners who use appropriate authority in a productive way can effectively *protect* mental health service users from the discriminatory barriers and restraints they experience in their lives caused by institutional discrimination, prejudice, stereotyping and stigma. If they use their authority in a limiting way, they merely reinforce and compound the negative life experiences of service users as they engage in *oppressive* practice.

Table 7.1 The social impacts of authority within the mental health field	
Productive	**Protective authority** is where practitioners act *with* vulnerable people to safeguard their interests and reduce unnecessary risks to them and/or others within a legislative framework that protects their rights to the least restrictive intervention, and supports their journey to longer-term recovery.
Limiting	**Oppressive authority** is where practitioners act consciously or unconsciously to uphold a discriminatory form of social organisation and a dominating style of professional practice which serves to contain, suppress and coerce individuals or social groups that may already be vulnerable or marginalised.

The use of power by mental health practitioners can hold greater risks than the exercise of appropriate authority, as it is not subject to any clear form of limitation or challenge. The abuse of power can easily lead to an autocratic and patronising style of working in which individual practitioners decide *for* people what is in their best interests and, consciously or unconsciously, impose their own personal agendas onto service users. This style of working is where coercion of vulnerable people and suppression of their viewpoints becomes more likely. It also inevitably leads to greater conflicts between practitioners and service users as service users resist coercion or manipulation by practitioners.

A working relationship that is defined by what the practitioner is authorised to do (and not to do) can lead to greater accountability of practitioners. Operating on the basis of such explicit authority can be liberating, in that it is clearer as to what is acceptable and unacceptable in practice. Practitioners have to bring more negotiation to their style of working and must be more mindful of people's rights. Having greater clarity about what is authorised and unauthorised behaviour enables a more open debate about the validity of the practitioner's authority and allows service users legitimate means to challenge that authority if they feel that they are being treated unfairly.

However, there are situations in which operating on the basis of power rather than authority may sometimes be justified, particularly in contexts such as that of institutional racism. Here, authority is corrupted. It may be underpinned by legislation that is oppressive, policy and procedures of organisations that are unfair and discriminatory, and leadership that is biased and unethical. Such authority can become a tool for oppression, and practitioners may struggle to use other forms of power in order to operate ethically and professionally in a discriminatory organisational environment.

The productive use of power by practitioners who are striving to combat the effects of a discriminatory mental health system can be empowering for individual service users in the short term. However, in the longer term, in relation to the service organisation, this approach can also be undermining of the checks and balances that go along with legitimated authority. If increasing numbers of practitioners in mental health services start to 'do their own thing' outside of any authorisation, those practitioners who choose to use power oppressively to dominate service users may increasingly do so with impunity.

Applying these concepts to the situations currently faced by Black service users, we may see the basis of much of the alienation described in *Breaking the Circles of Fear* (Keating *et al.*, 2002). Instead of seeing mental health practitioners to be authorised in ways that ensure their accountability and allow challenge if powers are abused, they tend to see an authority that is corrupted by institutional racism, one that effectively sanctions the systematic and excessive detention and compulsory treatment of Black people, and imposes a form of service provision that is culturally insensitive and denies them access to 'talking' therapies or support services that might give them more control over their lives. And what they fail to see, in sufficient quantity, are practitioners willing to 'stick their necks out' and use other forms of power to challenge and change this corruption of authority.

Equality and diversity

Valuing diversity involves understanding cultural differences. Culture is a complex concept and cannot be captured and represented by a few facts and bits of knowledge. A 'little learning' can certainly be 'a dangerous thing'. The temptation in training people about other cultures is to over-simplify and leave people with the false impression that they now 'know' about a particular culture. Such simplistic thinking leads to assumptions about individuals from a different culture and further compounds the problem of cultural stereo-typing. The process is particularly dangerous in mental health work where far-reaching decisions are made on the basis of interpretation of a person's behaviour as being atypical or 'anti-social' – essentially culturally determined and value-based judgements.

Cultural difference must be set within the current political and economic context of our society, if valuing diversity is to be meaningful. Witness the change in perception of the cultural difference of being a Moslem post 11 September 2001. Valuing diversity becomes just another vacuous phrase in policy documents if it is not linked to a wider strategy for promoting equal-ity that takes into account issues of power and structural inequality in communities.

The appropriate use of power and authority by practitioners is essential for good practice. Where practitioners exercise protective authority within an organisational context that respects diversity, people who are vulnerable to oppression are likely to feel positively valued and supported. Where power is used by practitioners outside the limits of their legitimated authority, it must be to engage in behaviours that value diversity, promote equality and chal-lenge discrimination – a deployment of co-operative power alongside service users in their struggle against an institutionally discriminatory service system. The process can be summarised in the following way:

$$\text{Protective authority and/or co-operative power} + \text{Diversity} \Rightarrow \text{Positive values and norms} \Rightarrow \text{Equality}$$

Professionalism

It is not only organisations that have to change to tackle racism; the whole concept of professionalism has to be re-evaluated and redefined. Profession-alism from a Black and anti-oppressive perspective primarily has to be about increasing service user autonomy. It is an outcome-oriented approach and not just about inputs such as technical expertise and knowledge, although these aspects of professionalism are still important. What is being posited here is an expansion of the concept of professionalism to respond to a more holistic and social model formulation of what professional practice should entail.

Achieving greater service user autonomy involves a different mode of operation for mental health professionals. It means defending a truly independent stance against forces that threaten the rights and interests of devalued and vulnerable groups. It is a stance that will not always be politically popular or in agreement with the government of the day, but professionals must be prepared to go the extra 'hard yards' if they are really committed to the values and purpose of their work. If mental health professionals are not prepared to share the struggle and pain of their service users, they should seriously question whether they are doing the right work.

At the heart of the transformation of professionalism there must be a commitment to critical self-reflection. Professionals must be prepared to question their basic assumptions and identify their own prejudices and stereotypes about people. They must be prepared to analyse their decision-making and make more explicit the criteria and values underpinning decisions. They must also be prepared to be challenged by service users and others and regard this as part of a learning process.

Capability of professionals must be judged in the context of diverse communities, and competencies for mental health work must be formulated with anti-oppressive practice as an integral part of good practice. There needs to be a clearer definition of professional authority and what constitutes the appropriate use of authority. Capability must also mean the proactive promotion of equality and the valuing of diversity and not just reactive anti-discriminatory practice.

Participation

Participation of service users in mental health services is a pre-requisite for any social model approach, but it is particularly important for a Black perspective as a safeguard against culturally inappropriate services. It should be recognised that there needs to be flexibility to allow for varying degrees of participation. Black service users initially may be quite reticent or cynical about participation, given past experiences of services. The credibility gap may take some time to bridge.

The first step is usually to build capacity for participation among Black service users. In the mental health field, there is no established track record of involving Black service users in any systematic or meaningful way in service development and delivery. This is also sadly true in the service user movement itself (Wallcraft and Bryant, 2003). Given this background, it is going to prove difficult to achieve genuine participation of Black service users in mental health services. However, this is precisely what is required across a range of areas in service provision (Ferns *et al.*, 2005). To make real progress in dealing with institutional racism in mental health services, Black service users need to participate in:

- policy development and implementation
- audit and quality assurance work
- service design and development
- training of practitioners
- research into services.

A holistic approach for Black service users and Black communities

Instead of the 'quick fix' approach discussed earlier, there is a need for an integrated and holistic way of working that does not attach undue importance to a person's medical diagnosis (Dutt and Ferns, 1998). The pre-requisites for social models discussed above form the elements of *how* change can be achieved. A holistic approach (see Figure 7.1) takes into account a wide range of interlinking social, economic, political and psychological factors that influence people's distress – and seeks to identify and bring about positive outcomes, not just in relation to people's symptoms, but in relation to all aspects of their family, social and cultural lives. Such an approach involves identifying discriminatory barriers in order to remove them – including institutional discrimination in services.

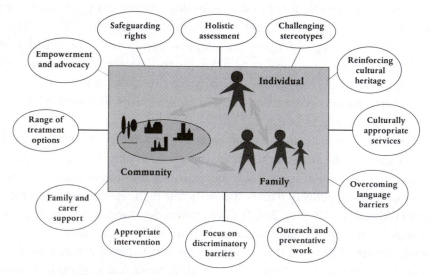

Figure 7.1 A holistic model of mental health

Five challenges for mental health services

Many years of talking to and working with Black service users and their families have highlighted specific themes about what is wanted from mental health services. These themes can be usefully expressed as challenges for services as Black people struggle to get assistance at times of distress. Mental health services must successfully meet these challenges if they are not to compound further the experiences of oppression, marginalisation and alienation that many Black people in mental distress face in society. The challenges represent an agenda for action to improve mental health services based on a social model approach for Black and ethnic minority people.

The five challenges are:

- humanity
- equality
- creativity
- accessibility
- practicality.

Humanity

> There was an older African nurse who walked with me. He talked to me like father to son. I respected him. I felt it in my heart. (Young African man)

> Because of the professionalism of the mental health people I felt that I was helped to understand my problems. People were genuinely interested in my welfare for the first time in my life. (Black British man)

> I used to work in hospitals. It was a big blow to be on the other side – very depressing. (Asian woman)

The quality of human relationships between service users and practitioners is an essential factor in any type of mental health intervention. No amount of technical expertise or even financial resources can compensate for a lack of trust, credibility or respect. Black service users have constantly asked for practitioners to be more in touch with their own humanity and vulnerability to distress. One Black service user put it to me that practitioners are always going on about the lack of 'insight' of service users but rarely seem to have 'insight' into their own behaviour.

Practitioner teams should enable team members to talk about their feelings in doing mental health work. Service organisations should publicly reflect the importance of human relationships in the work through explicit 'values statements' and policies. Continuity of working relationships in mental health services is of great concern to Black service users and practitioners may also find the work more rewarding if they are able to form longer-lasting relationships with service users as real people, rather than experiencing a string of human 'snapshots' of some 'diagnosis' or other.

There are many more things that connect us to someone from a different culture than separate us. White practitioners must not let the fear of racism de-skill them and must maintain faith in their own capability.

Equality

> They didn't really take my culture into account – one patient told me to think of Rama and line up for my medication. (Asian woman)

> In my culture we usually greet people by kissing them on the cheek. The doctor wouldn't take me off section until I stopped doing this as he said that I was being 'over-friendly'. (African-Caribbean woman)

> If I talked about spirituality to the doctor he would increase my medication. (African-Caribbean man)

One of the biggest challenges for the future is to develop truly inclusive mental health services that are appropriate for everyone, not only in terms of race and culture, but also in relation to gender, sexuality, spirituality, disability and age. A holistic approach to equality will avoid any hierarchies of oppression, while acknowledging the differences in causation and needs between the various groups in society who are vulnerable to oppression.

Service organisations need to pursue a strategic approach to equality, valuing diversity within professional teams, working with communities to remove discriminatory barriers to Black people, and helping those experiencing mental distress to be valued members of their own communities.

Creativity

> It meant a lot to me to perform a song for the other people at the day-centre. (Black British man)

> They need a Mother and Baby Unit locally so that kids and mums are not separated. (Asian woman)

> There should be some Indian movies or satellite TV on the ward. (Male Asian refugee)

Black service users need to have a greater range of service options available to them; therefore more creativity is required in service development and delivery. Practitioners must work with Black service users to come up with creative solutions to problems. This will lead to services being more responsive to Black service users and enable practitioners to individualise packages of assistance.

Teams can foster creativity by supporting practitioners in taking the risk of trying out something new. Service organisations can support creativity by ensuring that practitioners have sufficient authority to make decisions in part-nership with service users, and by working more closely with Black and ethnic minority communities to involve a wider range of people in helping to tackle mental distress in those communities.

Accessibility

> Someone told me when I was homeless that if I pretend to be mentally ill I will get accommodation. I pretended and they gave me a strong drug and locked my jaw. (Male African refugee)

> I went to the doctor (GP) and he thought that I was OK and he sent me home – I was seriously suicidal. (Chinese woman)

> I want more information – I've been in this country for two years and I've just found out about Meals-on-Wheels. (Asian woman)

Black and ethnic minority service users have had a long-standing problem of not getting adequate information about existing services and not having sufficient choice of culturally appropriate services when access is gained. Practitioners need to inform Black service users and families about what services are available using different formats and languages.

Organisations should review their systems for speed of response and eliminate any 'red-tape' that may slow down or restrict access for Black com-munities. Mental health services could be more proactive in training and educating other local community service providers to open up more ordinary community resources to Black people in mental distress.

Practicality

> The most brilliant help I got from the Social Services Department and the Trust was them finding a nursery for my one-year-old. In those days I got myself an education and eventually a job and all the while I was on medication. It gave me a chance to have a life. (Asian woman)

> One member of staff went out of his way to take me down to Abbey National to get some money out and help me to send some clothes and toys to my daughter. (African-Caribbean man)

All service users, including Black service users, give a high priority to a variety of practical forms of assistance to do with finances, employment, general health, accommodation, training and education. Practitioners must ensure that they advocate for Black service users in getting practical help, particularly as Black people have traditionally had poor access to a range of welfare and preventative services including information about welfare benefits.

Conclusion

> I can't trust anyone anymore; I've been betrayed so often – so many broken promises. (Woman refugee)

The failure to eradicate institutional racism from mental health services in the UK over the past 25 years has been little short of spectacular – and this has been highlighted again recently with the enquiry into the death of David 'Rocky' Bennett (Norfolk, Suffolk and Cambridgeshire Strategic Health Authority, 2003). Despite a great deal of rhetoric, and some pockets of excellent practice, the overall picture remains stubbornly the same. It can be argued that we have even taken a step backwards with the proposed reform of the Mental Health Act, which holds greater potential for discrimination against Black people, especially Black men who are most vulnerable to compulsory treatment under the Act.

We need to understand the historical roots of the current problems for Black people in mental health services or we will be condemned to repeating past mistakes. We must not waste the opportunity to formulate social models of mental health that incorporate a Black perspective, value diversity and promote equality for all. There have been numerous studies, local and national, that have laid out what Black service users want. Services must now meet the challenges that have emerged with actions not just words. There have been too many broken promises. If you lead people down too many false trails there comes a time when they will stop going along with you.

'Scientific bureaucracy' appears to be on the march once again in health and social services; we must not let the drive for 'evidence-based' approaches detract from putting service users at the centre of services. We need to listen even more closely to Black service users at this time of flux and transition in the development of mental health services. If we can get it right for groups of people that have been traditionally poorly served, then we can get it right for the vast majority of people. Let's stop and take direction from service users for once.

Acknowledgements

I am grateful to Premila Trivedi who generously gave her time in discussing many of these issues and ideas with me. All quotations from service users are taken from Ferns, 2003.

References

Balarjaran, R. and Soni Raleigh, V. (1993) *Ethnicity and Health*. London: Department of Health.

Beliappa, J. (1991) *Illness or Distress? – Alternative Models of Mental Health*. London: Confederation of Indian Organisations.

Bolton, P. (1984) 'Management of compulsorily admitted patients to a high secure unit.' *International Journal of Social Psychiatry 30*, 77–84.

Browne, D. (1997) *Black People and 'Sectioning': The Black Experience of Detention under the Civil Sections of the Mental Health Act*. London: Little Rock Publishing.

Butt, J. and Mirza, K. (1996) *Social Care and Black Communities – A Review of Recent Research Studies*. London: HMSO.

Chen, E., Harrison, G. and Standen, P. (1991) 'Management of first episode psychotic illness in Afro-Caribbean patients.' *British Journal of Psychiatry 158*, 517–522.

Cochrane, R. (1977) 'Mental illness in immigrants to England and Wales: an analysis of mental hospital admissions – 1971.' *Social Psychiatry 12*, 23–35.

Cochrane, R. and Sashidharan, S. (1996) 'Mental health and ethnic minorities: a review of the literature and service implications.' In NHS Centre for Reviews and Dissemination *Ethnicity and Health*. CRD Report 5. York: University of York.

Dean, G., Walsh, D., Downing, H. and Shelley, E. (1981) 'First admission of native-born and immigrants to psychiatric hospitals in South-East England, 1970.' *British Journal of Psychiatry 139*, 506–512.

Dutt, R. and Ferns, P. (1998) *'Letting Through Light' – A Training Pack on Black People and Mental Health*. London: Department of Health.

Fernando, S. (1995) *Mental Health in a Multi-ethnic Society*. London: Routledge.

Fernando, S. (1999) 'Ethnicity and mental health.' In M. Ulas and A. Connor (eds) *Mental Health and Social Work*. London: Jessica Kingsley Publishers.

Fernando, S. (2003) *Cultural Diversity, Mental Health and Psychiatry – The Struggle against Racism*. London: Routledge.

Fernando, S., Ndegwa, D. and Wilson, M. (1998) *Forensic Psychiatry, Race and Culture.* London: Routledge.

Ferns, P. (2003) *'Letting Through Light' – A Service User-led Audit in Ealing, Published by LitTle Project.* London: West London Mental Health NHS Trust and Ealing Social Services.

Ferns, P. (2004) *SPN Response to 'Delivering Race Equality'.* London: Social Perspectives Network. www.spn.org.uk

Ferns, P., Dutt, R., Trivedi, P. and Walker, D. (2005) *Journey to Participation – Letting Through Light 2.* Brighton: Pavillion.

Furnham, A. and Shiekh, S. (1993) 'Gender generational and support correlates of mental health in Asian immigrants.' *International Journal of Social Psychiatry 39,* 1, 22–33.

Harrison, G., Ineichen, B., Smith, J. and Morgan, H. (1984) 'Psychiatric hospital admissions in Bristol: social and clinical aspects of compulsory admission.' *British Journal of Psychiatry 145,* 605–611.

Keating, F., Robertson, D., McCulloch, A. and Francis, E. (2002) *Breaking the Circles of Fear: A Review of the Relationship Between Mental Health Services and African and Caribbean Communities.* London: Sainsbury Centre for Mental Health.

Littlewood, R. and Lipsedge, M. (1989) *Aliens and Alienists – Ethnic Minorities and Psychiatry.* Harmondsworth: Penguin.

Lloyd, K. and Moodley, P. (1992) 'Psychotropic medication and ethnicity: an inpatient survey.' *Social Psychiatry and Psychiatric Epidemiology 27,* 95–101.

MacCarthy, B. and Craissati, J. (1989) 'Ethnic differences in response to adversity: a community sample of Bangladeshis and their indigenous neighbours.' *Social Psychiatry and Psychiatric Epidemiology 24,* 196–201.

McGovern, D. and Cope, R. (1987a) 'First psychiatric admission rates of first and second generation Afro-Caribbeans.' *Social Psychiatry 22,* 139–140.

McGovern, D. and Cope, R. (1987b) 'The compulsory detention of males of different ethnic groups, with special reference to offender patients.' *British Journal of Psychiatry 150,* 505–512.

Nazroo, J. (1997) *The Health of Britain's Ethnic Minorities: Findings from a National Survey.* London: Policy Studies Institute.

Nazroo, J. and King, M. (2002) 'Psychosis – symptoms and estimated rates.' In K. Sproston and J. Nazroo (ed.) *Ethnic Minority Psychiatric Illness Rates in the Community (Empiric).* London: National Centre for Social Research, TSO.

Norfolk, Suffolk and Cambridgeshire Strategic Health Authority (2003) *Independent Inquiry into the Death of David Bennett.* Cambridge: Norfolk, Suffolk and Cambridgeshire Strategic Health Authority.

Reed Report (1990) *Race, Gender and Equal Opportunities.* London: HMSO.

Sangster, D., Shiner, M., Patel, K. and Sheikh, N. (2002) *Delivering Drug Services to Black and Ethnic-minority Communities.* London: Department of Health.

Sashidharan, S. (1989) 'Schizophrenia or just Black?' *Community Care, 783,* 14–15.

Smaje, C. (1995) *'Race' and Ethnicity: Making Sense of the Evidence.* London: King's Fund.

Soni Raleigh, V. (1995) *Mental Health in Black and Minority Ethnic People – The Fundamental Facts.* London: Mental Health Foundation.

Tew, J. (2002) *Social Theory, Power and Practice.* Basingstoke: Palgrave.

Wallcraft, J. and Bryant, M. (2003) *The Mental Health Service User Movement in England.* London: Sainsbury Centre for Mental Health.

Wilson, M. and Francis, E.J. (1997) *Raised voices: African Caribbean and African Users' Views and Experiences of Mental Health Services in England and Wales.* London: Mind.

CHAPTER 8

Women's Mental Health

Taking Inequality into Account

Jennie Williams

Introduction

This chapter takes social inequality as its starting point, and then maps some
of the important implications for women's mental health. The intention is to
demonstrate that it is both valid and useful to conceptualise women's mental
health problems as responses to damaging experiences that are rooted in their
lived experiences of inequality and abuses of power.

The continued existence of divisions in our society based on dimensions
such as gender, race and class can quickly be verified by a walk down any high
street or recourse to freely available government statistics (Dench *et al.*, 2003).
That these inequalities have important implications for mental health is
beginning to receive recognition nationally (Department of Health, 2002,
2003) and internationally (Wetzel 2000), though people with experience of
using mental health services have been telling us this for a long time
(Beresford, 2000; Trivedi, 2002). While mental health providers are beginning to share this basic premise, many are unclear about the implications for
their practice (Cann *et al.*, 2001: Williams, Scott and Waterhouse, 2001b).

Characteristics of social inequality

I shall begin by directing attention to some of the defining social
psychological characteristics and dynamics of inequitable social relations.
This analysis is informed by the work of feminists who have written about the
psychological implications of gender from an intergroup perspective

(Apfelbaum, 1999; Baker-Miller, 1976; Williams and Watson, 1988; Williams, 1999).

Social inequality describes a relationship between groups when one group is privileged at the expense of the less powerful group. A conflict of interests is embedded in all unequal intergroup relationships because the privileged or dominant group, by definition, is in the position to get what it wants at the expense of members of the subordinate group. To provide a specific example, patriarchy is a system that meets men's needs at women's expense. Inequalities are sustained by explanations and practices which shape social institutions as well as our daily life; they are a defining characteristics of the social context within which we live and give meaning to our existence. Social inequalities in our society means that attributes such as gender, race or class affect access to socially valued resources including money, status and power.

As Baker-Miller (1976) observed, some unequal relationships have movement towards equality as part of their rationale, even though this may be imperfectly achieved in practice. Examples include the parent/child and the teacher/student relationships. In contrast, inequalities that have a conflict of interests at their core are maintained by a range of processes and practices that function to maintain privilege while deflecting attention from injustice. This is achievable because dominance is associated with having the power to determine the ideologies, culture and practices of society. Through this influence, inequality is legitimised and made invisible and the conflict of interests at the heart of social relations is hidden. Dominant groups are, therefore, in the position to define what is 'normal' human behaviour and relationships. It is therefore normal to behave in ways which sustain inequality, and most of the time we are unaware of our participation in this undertaking.

About gender inequality

Gender inequality has particular significance for mental health. Families are the place in which females and males whose structural relationship is one of inequality live together, and where we construct our gender identities as children and adults. While other social inequalities are also important they are usually less central to our private lives and psychological functioning.

While the focus here is on damage to women, it is also important to acknowledge that men are also harmed by the practices which construct their interest and capacity to oppress women (Miller and Bell, 1996; New, 2001). Both the harm to men, and the oppressive behaviour of men, needs to be seen in the context of the gender system. However, members of dominant groups do not like to hear about or think about inequality in their social relations, and prefer the social world to be described in other ways. They prefer to believe that the status quo is right and good for all parties. Having power makes this easy. These dynamics find expression in the lack of force behind the comparatively small body of work linking gender relations to men's mental health, and the evident resistance to these ideas within the field of mental health. Ideologies of masculinity also make it difficult for men to consider their individual or collective psychological vulnerabilities.

I shall now map some of the important ways in which social inequality and gender inequality specifically, can be linked to women's mental health, focusing in turn upon the following interrelated factors and processes:

- access to resources that promote mental health
- greater exposure to mental health risks
- processes that maintain the status quo.

Access to resources that promote mental health

As Wetzel (2000) observes '…mental health even when biologically influenced, relates in large measure to the economic welfare and general resources of people in the context of their families and communities in which they live' (p.205). It is significant, therefore, that gender inequality creates the conditions under which women are treated less favourably than men; where they have less access to resources known to support and promote psychological well-being. Despite the evolution in the home and work roles of men and women over the last half century, women's restricted access to valued material and social resources continues to be a very striking feature of gender relations in contemporary society.

Money

The existence of inequalities in our society means that many women have restricted access to money. 'Gender rather than an individual's skills and abilities, continues to be a major determinant of individual economic prosperity' (Equal Opportunities Commission, 2000 p.7). To illustrate, when all sources are taken into account, overall, women's gross income is 49 per cent that of men's (Office for National Statistics, 2002). Older women and women who are lone parents are especially likely to live in poverty.

MENTAL HEALTH IMPLICATIONS FOR WOMEN

The positive association between poverty and mental health problems is one of the best established in all of psychiatric epidemiology. Research has consistently documented that low income is associated with high rates of mental disorder among women. Belle and Doucet (2003) provide a carefully detailed account of the processes by which women's mental health can be affected by low income; this includes the mediating effect of poor diet and food insufficiency (Siefert *et al.*, 2001). Belle and Doucet (2003) also draw attention to the fact that the most stigmatised forms of poverty involve reliance on state support; and that recipients 'often describe experiences of humiliation, dehumanisation, denigration, depression and shame' (p.108).

Work

Inequality distorts subordinate groups' understandings of their qualities and capabilities; women encounter a stream of misinformation about their capacities and liabilities (New, 2001 p.734). They are steered away from ambitions and activities that might challenge the status quo, towards those that meet the needs of dominant groups. As Baker-Miller observed (1976), this typically means providing services that members of the dominant group do not want to perform for themselves: the roles and tasks that are less socially valued, and financially rewarded. Occupational segregation is still very evident in the world of work. Women are concentrated in lower-skilled and lower-paid jobs than men, with less access to vocational training and education (Equal Opportunities Commission, 2003).

MENTAL HEALTH IMPLICATIONS FOR WOMEN

There is good evidence that women's physical and mental health can be enhanced by employment outside the home (Doyal, 2000). Paid work is a potential source of important determinants of mental health including self-esteem, financial and emotional independence, and social support. However, moving beyond the boundaries of sex-segregated occupations can be associated with psychological costs. Studies of high-achieving women suggest that feelings of 'precariousness' 'vulnerability' and 'lack of entitlement' are commonplace. Apfelbaum suggests that these are psychological indicators that women 'remain at the margins of the places where power is being handled, exchanged and distributed' (1993 p.417).

Doyal (2000) also makes the point that work can be a source of stress when it is poorly paid, of low status, a source of high demands, and offers the person little opportunity for control. It is those women whose lives are already most disadvantaged by social inequalities, defined by class, race and age who are most likely to experience the psychological disadvantages, and least likely to experience the psychological advantages of paid work.

Status and value

Gender inequalities mean that women's lives, work and activities are systematically accorded less status and value than men, the consequences of which are ameliorated or accentuated by the interactive effects of other aspects of a woman's life such as her class, race and age.

MENTAL HEALTH IMPLICATIONS FOR WOMEN

Low social status is associated with health-damaging emotional and physiological consequences (Belle and Doucet, 2003), and it is unsurprising that feelings of sadness and depression are common among women. In personal and social life this is evident in the disrespect often shown to women, which may be internalised as feelings of being unvalued and unworthy – 'I'm just a housewife'. Cultural norms about the relative lower worth of women are also detectable in the pervasive belief held by some women that they are not entitled to have their needs met, to be valued, or to be treated respectfully. Such beliefs make women vulnerable to exploitation and use by others, and make it difficult for them to act on their own behalf, for example to leave a violent relationship (Patzel, 2001).

While families may offer some protection against these processes, they can also be the place where girls and women are exposed to extreme forms of demeaning criticism and emotional abuse (Atwood, 2001). The likelihood of being exposed to disrespect and contempt is also heightened for some groups of women, for example those who use mental health services, are poor, or are from a minority group. Increasing age also brings vulnerability. As long as women are primarily charged with the task of reproduction, nurturing and the transmission of values to the next generation, they risk being perceived as socially redundant and of limited social value when that work ends. The significance placed on youth, appearance and reproductive capacity also undermine the position of women in mid and later life, fuel a negative image of their roles and marginalise their views and position in a range of economic and social contexts (Milne and Williams, 2003).

The lower value placed on women is also a determinant of the quality of care women receive from mental health services. Evidence from a range of sources suggest that women are more likely to have their mental health needs minimised, trivialised and marginalised (Beal and Gardner, 2000; Nehls, 1998; Williams, Scott and Bressington, 2004). Misogyny is easily detected in the everyday language used to speak about women who use mental health services (Williams *et al.*, 2004).

Ingroup relations

The effects of social inequalities on women's access to material, social and psychological resources are typically detrimental. However, an exception to this is their potential access to valued relationships with other women. Like members of any disadvantaged group, women are well placed to seek support and value from each other.

MENTAL HEALTH IMPLICATIONS FOR WOMEN

It is well documented that women's relationships with each other, both within and outside of mental health services, can be a source of therapeutic support (Bernardez, 1996; Harris, 1998; Watson, Scott and Ragalsky, 1996). Opportunities to share experiences can enable women to see commonalities among their difficulties, and to have their own experiences and feelings validated. This is particularly important when diagnosis has made it difficult for women to see commonalities with other women, and robbed them of the chance to find shared realities. Groups can help women to shift from believing their distress is a function of their personal inadequacy, to viewing it as an understandable reaction to the hardship, trauma and injustice in their lives. In contradistinction, this type of resource is less readily available to men because of the constraints placed on men by ideologies of masculinity (Miller and Bell, 1996).

Greater exposure to mental health risks

Devalued and unpaid work

HOUSEWORK

Women are now allowed to work outside as well as inside the home. However, they earn less, hold less prestigious jobs, and accumulate lower pensions, while carrying out more of the household tasks, including childcare and housework. Research consistently demonstrates that married men do less housework than their partners (Pilcher, 2000; Seymour, 1992), and reports gender differences in the quality as well as the quantity of free time. Women's free time is often fragmented: personal or spare time is conflated with household tasks and many feel they have 'no time to call my own' (Seymour, 1992).

Mental health implications for women

Women's home roles are often characterised by over-work, extensive responsibilities and a lack of power and value: there is now ample evidence that these exact a mental health cost from women (Bird, 1999; Brown and Harris, 1978). In mid and later life women who have primarily worked within the home appear more likely to experience depression than women who have also been employed, an outcome which is suggested to be mediated by low self-esteem, helplessness and poverty (Milne and Williams, 2003).

UNPAID CARE

The responsibility for caring for sick and incapacitated relatives falls predominantly on women (Maher and Green, 2002). Two thirds of carers are women and women predominate in those groups with the heaviest commitments. Married people not in paid work, part-time employees and those in low-status, poorly paid jobs are more likely to become carers than more advantaged groups; most of these are women. While being employed does not affect whether or not women start care giving, women who do start are more likely to reduce employment hours or stop work altogether (Pavalko and Artis, 1997). Research indicates that carers providing substantial amounts of care face much financial hardship; half of these carers' incomes are within the lowest two fifths of income distribution; and one in five intensive carers has difficulty paying for essentials such as fuel bills (Carers National Association, 2000). Many women also lose the opportunity to make proper pension provision; one of the key reasons for this is interruptions to employment by periods of caring. This may be a second interruption following an earlier break for child rearing. Those carers who begin caring when they are employed, compromise their earning capacity for the remainder of their working lives as well as for retirement.

Mental health implications for women

Research is now making explicit the interlinked and cumulative nature of the range of effects caring has on carers' health and well-being. This includes effects on mental health that are mediated by the impact that caring can have on employment, income and pension in later life (Milne and Williams, 2003).

Caring can also have social and personal costs. Leading a life constrained by caring is described by Twigg as 'restrictedness' (1994). This refers to facing a timetable of caring tasks, worrying about leaving the cared-for person alone as well as broader constraints such as a limited social life. Working carers often experience a 'time bind' resulting in less time for themselves and their family (Milne and Williams, 2003).

The work of women carers is typically under-valued, associated with powerlessness, isolation, and financial hardship: all known determinants of mental health difficulties. Evidence from the General Household Survey (Office for National Statistics, 2002) suggests that compared to women in general, women carers are 23 per cent more likely to have symptoms of psychological stress (Singleton *et al.*, 2002). Research using the British Household Panel Survey offers further confirmation that caring has a significant negative impact on the emotional health of carers (Henwood, 1998).

Intimate relations with men

Women's lives are changing: access to employment and money provide them with choices they did not have in the past. However, as the evidence reviewed above shows, there is little to suggest that these gains in autonomy have been accompanied by more egalitarian relations with their male partners. While most of us can cite examples where change has taken place, there is still inequality between the sexes in families and close relationships. Men in these contexts do not want to give up the benefits of male privilege; requests for change may invoke feelings of insecurity and anxieties about the possibilities of power reversal. Women too may be ambivalent about change in the only domain where they are entitled to claim an identity and exercise some forms of power and control (Williams and Watson, 1988).

MENTAL HEALTH IMPLICATIONS FOR WOMEN

There are indications that many women are unhappy with their close relationships with men, and married life in particular (Walters, Avotri and Charles, 1999); almost three quarters of divorces are initiated by women. Married women are the most depressed segment of the population. This includes women who are demoralised by the experience of being betrayed, abused, disrespected, and abandoned by their partners, and who find it difficult to believe in their own value, and right to control over their lives (Hurst, 1999).

Abuse and violence

The existence of structural inequalities creates opportunities for very serious abuses of power. Gender inequality underpins commonly held beliefs among men that they should have their needs – including their sexual needs – met by women (Hill and Fischer, 2001): that what they do or want takes precedence over the needs of women, and that their prerogatives should not be questioned. This sense of entitlement has been linked to rape, domestic violence, sexual abuse of children and sexual harassment. The constraint that gender inequality places on the characteristics and qualities deemed appropriate in men has also been identified as a contributing factor here. In the interests of gender inequality men are encouraged to be independent, emotionally inexpressive, and goal-orientated with the attendant possibility of becoming out of touch with their own emotions and the emotions of others.

Physical and sexual violence and abuse, perpetrated overwhelmingly most frequently by men is a common and sometimes covertly sanctioned means of expressing and maintaining dominance in family and community settings. It is estimated that globally, one third of women have been beaten, coerced into sex, and subjected to extreme emotional abuse (Heise, Ellsberg and Gottemoeller, 1999). Research shows that between 1 in 10 and 1 in 3 girls experience sexual abuse in childhood – depending on the definition of abuse and at what age childhood is deemed to end. Violence can and does occur over the lifespan, from childhood to old age, with elder abuse being the most recent aspect of domestic violence to receive sustained research attention. The lifetime prevalence rates for women experiencing domestic violence is 1 in 4, and the peak incidence of physical and sexual violence occurs among young women (Domestic Violence Data Source, 2002).

MENTAL HEALTH IMPLICATIONS FOR WOMEN

The mental health implications of these forms of power abuse are now well substantiated (Goodman *et al.*, 1999; Harris and Landis, 1997; World Health Organisation, 2000). Indeed, physical and sexual assault are normative experiences in the lives of women who have serious mental health problems, who are homeless or living in secure psychiatric services. By mid life substantial numbers of women will have experienced these kinds of trauma often in conjunction with other forms of exploitation and oppression. Those that have had the resources and opportunity to work through their psychological impact will be well placed to make the best of their futures. However, many will not be so fortunate; not least because most statutory mental health services are ill equipped to support women in finding resolution to these profound experiences of disempowerment (Williams and Scott, 2002).

There is evidence (Byrne *et al.*, 1999) that women who live below the poverty line are at increased risk of violence, and that physical and sexual assault increases the risk of poverty, divorce and unemployment. These dynamics and the effects of these cumulative risks are very evident in the backgrounds and life stories of women using mental health services (Goodman *et al.*, 2001; Williams *et al.*, 2004).

Processes that maintain the status quo

To maintain advantage the dominant group needs to use its power systematically to safeguard its position, and keep the subordinate group in its place. Considered below are some of the important ways in which these processes are implicated in women's mental health.

Femininity and masculinity

It is well noted (Baker Miller, 1976) that people from subordinate social groups are socialised to develop psychological characteristics that are pleasing to the privileged and which foster compliance rather than rebellion. These characteristics include: submissiveness, passivity, deference and lack of assertion. Women are also often deemed to be irrational, incapable and incompetent – all characteristics which suggest that women are ill suited to acting autonomously or to exercising power. More subtle processes can also be detected. In addition to negative characteristics, women's subordinate status is justified and maintained by the attribution of positive qualities such as nurturance and warmth – the 'women are wonderful' factor. This benevolent sexism protects the self-concepts of sexist men by allowing them to see themselves as the protectors, admirers and intimates of women, rather than their hostile dominators. However, both hostile and benevolent sexism function to keep women in their place (Glick *et al.*, 2000). Data collected by Glick *et al.* (2000) suggest that many women avoid the hostility they could encounter if they reject conventional female roles, by conforming to these roles and being rewarded by men's benevolence.

MENTAL HEALTH IMPLICATIONS FOR WOMEN

Being a good woman

The risks to women of being brought up to please men and to accommodate the wishes of others, is of neglecting their own needs and losing the sense of their own entitlement. Jack (1991) calls this 'silencing the self'. Women are also placed in a double bind because caring for others and being nurturant are socially under-valued activities. Should they feel angry about their lives and experiences, 'good women' are expected to stifle rather than express these feelings. The psychological costs of this toxic combination of social expectations and injunctions are revealed in the accounts that some women offer of their lives (Hurst, 1999). A common theme in the lives of many women is that of 'getting on with it' and working very hard to 'hold it altogether', including minimising, normalising and coping with disappointment and distress in the service of being a 'good woman' (Scattolon and Stoppard, 1999). 'Good women' measure their self-worth through the success or failure of their relationships, and they can feel obligated to preserve those relationships even if it exacts a terrible personal cost (Rodman, Aronson and Schaler Buchholz p.115).

What is healthy?

Gender and other social inequalities also have discernable effects on understandings and definitions of mental health. So, even though femininity is demonstrably linked to clear mental health risks, studies find that women who have internalised these characteristics are generally considered to be normal and mentally healthy (Penfold and Walker, 1984). Derogatory and discouraging terms such as 'mad', 'bad', 'weak', 'sick' and 'crazy' are terms that are generally reserved for those women whose behaviour, sexual choices and lifestyles do not appear to be governed by expectations of femininity or which might be 'read' as an indictment of injustice. This is particularly the case for women when they are outside their home and are therefore 'out of place' (Unger, 1988). In contexts and institutions where there is no rationale or incentive for attributing 'good' (or useful) characteristics to women, then hostility can be unchecked. This is particularly the case for women using psychiatric services who are usually a poor match for the stereotype of a 'good' women or even a 'good' patient. Misogyny is widespread and painfully evident in the language used to describe women, their behaviour and needs.

Managing anger

For some women, the dominant themes in their lived experience of inequalities are those of abandonment, betrayal, abuse, disappointment and frustration – experiences which assault the self and which are a source of powerful emotions including great sadness, anger and rage. Yet, one of the injunctions that support the perpetuation of gender inequality is that women should not be angry. It is men in our society who are authorised to be angry and violent. The obvious implication for mental health services is that they should enable women to give voice to their experiences, and to find safe ways to express their anger and rage. Yet, mental health services typically function to suppress emotion through medication.

Victim blaming

Victim blaming is a widely used device for deflecting attention from the causes of a problem which lie elsewhere. Within the context of gender relations women are blamed for social and family problems as well as for their own distress and efforts to survive these feelings (Penfold and Walker, 1984). Psychiatry makes its own particular contribution to this discourse, with its emphasis on diagnosis, individual pathology and medicalised responses to distress. In these ways, the connections between a woman's behaviour and distress and her lived experience are severed, and without these understandings her behaviour is easily understood as meaningless, out of control and dangerous.

MENTAL HEALTH IMPLICATIONS FOR WOMEN

There is plentiful evidence of the ways in which women struggle to manage and survive damage rooted in gender and other social inequalities. Dissociation, self-harm, eating distress, embodiment, the use of prescribed and non-prescribed drugs, assault and fire-setting, are all common ways in which women manage unbearable feelings of anger, anxiety, depression and loss when they have limited control, and when they do not feel entitled to speak or safe enough to do so (Bear, 1999; Lart *et al.*, 1999; see also Chapter 6). Yet, in the context of mental health services where power rests largely with the service providers, a woman is likely to be judged, blamed and often punished. Mental health services are no different from other social institutions in having rules and practices that serve the interest of privilege; and the absence of understanding of past experiences of disempowerment is often compounded. Women are unlikely to receive opportunities for acknowledgement, understanding and change when mental health staff have not been enabled to understand their disempowerment, or when the dominance of psychiatric ideologies means that they lack the knowledge and skills to detect or intervene effectively (Cann *et al.*, 2001; Williams *et al.*, 2004).

Dynamics of change

There is huge reticence within mental health services towards taking social inequalities seriously when it is quite obvious – even from the modest resumé of the evidence presented here – that they are very significant determinants of mental health and the quality and safety of services. An appreciation of the social psychological dynamics associated with inequalities helps make this reticence understandable. In short, it is functional for the status quo, and privilege, if the considerable psychological distress and damage created by social inequalities is not recognised as such. Those who challenge this often find themselves undermined (e.g. Chesler, 1994), and it is no accident that recent efforts to give policy attention to women with mental health needs is called 'Into the Mainstream' (Department of Health, 2002). It is also less personally challenging to minimise the significance of social inequalities. We do not have to ask ourselves how we benefit materially and psychologically from existing social relations, or query the morality of our personal strategies for satisfaction and survival within this context. Neither do we have to listen carefully to what people with mental health needs have to say about their lives and experiences, and learn in graphic and painful detail about chronic and traumatic forms of oppression.

However, in addition to processes and interests that work to perpetuate inequalities, there are those that expose inequality and throw into question the basis for its existence. Naming the problem is an essential first step.

Conclusion

An intergroup analysis of social inequalities provides a framework that can help us to identify, understand and address important implications for mental health. This level of analysis continually confronts us with issues of power, and simultaneously reminds us that issues of power have been either ignored or misrepresented within the field of mental health. As I have noted elsewhere, this framework has obvious implications for policy (Scott and Williams, 2002; Williams, LeFrancois and Copperman, 2001a), training

(Scott and Williams, in press) service provision (Williams and Scott, 2002) and clinical practice (Williams and Watson, 1988; Watson and Williams, 1992). However, it should never be used as a substitute for talking to individual women about their lives and experiences. In the final analysis, the efficacy of mental health services rests on their capacity to provide respectful and safe relationships within which women can tell their own stories of disempowerment and survival.

References

Apfelbaum, E. (1993) 'Norwegian and French women in high leadership positions: the importance of cultural contexts upon gendered relations.' *Psychology of Women Quarterly, 17*, 4, 409–429.

Apfelbaum, E. (1999) 'Relations of domination and movements for liberation: an analysis of power between groups (abridged).' *Feminism and Psychology, 9*, 3, 267–272.

Atwood, N. C. (2001) 'Gender bias in families and its clinical implications for women.' *Social Work 46*, 1, 23–36.

Baker Miller, J. (1976) *Towards a New Psychology of Women.* London: Sage.

Beal, B. A. and Gardner, C. B. (2000) 'Gendered advice and mental health practices.' *Perspectives on Social Problems 12*, 203–216.

Bear, Z. (ed.) (1999) *Good Practice in Counselling People Who Have Been Abused.* London: Jessica Kingsley.

Belle, D. and Doucet, J. (2003) 'Poverty, inequality, and discrimination as sources of depression among US women.' *Psychology of Women Quarterly 27*, 101–113.

Beresford, P. (2000) 'Service users' knowledges and social work theory: conflict or collaboration?' *British Journal of Social Work 30*, 4, 489–503.

Bernardez, T. (1996) 'Women's therapy groups as the treatment of choice.' In B. DeChant (ed.) *Women and Group Psychotherapy: Theory and Practice.* London: Guilford Press.

Bird, C. E. (1999) 'Gender, household labor, and psychological distress: the impact of the amount and division of housework.' *Journal of Health and Social Behavior 40*, 1, 32–45.

Brown, G. W. and Harris, T. (1978) *Social Origins of Depression.* London: Tavistock Publications.

Byrne, C. A., Resnick, H.S., R., Kilpatrick, D. G., Best, C. L. and Saunders, B. E. (1999) 'The socioeonomic impact of interpersonal violence on women.' *Journal of Consulting and Clinical Psychology 67*, 3, 362–366.

Cann, K., Withnell, S., Shakespeare, J., Doll, H. and Thomas, J. (2001) 'Domestic violence: a comparative survey of levels of detection, knowledge and attitudes in healthcare workers.' *Public Health 115*, 89–95.

Carers National Association (2000) *Caring on the Breadline: The Financial Implications of Caring.* London: Carers National Association.

Chesler, P. (1994) 'Heroism is our only alternative.' *Feminism and Psychology 4*, 2, 298–306.

Cosgrove, L. (2000) 'Crying out loud: understanding women's emotional distress as both lived experience and social construction.' *Feminism and Psychology 10*, 2, 247–267.

Dench, S., Astam, J., Evans, C., Meager, N., Williams, M. and Willison, R. (2003) *Key Indicators of Women's Position in Britain.* London: Women and Equality Unit.

Department of Health (2002) *Women's Mental Health: Into the Mainstream – Strategic Development of Mental Health Care for Women.* London: Department of Health. www.doh.gov.uk/mentalhealth/women.htm.

Department of Health (2003) *Mainstreaming Gender and Women's Mental Health: Implementation Guidance.* London: Department of Health. (Free of charge from Department of Health, PO Box 777, London SE1 6XH or download from www.doh.gov.uk/mentalhealth).

Domestic Violence Data Source (2002) *Factsheets 1–5.* www.domesticviolencedata.org/4_faqs/facts.htm

Doyal, L. (2000) *Health and Work in Older Women: A Neglected Issue.* London: The Pennell Initiative for Women's Health.

Equal Opportunities Commission (2000) *Women and Men in Britain: The Labour Market.* London: Equal Opportunities Commission.

Equal Opportunities Commission (2003) *Facts about Women and Men in Great Britain.* London: Equal Opportunities Commission.

Glick, P., Fiske, S.T., Mladinie, A., Saiz, J.L., Abrams, D., Masser, B. *et al.* (2000) 'Beyond prejudice as simple antipathy: hostile and benevolent sexism across cultures.' *Journal of Personality and Social Psychology 79*, 5, 763–775.

Goodman, L. A., Thompson, K. M., Weinfurt, K., Corl, S., Acker, P., Mueser, K. T. *et al.* (1999) 'Reliability of reports of violent victimization and posttraumatic stress disorder among men and women with serious mental illness.' *Journal of Traumatic Stress 12*, 4, 587–599.

Goodman, L. A., Salyers, M. P., Mueser, K. T., Rosenberg, S. D., Swartz, M., Essock, S. M., *et al.* (2001) 'Recent victimization in women and men with severe mental illness: prevalence and correlates.' *Journal of Traumatic Stress 14*, 4, 615–632.

Harris, M. (1998) *Trauma Recovery and Empowerment: A Clinician's Guide for Working with Women in Groups.* New York: The Free Press.

Harris, M. and Landis, L. L. (1997) *Sexual Abuse in the Lives of Women Diagnosed with Serious Mental Illness.* London: Harwood Academic.

Heise, L., Ellsberg, M. and Gottemoeller, M. (1999) *Ending Violence Against Women (Population Reports, Series, L, 11).* Baltimore: Johns Hopkins University School of Public Health.

Henwood, M. (1998) *Ignored and Invisible: Carers' Experience of the NHS.* London: Carers National Association.

Hill, M. S. and Fischer, A. R. (2001) 'Does entitlement mediate the link between masculinity and rape-related variables.' *Journal of Counseling Psychology 48*, 1, 39–50.

Hurst, S. A. (1999) 'Legacy of betrayal: a grounded theory of becoming demoralized from the perspective of women who have been depressed.' *Canadian Psychology 40*, 2, 179–191.

Jack, D. C. (1991) *Silencing the Self: Women and Depression.* Cambridge, MA: Harvard University Press.

Lart, R., Payne, S., Beumont, B., MacDonald, G. and Mistry, T. (1999) *Women and Secure Psychiatric Services: A Literature Review.* York: University of York, NHS Centre for Reviews and Dissemination.

Maher, J. and Green, H. (2002) *Carers 2000.* London: The Stationery Office.

Miller, J. and Bell, C. (1996) 'Mapping men's mental health.' *Journal of Community and Applied Social Psychology 6*, 5, 317–327.

Milne, A. and Williams, J. (2003) *Women in Transition – A Literature Review of the Mental Health Risks Facing Women in Mid-life.* London: Pennell Initiative for Women's Health.

Nehls, N. (1998) 'Borderline personality disorder: gender stereotypes, stigma, and limited system of care.' *Issues-in-Mental-Health-Nursing 19*, 2, 97–112.

New, C. (2001) 'Oppressed and oppressors? The systematic mistreatment of men.' *Sociology 35*, 3, 729–748.

Office for National Statistics (2002) *Social Trends.* London: The Stationery Office.

Patzel, B. (2001) 'Women's use of resources in leaving abusive relationships: a naturalistic inquiry.' *Issues in Mental Health Nursing 22*, 729–747.

Pavalko, E. K. and Artis, J. E. (1997) 'Women's caregiving and paid work: causal relationships in late midlife.' *Journals of Gerontology: Series B: Psychological Sciences and Social Sciences 52b*, 4, S170–S179.

Penfold, P. S. and Walker, G. A. (1984) *Women and the Psychiatric Paradox.* Milton Keynes: Open University Press.

Pilcher, J. (2000) 'Domestic divisions of labour in the twentieth century: "change slow a-coming".' *Work, Employment and Society 14*, 4, 771–780.

Rodman Aronson, K.M. and Schaler Buchholz, E. (2001) 'The post-feminist era: still striving for equality in relationships.' *American Journal of Family Therapy 29*, 109–124.

Scattolon, Y. and Stoppard, J. M. (1999) '"Getting on with life": women's experiences and ways of coping with depression.' *Canadian Psychology 40*, 2, 205–219.

Scott, S. and Williams, J. (2002) 'Incorporating women's views and priorities in core policy decisions.' In *Health in the Commonwealth: Priorities and Perspectives 2001/2002.* London: Commonwealth Secretariat.

Scott, S. and Williams, J. (in press) 'Staff training and support.' In N. Jeffcote and T. Watson (eds) *Working Therapeutically with Women in Secure Settings.* London: Jessica Kingsley.

Seymour, J. (1992) '"No time to call my own": women's time as a household resource.' *Women's Studies International Forum 15*, 2, 187–192.

Siefert, K., Heflin, C. M., Corcoran, M. E. and Williams, D. R. (2001) 'Food insufficiency and the physical and mental health of low-income women.' *Women and Health 32*, 1–2, 159–177.

Singleton, N., Maung, N. A., Cowie, A., Sparks, J., Bumpstead, R. and Meltzer, H. (2002) *Mental Health of Carers.* London: The Stationery Office.

Trivedi, P. (2002) 'Racism, social exclusion and mental health: a Black user's perspective.' In K. Bhui (ed.) *Racism and Mental Health.* London: Jessica Kingsley.

Twigg, J. A. K. (1994) *Carers Perceived: Policy and Practice in Informal Care.* Buckinghamshire: Open University Press.

Unger, R. K. (1988) 'Psychological, feminist and personal epistemology.' In M. M. Gergen (ed.) *Feminist Thought and the Structure of Knowledge.* New York: New York University Press.

Walters, V., Avotri, J. Y. and Charles, N. (1999) '"Your heart is never free": women in Wales and Ghana talking about distress.' *Canadian Psychology 40*, 2, 129–142.

Watson, G., Scott, C. and Ragalsky, S. (1996) 'Refusing to be marginalized: groupwork in mental health services for women survivors of childhood sexual abuse.' *Journal of Community and Applied Social Psychology 6*, 5, 341–354.

Watson, G. and Williams, J. (1992) 'Feminist practice in therapy.' In J. Ussher and P. Nicolson (eds) *Gender Issues in Clinical Psychology.* London: Routledge.

Wetzel, J. W. (2000) 'Women and mental health: a global perspective.' *International Social Work 34*, 2, 205–215.

Williams, J. (1999) 'Social inequalities, mental health and mental health services.' In C. Newnes, G. Holmes and C. Dunn (eds) *Thinking About Psychiatry and The Future of the Mental Health System*. Ross-on-Wye: PCCS Books.

Williams, J., LeFrancois, B. and Copperman, J. (2001a) *Mental Health Services that Work for Women: Survey Findings*. Canterbury: Tizard Centre, University of Kent.

Williams, J. and Scott, S. (2002) 'Service responses to women with mental health needs.' *Mental Health Review 7*, 1, 6–14.

Williams, J., Scott, S. and Bressington, C. (2004) 'Dangerous journeys: women's pathways through secure services.' In N. Jeffcote and T. Watson (eds) *Working Therapeutically with Women in Secure Settings*. London: Jessica Kingsley.

Williams, J., Scott, S. and Waterhouse, S. (2001b) 'Mental health services for "difficult" women: reflections on some recent developments.' *Feminist Review 68*, Summer, 89–104.

Williams, J. A. and Watson, G. (1988) 'Sexual inequality, family life and family therapy.' In E. Street and W. Dryden (eds) *Family Therapy in Britain*. Milton Keynes: Open University Press.

World Health Organisation (2000) *Women's Mental Health: An Evidence Based Review*. Geneva: World Health Organisation.

CHAPTER 9

'The Sickness Label Infected Everything we Said'

Lesbian and Gay Perspectives on Mental Distress

Sarah Carr

Thus psychiatry has its own blind spot. It may see only one dimension of the doctor–patient dialectic: the disease or demon within the sufferer. What patients' narratives particularly highlight are the demons without, amongst which the madhouse-keeping psychiatrist himself, his techniques and his milieux, may well all too readily figure as the final instance.

Roy Porter (1999)

Mental health professionals in Britain should be aware of the mistakes of the past. Only in that way can we prevent future excesses and heal the gulf between gay and lesbian patients and their psychiatrists.

King and Bartlett (1999)

Introduction

In this chapter I present an account based on several sources of knowledge, one of which is lived experience. By presenting what I call a 'personal case study' alongside historical accounts and recent research, I hope to humanise the issues being discussed, partly to counter the dehumanisation that comes with being pathologised. However, this 'case study' involves the practice rather than the patient coming under scrutiny, with the patient observing and diagnosing from their own perspective and recording this in a narrative account. After presenting this account, I will then attempt to understand it within an historical framework. Following this, I will move into the present context to examine the contemporary experiences of lesbians and gay men who use mental health services, and the risk of discrimination within those services. I will be concentrating on those who identify as lesbian or gay, although some of the issues discussed here will relate to bisexual, trans-gendered and transsexual people too. When I use the phrase 'gay people', I am referring to both gay men and women. However, I do recognise that gay men and lesbians have specific issues relating to our gender as well as our sexuality that cannot be discussed in detail within the parameters of this study. Finally, I will argue that a recognition of personal, social and cultural influences can enhance and transform the way in which the needs of gay men and women are understood and addressed within mental health services.

A personal case study

When I was 18 I was unwell: I was self-harming, neglecting to eat properly, wandering and experiencing the feeling that I was becoming transparent or physically disappearing. Social relationships and sometimes even moving and speaking were difficult for me. During my first term at university the execution of my plan to kill myself was, now thankfully, interrupted. It never occurred to me to visit a doctor because I did not regard myself as being ill, but eventually a friend persuaded me to seek the help of a psychotherapist. This was my first encounter with therapy 'proper' and I had no idea of what to expect; I was also very vulnerable. By the end of the first consultation the therapist had discovered my sexual orientation, which provided him with the disease to cure and because I was not all that happy about my sexuality at that stage, I complied with him. Thus our therapeutic project became my 'heterosexualisation', the idea being that if I became heterosexual then I would be cured of my mental distress. So, my homosexuality was my illness.

My therapist's method for diagnosing my 'latent heterosexuality' was novel to say the least. He showed me several examples of top-shelf pornography designed for heterosexual men and concluded that because I did not find these images sexually appealing, I could not really be gay. This strategy bears some relation to traditional methods of aversion therapy: up to the late 1960s gay people, men in particular (who were sometimes referred by the criminal courts for treatment), were given aversion therapy which consisted of electric shocks or nausea-inducing drugs coinciding with the presentation of homoerotic images (this is something that will be discussed in more detail later on). My therapist showed me pornographic images of women to which I had an inherent aversion and he tried to use hypnosis to reinforce and generalise this feeling in an effort to coax my 'repressed heterosexuality' into returning. However, my resistance to his attempts to hypnotise and avert me into a more 'healthy' state of *at least* bisexuality forced him to conclude that I had some sort of personality disorder.

I may have been spared the horror of aversion therapy, but the fundamental idea was still the same: homosexuality is a disease of the mind and is the biomedical cause of mental illness, if not the illness itself. To me, the medical model of homosexuality to which I was subjected during my treatment was actually harmful and eventually I found it less damaging to continue coping with my distress by self-harming. It was 1990 and at that point in time my therapist was not just following his own idiosyncratic approach; this method could be endorsed by reference to the World Health Organisation's International Classification of Disease, which, until 1992, classified homosexuality as a disease under Section 302 – 'sexual deviations and disorders'. It was finally removed from the British central database of mental illnesses in 1994.

Even after homosexuality had been officially removed from international disease classification, I still found it difficult to find the support I needed. In fact, my experiences taught me to avoid mental health services when I became unwell and at times I have felt too vulnerable to risk seeing a doctor. The fact is that many mental health practitioners still operate using the disease model of homosexuality because it is integral to their inherited clinical thought and practice. The authors of a major historical review of this subject concluded that 'the conservative social bias inherent in psychiatry and psychology [has] damaged the lives of gay men and lesbians and provided grounds for discrimination' (King and Bartlett, 1999 p.111). This can then be compounded by the personal religious beliefs or moral prejudices of the individual. For example, my therapist was a Roman Catholic man and so, I believe, had an additional religious motivation for curing me. From the nature of my treatment I got the impression that, obscurely, he felt me to be a wasted womb. For him, therefore, my mental distress came from my inability to recognise that I was not complete without a male sexual partner. Such experiences have led me to believe that the claim of therapists and doctors to professional objectivity can often be a false one. As one author has observed, 'medical treatment often has more to do with doctors' values and attitudes than with objective realities' (Rose, 1994 p.586). I have met with practitioners whose religious, moral and social prejudices have prevented them from recognising me as a human being trying to manage difficult and complex experiences. As a consequence some have been unable to resist trying to cure me through the manipulation of my sexuality. Sadly, my experiences seem to exemplify a general situation and reflect the residual traces of a period in the history of psychiatry characterised by medicalisation and often inhumane clinical practice.

A brief psychiatric history of homosexuality

Social historians have argued convincingly that 'the homosexual' is a nineteenth-century social construct, originally invented not by gay people themselves but by the medical establishment in order to classify and control people who were considered to be a social and moral threat. In his work, *The History of Sexuality*, Michel Foucault describes how nineteenth-century science constructed 'the homosexual' as

> a personage, a past, a case history and a childhood... Nothing that went into his total composition was unaffected by his sexuality. It was everywhere present in him: at the root of all his actions... It was consubstantial with him, less a habitual sin than as a singular nature... The sodomite had been a temporary aberration; the homosexual was now a species. (Foucault, 1990 p.43)

In other words, homosexuality came to be seen as something a person *is* rather than something that they *do*. It became the externally imposed defining principle for an individual. Further, the historian Roy Porter has argued that 'modern sexual science shifted attention from practices to bodies, genes, brains and psyches, and systematically pigeon-holed such people as "deviants", inverts or homosexuals...' (Porter, 1997 p.703). He also recognised that this enabled the Victorian social and medical establishment to use such classifications to treat people and control their behaviour:

> Our discourses specifying male and female roles, heterosexuality and homosexuality stem largely from late nineteenth century medicine and psychiatry... Sexology provided the classificatory and diagnostic systems required to administer the asylums, hospitals, reformatories and jails... (Porter, 1997 p.702)

As a result of this (in the words of Barbara Gittings, one of the founders of the US gay liberation movement during the late 1950s):

> Psychiatrists were one of the three major groups that had their hands on us. Religion and law were the other two. So besides being sick we were sinful

and criminal. But the sickness label infected everything we said and made it difficult to gain any credibility for anything we said for ourselves. The sickness label was paramount. (quoted in Marcus, 1993 p.221)

This notion of homosexuality as sickness, the behavioural symptoms of which must be subject to social control and medical cure, is one which still haunts the mental health system today. Although gay people in Britain are no longer subjected to the barbaric physical treatments which will be described next, it is vital to be aware of past practices if the present situation is to be understood and addressed.

In his history of the Royal Victoria Military Hospital at Netley, near Southampton, Philip Hoare describes some of the treatments administered at the 'D-Block' psychiatric wing during the mid twentieth century. It was here that the famous 'anti-psychiatry' practitioner, R.D. Laing, was on placement in the 1950s. Some of the soldiers incarcerated in D-Block were there because of their sexual orientation:

> Then regarded as a psychiatric disorder, according to one orderly working at Netley around Laing's time there, homosexuality was a case for treatment in itself: '…Sometimes a chap would be so distressed, he could be suicidal. They tried very often to wean them off it [homosexuality] a bit. They used to show them pictures of women, of men, and give them electric shocks'. (Hoare, 2002 p.320)

Such treatment was not confined to the military hospital. Harrowing accounts exist of behavioural treatments practised in NHS hospitals during the 1950s and 1960s when

> the mainstream still saw homosexuality as an aberration to be corrected. Doctors had come up with a number of different methods for 'treating' homosexuality. There were two forms of aversion therapy – the use of emetics [vomit-inducing drugs] and, if that failed…electro-convulsive shock treatment. Lobotomies were also performed in some cases [and]…chemical castration was not only permitted but…encouraged. (Jivani, 1997 p.122)

Peter Price, a gay man who received the 'slide and emetic' aversion therapy for homosexuality (a 'Pavlovian' behavioural treatment designed to link homoerotic stimulation [pictures or slides] with revolting physical experiences) in an NHS hospital in the early 1960s describes his ordeal:

> …for seventy-two hours I was injected, I drank, I was sick…I just had to sit in my own vomit and excrement…I was in a terrible state. What was going

through my mind was not the fear of being gay; it was the fear of not coming out of the psychiatric wing alive… (quoted in Jivani, 1997 p.125)

Luchia Fitzgerald, a young lesbian who was seeing a probation officer during the 1960s, was sent by the officer to see a psychiatrist, because it was thought that she had a problem with her sexuality:

> They were discussing how they could put it right and he made suggestions of a part of my brain not being developed right and that really the only way forward was to have surgery… I was thinking to myself maybe these people are right because they're professionals, they know what they're doing… I thought maybe if I was heterosexual, I could go home, settle down and be like everyone else. (quoted in Jivani, 1997 pp.126–127)

Up until 1967 in Britain, sexual acts between men were a criminal offence punishable by imprisonment (sexual acts between women had not been considered possible, so were not covered by legislation) but the judiciary often treated gay men more leniently if they agreed to undergo treatment. One of those men was Alan Turing, Britain's most famous mathematician who had been awarded an OBE for breaking the German Enigma Code during World War II. In 1952 he was prosecuted for having sex with another man and agreed to a course of hormone therapy instead of probation. Because this treatment resulted in nothing but distressing physical changes and severe depression 'a year after his ordeal by oestrogen ended, Turing killed himself by eating an apple dipped in cyanide' (Jivani, 1997 p.123). Regarding Turing's work it is a tragic irony that what was occurring in post-war Britain had also occurred in Nazi Germany. In his history of the persecution of gay men and women in Germany during the Third Reich, Günter Grau cites documented medical experiments on gay men at Buchenwald concentration camp. These experiments were designed 'to investigate whether implantation of the "artificial male sex gland" can normalize the sexual orientation of homosexual persons' (Grau, 1995 p.286). Despite past efforts of the medical establishment to control and cure gay people, it appears that none of the essentially experimental interventions proved successful in turning a homosexual person into a heterosexual person. They could however turn otherwise mentally well individuals into people with major mental health problems (King and Bartlett, 1999).

The present situation

Given this history it is not surprising that gay men and lesbians have difficulties with mental health services even though some research shows that we may be high users of them:

> Gay men and lesbians are greater users of mental health services in primary and secondary care than heterosexual men and women. We need to know more about the quality of treatment they receive, particularly because mental health professionals may be insensitive or even hostile to their needs. (King *et al.*, 2003 p.557)

General research from the US has revealed that fewer than half of lesbian, gay, bisexual and transgender adults surveyed had disclosed their sexual orientation to their healthcare provider (Harris Interactive, 2002). For those that have sought help from mental health services in the UK, one survey showed that half of the respondents reported that their sexuality had been inappropriately used to explain the cause of mental distress (Golding, 1997). The ground-breaking study by Linda McFarlane on the experiences of lesbians, gay men and bisexuals in UK mental health services concluded that 'lesbian, gay and bisexual mental health service users are discriminated against and oppressed, not only by the attitudes and behaviour of society at large, but also from within mental health services' (McFarlane, 1998 p.117). The report found that, like me, other gay people sometimes choose to avoid mainstream mental health services because they are afraid of being 'pathologised, negatively judged or stigmatised' (McFarlane, 1998 p.117). A 1997 Mind survey reported that 78 per cent of lesbian and gay respondents 'expressed reservations about feeling safe enough to disclose their sexuality within a mainstream mental health service' (Golding, 1997 p.28), and 84 per cent said that they 'feared prejudice, discrimination or that their sexuality would be pathologised' (Golding, 1997 p.8). Eighty-eight per cent of respondents who experienced prejudice and discrimination within mental health services felt too vulnerable to challenge it (Golding, 1997).

Treatments available in modern mental health services such as psychotherapy have often proven to be biased and research published in the *British Journal of Psychiatry* in 2001 indicated that lesbian and gay patients 'may encounter overt or covert bias, including the pathologisation of homosexuality *per se*', when receiving psychotherapeutic treatment on the NHS (Bartlett, King and Phillips, 2001 p.545). Furthermore 'gay men and lesbians continue to be treated almost exclusively by heterosexual psychotherapists, whose theoretical training has been, by today's standards, homophobic' (King and

Bartlett, 1999 p.110) and 'the history of pathologizing homosexuality is recent enough to have affected the training of most mental health practitioners' (Rothblum, 1994 p.214).

It appears that mental health services continue to be characterised by a cultural and institutional bias against gay people. And, as my personal experience has shown, some of the individual professionals within the service can have personal prejudices that affect the quality of treatment and response. Only 11 per cent of gay mental health service users in a UK Mind survey reported that they received a completely positive reaction after coming out to mental health workers and other service users (Golding, 1997). Researchers have reported that counsellors' opinions paralleled those of the larger society, with individuals tending to pathologise to a greater degree gay men and lesbians than they would heterosexuals (Bieschke, McClanahan and Tozer, 2000). Other research on the attitudes of mental health service staff has shown that 'although the majority of providers do not view homosexuality as being pathological, they still frequently evidence both attitudinal and behavioural responses to sexual minority clients that may not be conducive to positive outcomes' (Cochran, 2001 p.939). A large US study on the attitudes of social work and counselling postgraduates revealed that a significant minority still expressed negative attitudes towards lesbians and gay men, with 'males, heterosexuals, African Americans and conservative [Christians] reflect[ing] the demographics of those who tended to express the least acceptance' (Newman, Dannenfelser and Benishek, 2002 p.280). As these service user experiences and academic research studies show, the mental health profession would benefit from training and education to ensure that their lesbian and gay clients are better served.

In order to improve mental health services for gay people it would seem that professional training should not only incorporate issues of diversity and awareness, but also the structured and supported examination of personal prejudice and its influence on professional values and ethics.

> The resolution of conflicts between religious or moral beliefs with codes of ethics and professional roles is something that [should be] part of every social work or counselling curriculum…[trainers] will need skills and strategies that increase the well-being and acceptance of lesbian and gay clients. (Newman et al., 2002 pp.283–284)

Lesbian and gay issues have been found to be poorly addressed in social work training, and although equal opportunities policies exist in social work departments, active implementation with regard to gay staff and clients is rare (Price, 1997).

With specific reference to psychotherapy practitioners in the NHS, it has been recommended that

> in line with its policy on equal opportunities, NHS psychotherapy departments should scrutinize the training and experience of applicants for posts to ensure they are equipped to meet the needs of a wide cross-section of the community, including gay and lesbian clients. (Bartlett *et al.*, 2001 p.548)

Referring to work by Man (1994), Mind have stated that

> prior to working with lesbians and gay men, counsellors need to work through their own attitudes, myths, stereotypes and sexual feelings (both attractions and aversions) towards persons of the same or opposite sex... In order to work effectively with lesbians and gay men, counsellors need to be aware of how the values and beliefs of their client differ from their own; if they cannot respect these differences they should not be in a position to offer a service. (Mind, 2001 p.13)

Professionals should therefore be encouraged to examine the complex interplay of personal and professional opinion, their prejudice and practice. They need to be aware that mental health services can contribute to a gay person's sense of alienation and oppression. This requires some understanding of perspectives that incorporate the social and psychological aspects of mental distress: 'Contexts – social, political and cultural – are central to the understanding of mental health problems' (Double, 2002 p.26).

The mental health of gay people: social and cultural contexts

The truth is that gay people can experience mental distress because of their sexual orientation, but this has nothing whatsoever to do with diseases of the mind. In 1994, Mind's Equalities Group issued this statement: 'The myth that sexual identity alone is either a cause or symptom of mental distress must be revealed and repudiated. We recognise the cumulative effect of discrimination in all our social systems...' (quoted in Mind, 2001 p.5). The medical model which pathologises lesbians and gay men can be seen as one of the many social factors that can impact on our mental well-being and sense of self. Linda McFarlane's study showed that there *can* be a connection between sexual orientation and mental health problems, but it needs to be understood in social and cultural rather than medical terms. The report showed that homophobia (prejudicial behaviour towards, abuse of, or discrimination against gay people) and heterosexism (the assumption that everyone is, needs or wants to be heterosexual) have an impact on mental health. She writes that, 'difficulties in coming out compounded feelings of loneliness and isolation, guilt and fear and led in some instances to feelings of depression, self-harm and attempted suicide' (McFarlane, 1998 p.117). Elsewhere large-scale studies and research reviews have shown that gay people:

- had significantly worse mental health (particularly for suicidality), greater childhood adversity and less positive support from family than their heterosexual counterparts (Jorm *et al.*, 2002)

- suffered from victimisation and low self-esteem leading to major depression (Otis and Skinner, 1996)

- had an increased risk of major depression, suicidal ideation, suicide attempts, substance misuse and self-harm (Cochran, 2001; King *et al.*, 2003).

Gay people continue to lack the level of social support and affirmation enjoyed by their heterosexual counterparts, which many believe has a deep effect on our mental health and psychological well-being:

> Cultural heterosexism is pervasive in our cultural institutions and operates to deny the legitimacy of alternative sexual orientations. At the same time, psychological heterosexism is part of a set of values and beliefs imparted to us through socialization that stigmatizes and denigrates alternative sexual orientations. (McFarlane, 1998 p.97)

Further to this

> the problematization of their own lifestyle (indeed more broadly, their way of life) has been based on a conscious imperative among lesbians and gay men to invent the self and ways of relating to others...lesbians and gay men must create a self out of (or despite) the heterosexual self that is culturally given to them... They must invent ways of relating to each other because there are no ready-made cultural or historical models or formulas for same-sex relationships, as there are for different-sex relationships. (Blasius, 1994 p.191)

Like some disabled people, and in contrast to many people from Black and ethnic minority groups:

> as minorities, [gay people] are also somewhat unique in that they represent a marginalized segment of our society whose parents do not share their

minority status. Consequently, they are confronted with the additional challenge of not only being stigmatized by society at large but also the prospect of being an outcast in their own homes. (Goldfried and Goldfried, 2001 p.684)

For young people:

at a time when other adolescents are discovering how to express themselves socially, those youth who identify as lesbian or gay, but wish to remain hidden, are learning to conceal large parts of themselves from their family and friends. (Rivers and Carragher, 2003 p.382)

Gay mental health service users who have said they sometimes wished they were heterosexual often did so because they felt that life within their family and society would be easier without the threat of prejudice, discrimination, harassment or violence (Golding, 1997). Additional oppression exists for gay men and women from Black and ethnic minority groups in wider society, within family and community and within mental health services (Greene, 1994; Harris and Licata, 2000; Hayfield, 1995). As the first generation of self-defined gay people matures, issues about appropriate support for older gay people are emerging (Age Concern, 2002), particularly regarding professional assumptions about heterosexual family patterns, partnerships and support networks (Heaphy and Yip, 2003). The extent of the exclusion of gay people at both micro and macro levels, from family, community and society, has led one author to conclude that we are especially at risk of suicide as defined in Emile Durkheim's classic sociological theory (Durkheim, 1997), which highlighted the role of social factors and the extent of individual integration into society (Millard, 1995).

School is often the site of exclusion and harassment for young gay people who already have an elevated risk of poorer mental health and suicide (Fergusson, Horwood and Beautrais, 1999; Rivers and Carragher, 2003). As well as the stigmatising and isolating effect of heterosexism in teenage culture, the psychological effects of homophobic bullying in a non-protective or discriminatory environment can be profoundly damaging to mental well-being in both the short and long term (Rivers and Carragher, 2003). Homophobic abuse in mainstream schools is commonplace and is often unchallenged or even encouraged by teaching staff (Buston and Hart, 2001; Rivers, 1995; Rivers, 1994; Warwick, Aggleton and Douglas, 2001). One Scottish observational study found that 22.5 per cent of sex education lessons under scrutiny contained instances of overt teacher homophobia, with pathologisation being one example (Buston and Hart, 2001). The children and young people who are targets for homophobic abuse are not necessarily gay, but for those that are, the result can be suicidal or self-harming behaviour (Rivers, 1994). 'For the lesbian and gay adolescent, the added pressure of victimisation or possible victimisation together with the adoption of a stigmatised identity can result in extremely low self-esteem and profound self-loathing' (Rivers and Carragher, 2003 p.379).

Although some reports on self-harm identify bullying as a risk factor, they have neglected to take the analysis further to include the needs of lesbian and gay young people (Royal College of Psychiatrists, 1998). One study of homophobia in the UK found that one quarter of gay respondents under 18 had been subjected to physical violence, 20 per cent to severe physical attack, and 79 per cent had experienced verbal abuse (Mason and Palmer, 1996). Despite this, only 6 per cent of bullying policies in surveyed UK schools made mention of homophobic bullying, and 38 per cent thought it inappropriate to provide any support and information for lesbian and gay pupils (Warwick *et al.*, 2001). Government initiatives to promote healthy schools and reduce bullying have sometimes been found to ignore the issue of sexual diversity (Warwick *et al.*, 2001) and sex education has also been found to be inadequate at addressing issues of sexual diversity (Buston and Hart, 2001). It is likely that schools have been inhibited by Section 28 of the Local Government Act 1988 (finally repealed in late 2003), which made it unlawful for local authorities to '(a) intentionally promote homosexuality or publish material with the intention of promoting homosexuality, (b) promote the teaching in any maintained school of the acceptability of homosexuality as a pretended family relationship' (Warwick *et al.*, 2001). It is also likely that oppressive culture and practice in schools has been influenced by the pervasive myth that homosexuality cannot be established before early adulthood, a general misconception that has its origins in psychoanalytic theory (King and Bartlett, 1999). This emerging picture of social oppression as the cause of mental distress in young gay people suggests that the issues for adult mental health services could be extended to multi-agency child and adolescent mental health provision.

Conclusion

Before I could afford to pay for treatment with a lesbian therapist of my choosing, I had never been encouraged to explore how social and cultural experiences of being gay may have shaped my sense of self, and influenced my mental health. I had never felt safe or supported enough to do so in any statutory mental health service context. It was even tempting to avoid the topic altogether or deny I had any negative feelings about being gay. As one therapist observed about a gay client:

> I saw the client for six years. Initially he denied absolutely that his sexual preference was an issue...it seems an understandable defensiveness in the context of the pathologising of gay sex...only after two or three years were we able to look at what it meant to be gay... Ultimately we reflected long and often on how his personality had been influenced by both his culture's hostility to homosexuality and the identity he often felt forced to adopt by his own cultural gay norms. (Bartlett *et al.*, 2001 p.547)

Recognising the social issues that connect with my own mental health problems has helped me to stop blaming myself entirely for the distress I feel. Unfortunately, even statutory mental health services do not often help gay people in this process of recognition and can add to mental distress.

Mental health services should encourage self-acceptance and the construction of a positive sexual identity rather than promoting self-loathing and the compulsion to change. Both academic research and service user knowledge indicates that it is the experiences of rejection, isolation, discrimination and oppression that can make gay people vulnerable to mental distress. Instead of helping to alleviate it, mental health professionals can actively add to this distress. The Department of Health recently issued a document detailing plans for the strategic development of mental health care for women, which included explicit reference to the vulnerability of lesbian and bisexual women. The analysis was not based on a medical model, but rather recognised the influence of social factors on mental health. The document states that 'women who do not define themselves as heterosexual may have added stressors in their lives given the degree of stigma prevalent in society' (Department of Health, 2002a p.18). Further, the guidance says that 'it is important that practitioners do not make assumptions or value judgements regarding women's sexual identity, sexual behaviour and/or the choices they make regarding their sexuality... Irrespective of a woman's sexual orientation, respect and sensitivity should be accorded at all times' (Department of Health, 2002b p.14). This is a promising start, but in mental health practice the disease model of homosexuality still needs to be challenged on a fundamental level for both gay women and men. Mental health professionals need to be educated about the social influences on the mental health of gay people and to recognise that their practice can be compromised by personal or religious prejudice. Through the work of gay and service user researchers, campaigners and specialist mental health agencies like the Project for Advocacy, Counsel-

ling and Education (or PACE) (Gildersleeve and Platzer, 2003), the mental
health needs of gay people are slowly being recognised. How these needs will
be addressed in the long term within statutory mental health services remains
to be seen, but to conclude, perhaps these recommendations on professional
competency from the Bristol Royal Infirmary Inquiry are worth considering:

> The needs of the patients must be the driving concern... It calls for a
> commitment to respect patients, and to be honest and open towards them.
> And here, honesty includes the obligation of professionals to be honest with
> themselves about their abilities... It calls for retaining and conveying a sense
> of open-mindedness in the dialogue which is the patient's journey. Perhaps
> most important of all, it calls for a sense of shared humanity, sympathy,
> understanding, an ability to engage with the patient on an emotional level...
> (Kennedy, 2001 p.326)

References

Age Concern (2002) *Opening Doors to the Needs of Older Lesbians, Gay Men and Bisexuals: Report of a One Day Conference.* London: Age Concern.

Bartlett, A., King, M. and Phillips, P. (2001) 'Straight talking: an investigation of the attitudes and practice of psychoanalysts and psychotherapists in relation to gays and lesbians.' *British Journal of Psychiatry 179*, 545–549.

Bieschke, K., McClanahan, M., Tozer, E. (2000) 'Programmatic research on the treatment of lesbian, gay and bisexual clients: the past, the present and the course for the future.' In R. Perez, K. DeBord and K. Bieschke (eds) *Handbook of Counseling and Therapy with Lesbian, Gay and Bisexual Clients.* Washington: American Psychological Association.

Blasius, M. (1994) *Gay and Lesbian Politics: Sexuality and the Emergence of a New Ethic.* Philadelphia: Temple University Press.

Buston, K. and Hart, G. (2001) 'Heterosexism and homophobia in Scottish school sex education: exploring the nature of the problem.' *Journal of Adolescence 24*, 95–109.

Cochran, S. D. (2001) 'Emerging issues in research on lesbians' and gay men's mental health: does sexual orientation really matter?' *American Psychologist 56*, 11, 931–947.

Department of Health (2002a) *Women's Mental Health: Into the Mainstream. Strategic Development of Mental Health Care for Women.* London: Department of Health.

Department of Health (2002b) *Summary. Women's Mental Health: Into the Mainstream. Strategic Development of Mental Health Care for Women.* London: Department of Health.

Double, D. B. (2002) 'Redressing the imbalance.' *Mental Health Today September 2002*, 25–27.

Durkheim, E. (1997) *Suicide: A Study in Sociology.* New York: Simon & Schuster Inc.

Fergusson, D.M., Horwood, L.J. and Beautrais, A.L. (1999) 'Is sexual orientation related to mental health problems and suicidality in young people?' *Archives of General Psychiatry 56*, 10, 876–880.

Foucault, M. (1990) *The History of Sexuality Volume 1: An Introduction.* London: Penguin.

Gildersleeve, C. and Platzer, H. (2003) *Creating a Safe Space: Good Practice for Mental Health Staff Working with Lesbians, Gay Men and Bisexuals.* Brighton: Pavilion.

Goldfried, M. and Goldfried, A. (2001) 'The importance of parental support in the lives of gay, lesbian, and bisexual individuals.' *Clinical Psychology 57*, 5, 681–693.

Golding, J. (1997) *WithOut Prejudice: Mind Lesbian, Gay and Bisexual Mental Health Awareness Research.* London: Mind Publications.

Grau, G. (1995) *Hidden Holocaust?* London: Cassell.

Greene, B. (1994) 'Ethnic-minority lesbians and gay men: mental health and treatment issues.' *Journal of Consultant Clinical Psychology 62*, 2, 243–251.

Harris, H.L. and Licata, F. (2000) 'From fragmentation to integration: affirming the identities of culturally diverse mentally ill lesbians and gay men.' *Journal of Gay and Lesbian Social Services 11*, 4, 93–103.

Harris Interactive (2002) 'Press release: fewer than half of all lesbian, gay, bisexual and transgender adults surveyed say they have disclosed their sexual orientation to their health care provider.' www.harrisinteractive.com/news/allnewsbydate.asp?NewsID=555

Hayfield, A. (1995) 'Several faces of discrimination.' In V. Mason-John (ed.) *Talking Black: Lesbians of African and Asian Descent Speak Out.* London: Cassell.

Heaphy, B. and Yip, A. (2003) 'Uneven possibilities: understanding non-heterosexual aging and implications of social change.' *Sociological Research Online 8*, 4. www.socresonline.org.uk/8/4/heaphy.html

Hoare, P. (2002) *Spike Island: The Memory of a Military Hospital.* London: Fourth Estate.

Jivani, A. (1997) *It's Not Unusual: A History of Lesbian and Gay Britain in the Twentieth Century.* London: Michael O'Mara Books Ltd/BBC.

Jorm, A., Korten, A., Rodgers, B., Jacomber, P. and Christensen, H. (2002) 'Sexual orientation and mental health: results from a community survey of young and middle-aged adults.' *British Journal of Psychiatry 180*, 423–427.

Kennedy, I. (2001) *Learning from Bristol: The Report of the Public Inquiry into Children's Heart Surgery at the Bristol Royal Infirmary 1984 –1995.* Command Paper: CM 5207.

King, M. and Bartlett, A. (1999) 'British psychiatry and homosexuality.' *British Journal of Psychiatry 175*, 106–113.

King, M., McKeown, E., Warner, J., Ramsay, A., Johnson, K., Cort, C., Wright, L., Blizard, R. and Davidson, O. (2003) 'Mental health and quality of life of gay men and lesbians in England and Wales: controlled, cross-sectional study.' *British Journal of Psychiatry 183*, 552–558.

Man, L. (1994) 'Working with lesbian and gay clients.' *Journal of the British Association for Counselling 5*, 1.

Marcus, E. (1993) *Making History: The Struggle for Gay and Lesbian Equal Rights 1945–1990 – An Oral History.* New York: HarperCollins.

Mason, A. and Palmer, A. (1996) *Queer Bashing: A National Survey of Hate Crimes Against Lesbians and Gay Men.* London: Stonewall.

McFarlane, L. (1998) *Diagnosis: Homophobic. The Experiences of Lesbians, Gay Men and Bisexuals in Mental Health Services.* London: PACE.

Millard, J. (1995) 'Suicide and suicide attempts in the lesbian and gay community.' *Australian and New Zealand Journal of Mental Health Nursing 4*, 4, 181–189.

Mind (2001) *Lesbians, Gay Men, Bisexuals and Mental Health Factsheet.* London: Mind Publications. available at www.mind.org.uk/information/factsheets

Newman, B., Dannenfelser, P. and Benishek, L. (2002) 'Assessing beginning social work and counseling students' acceptance of lesbians and gay men.' *Journal of Social Work Education* 38, 2, 273–288.

Otis, M.D. and Skinner, W.F. (1996) 'The prevalence of victimization and its effect on mental well-being among lesbian and gay people.' *Journal of Homosexuality 30*, 3, 93–121.

Porter, R. (1997) *The Greatest Benefit to Mankind: A Medical History of Humanity from Antiquity to the Present.* London: Fontana.

Porter, R. (1999) *A Social History of Madness.* London: Everyman.

Price, J. (1997) *Queer in the Head: An Examination of the Response of Social Work Mental Health Services to the Needs and Experiences of Lesbians and Gay Men.* Surbiton: University of Warwick and SCA (Education).

Rivers, I. (1994) 'Protecting the gay adolescent at school.' Paper presented at the 'Adolescence and Family': Second International Congress on Adolescentology, Milan, Italy, 18–19 November.

Rivers, I. (1995) 'Mental health issues among young lesbians and gay men bullied at school.' *Health and Social Care in the Community 3*, 6, 380–383.

Rivers, I. and Carragher, D. (2003) 'Social-developmental factors affecting lesbian and gay youth: a review of cross-national research findings.' *Children and Society 17*, 374–385.

Rose, L. (1994) 'Homophobia among doctors.' *British Medical Journal 308*, 6928, 586–587.

Rothblum, E.D. (1994) '"I only read about myself on bathroom walls": the need for research on the mental health of lesbians and gay men.' *Journal of Consultant Clinical Psychology 62*, 2, 213–220.

Royal College of Psychiatrists (1998) *Managing Deliberate Self-harm in Young People – Council Report CR64.* London: Royal College of Psychiatrists.

Warwick, I., Aggleton, P. and Douglas, N. (2001) 'Playing it safe: addressing the emotional and physical health of lesbian and gay pupils in the UK.' *Journal of Adolescence 24*, 1, 129–140.

CHAPTER 10

Approaches to Risk in Mental Health

A Multidisciplinary Discourse

Shulamit Ramon

The discourse on risk in mental health is presently prolific. Most conferences on mental health in English-speaking countries will have sessions on *risk avoidance*, its assessment and management. Most books on mental health written by English speakers will echo the same emphasis. However, continental European conferences and publications would be unlikely to have such a focus. How come? Do they have less violent incidents? Do they have less violent patients? Or do they take a different approach to the discourse on risk in mental health? Do different mental health disciplines share the same approach to risk? Do users and carers share the same perspective?

Does *risk taking* play a part in mental health work and in the lives of users of mental health services? Logically the other side of risk avoidance, risk taking, is hardly mentioned, let alone being given serious consideration and perceived as worthy of being implemented in practice (Furedi, 1997). These are the issues to be looked at in this chapter.

The context

The discourse about risk is far from being conducted solely within the mental health system. It originates at the conceptual level in sociology, where it is closely related to the discourse on modernity and post-modernity, freedom and control, citizenship, exclusion and inclusion, health and illness, crime and deviance (Beck, 1992; Furedi, 1997; Giddens, 1991; Rose, 2000). The view of some prominent sociologists is that the increasing uncertainty of living in this epoch has led to greater emphasis on risk regulation and risk technology. The discourse around risk is to enable us to 'tame' it, as well as to confront it in the present and the future. The sociological literature discusses risk in terms of aversion and avoidance, perhaps because of the preoccupation with it as a threat to social stability and hence the interest in its suppression; it is indeed surprising that it is never perceived to be a stimulating factor in human lives. Merton's typology of innovation as a type of deviance (Merton, 1958), constructed in the middle of the twentieth century, is thus further caricatured by the prevailing view of societies as being interested only in tamed people.

The sociological argument is that societies seek to regulate people along the lines of the dominant ideologies of a given historical period and culture. The risk discourse is particularly developed within Anglo-Saxon societies, where it is assumed that the ideology of individual freedom and autonomy is based on *regulation from within*, in which those who do not conform are regulated through a series of inclusionary and exclusionary mechanisms and processes (see Chapter 4). It is further assumed that the inclusionary discourse of people with disabilities (e.g. inclusion within education and employment), including those with mental illness, is no more than an attempt to ensure their conformity and hence the reduction of risk to their society and to themselves. Within this perspective, empowerment is no more than a fiction, because it is aimed to offer the illusion of being in control over one's life, when one is merely toeing the line of being a good – that is a conforming – citizen.

Given this line of argument, it is not surprising that people who embody mental illness are perceived as a threat to social cohesion and hegemony. Professionals working with them are seen as mandated to ensure the reduction of the threat, the return to the fold of responsible, self-regulated citizens – and if this is not possible, then the application of exclusionary sanctions follows. The fascination within post-modernity, in particular with courting the irrational, expressed in literature, films, plays, poetry and the visual arts, cuts across this modernist focus on social order – as do empathic approaches to understanding mental illness and the (temporary) excitement/liberation it offers, side by side with suffering, to those experiencing it. Even the likely co-existence of the threat with the excitement is not recognised, let alone that of crediting users with having valuable expertise in experiencing this ambiguity to offer to the rest of us.

The risk discourse is also prominent among politicians, where it focuses on maintaining law and order, punishing those transgressing acceptable rules of conduct – and in which the politician emerges as the saviour of 'good' (i.e. conforming) people from the wrongdoing of 'bad' (non-conforming) people. Public safety was always a political issue, but became even more so towards the end of the twentieth century. Post 11 September 2001, *terrorism* has become the icon of the new risk discourse, in which the notion of *evil* is re-introduced.

There are compelling reasons for focusing on risk avoidance in mental health, which include:

- fear of others being hurt by people suffering from ill mental health
- fear of harm to self due to mental ill health (much more frequent than the risk to others).

Politicians in the western world are perceiving risk policies and measures as one of the two most important core issues of mental health policy, the other being cost containment (Shera *et al.*, 2002). The current debate in the UK on the proposals for the introduction of community treatment orders and of the preventive removal from the community of people diagnosed as having anti-social personality disorder highlights the direction in which the British government wishes to go, following many North American states and Australia in relation to community treatment orders (Brophy, Campbell and Healy, 2003; Hiday and Scheid-Cook, 1989; Home Office and the Department of Health, 1999).

Yet politicians in continental Europe do not demonstrate a similar preoccupation, highlighted by the fact that no EU country apart from Britain has legislated for community treatment orders, and the issue of risk avoidance does not seem to preoccupy their professionals, or informal carers. The statistics of self-harm and harm to others are often unreliable, but there is little to suggest that the rate of such incidents is lower in other western European countries. Some of them – for example the Netherlands and the Scandinavian countries – have more developed alternatives to hospitalisation in a crisis, while others do not (e.g. Spain, France, Germany, Greece). Some countries – such as Italy – have developed more extensive methods of both solidarity and attention to underlying social issues, even though the level of financial benefits is lower than in northern Europe. These approaches explain some of the reasons for the relative lack of interest in risk avoidance, but not all. There is some evidence that the media in these countries is less prone to demonise people with severe mental illness (Ramon and Savio, 2000). The difference in approach to risk avoidance may be related to cultural attitudes towards the irrational and towards law and order. Societies less tolerant of breaches of law and order, and less tolerant of the irrational, are less likely to tolerate the co-existence of people with mental illness in their midst, while being more likely to be keen on excluding them from everyday life – even at a time of closure of many psychiatric institutions and amidst an ideology of care in the community for those who used to be their residents.

Media coverage of the relatively few killings, albeit each lamented as a tragedy, committed by people diagnosed as suffering from either schizophrenia or personality disorder, has fuelled a political climate in which it is assumed that there has been an increase in such killings due to the policy of community care. However, Taylor and Gunn (1999) have convincingly demonstrated that the number of such killings has in fact gone down during the period of hospital closure, while the number of murders among those not diagnosed as mentally ill has gone up. However, neither their study nor their eminence (both are professors of forensic psychiatry and Taylor was the manager of the special health authority responsible for the British special hospitals) has dented the furore and zeal with which the politicians continue to treat this subject.

Interestingly the opposition to the preventive detention of people with personality disorder has increased among *all* mental health professions, leading their professional bodies to come out with statements to this effect. The government has delayed bringing forward a final version of the new Mental Health Bill, but does not show any sign of agreeing to take this measure out of what is being proposed.

Professional stakeholders

All mental health professionals are socialised to focus on the care function of their work – its controlling aspect kept either as a facet of caring, or of protecting the public and the client. As a result, the debate on risk avoidance and risk taking is stifled and discouraged. Focusing on the suffering experienced by mental health service users is discouraged too (Brandon, 1991).

Everyday practice of mental health workers in hospital wards and secure facilities is often dominated by risk avoidance activities, reflecting the fear of risk dominating politicians' concerns. Attitudes towards patients defined as at high risk are polarised between negative and positive stances which are derived from the individual professional's belief system (Bowers, 2002) and from whether or not the patient is seen as 'manipulative' – that is, covertly attempting to wrest control of the situation from the professional (Lewis and Appleby, 1988). For many professionals risk avoidance is the least attractive component of their work, but one they view as inevitable (Bracken and Thomas, 1998).

Risk avoidance work is now an increasing part of community mental health work. For example, in England, Approved Social Workers have had, since 1983, a key legal role in compulsory admission processes, in conjunction with psychiatrists and General Practitioners (Barnes, Bowl and Fisher 1990). Insufficient time is left to engage even in the other tasks required by the legislation, such as follow-up, let alone in risk taking professional activities. The social worker would need to calculate the risk from the admission itself to the client – in terms of personal and social identity, relationships with others, the deprivation of civil rights during the admission, and the likelihood of drifting into a cycle of admissions and chronicity.

In the minority of cases in which the social worker did not recommend compulsory admission, s/he had to calculate – and take – the risk of what will happen to the client without such an admission, to relatives and friends near to him/her, and to unknown others.

On the whole, professionals across the western world have responded to the challenge of risk avoidance by becoming more formal in their approach to risk assessment and management, and by being more defensive in their clinical practice.

Risk avoidance practice and policy issues for professionals, users and carers

Issues for professionals

These include managing users at risk to themselves and to others within restrictive settings (Lowe, 1992; Weijers and Manders, 2002); handling situations in which agreements are not kept for a variety of reasons (Pilgrim and Rogers, 1996); and managing violent incidents. A recent analysis of the latter (Benson et al., 2003) has highlighted that:

- Participants attributed blame to other parties and exonerated themselves, often doing so subtly.
- 'Zero tolerance' regimes foster a culture of blame and make it difficult to develop a culture of openness.
- Staff were unavailable to users on the ward.

- Specific attention to a user at risk was perceived as 'doing my routine work'.

- Power struggles took place between users and staff.

- Little attempt was made to look at the world through the user's eyes.

- In half of the incidents, nobody sat down with the users afterwards to talk about what had happened.

- Only reduced engagement with the user is seen as a preventive measure.

- Staff shortages, inability to take a break, and working long days contributed to a tense atmosphere.

- Poor communication, fear, and lack of reflection added to the poor outcomes.

It would therefore seem that the *organisational facet* is of central importance, as are communication patterns between professionals, users and carers (Rapaport, 2003).

The importance of the physical environment to the sense of safety and consequently to feeling empowered has come out as one of the most significant dimensions in a study of empowerment components on different wards (acute, rehabilitation, long-term), in which the dimensions originated from interviews with users (Schafer, 2003).

The realisation that the high tariff settings are not the most effective for the purpose of risk reduction has led to the introduction of community orders in Australia, Canada, New Zealand, the US and the UK (where there are currently supervised discharge and guardianship orders). These are compulsory orders that focus on where people should live, their presence in intervention settings, their daily activities, the control of their finance, and their entitlement to additional support over and above that provided to other people with mental health problems who are not subject to these orders. The major sanction if disobeyed is the return to hospitalisation. It is argued that the introduction of a clear structure to hitherto chaotic lives, plus more focused professional attention, enables people at high risk to reduce the degree of risk in their lives. The evidence concerning the efficacy of community treatment orders is rather mixed (Brophy *et al.*, 2003). Some of it indicates that they work well for people at a low to medium level of negative risk, for whom the order is establishing a structure and a level of stability their lives lacked before (Foster, 2001; Hiday and Scheid-Cook 1989). There is no evidence that the fear of hospitalisation is a meaningful component in the package for these people. However, there is also evidence that community treatment orders do not work that well for people with a violent past either towards themselves or others. In addition there is an ongoing debate as to the moral standing of community treatment orders which deprive citizens assessed as capable of living in the community of their freedom.

Issues for users and carers

In general, many users have opposed the compulsory nature of risk avoidance strategies, even when acknowledging being ill and in need of a safe place (Brennan, 2000). Mental health service users in all of the countries which have established community treatment orders of one type or another oppose this new invention, primarily on the grounds of the deprivation of civil liberties. They see them as yet another facet of the medicalisation of mental distress, as well as a mechanism of greater coercive control, and would like to see interventions which focus more on personalised relationships between staff and users, mutual support, and safe crisis facilities in the community as alternatives to hospitalisation and to what they see as the excessive use of medication (May, Hartley and Knight, 2003).

Women users have been vocal in expressing their views about acute admission wards and high secure hospitals as unsafe places for women (Mental Health Media, 2003). Since 1997, the British government has promised the end of wards in which accommodation is shared by men and women, or forcing women to socialise with men on such premises. Thus far, progress has been slow in phasing out mixed wards.

Black users and carers' associations, and a number of both Black and White professionals, have protested since the 1980s against the fact that Black people, especially young Black men, are more likely to be compulsorily admitted and in secure provisions than White people (Thomas *et al.*, 1993; see also Chapter 7). There has been no change in this disproportionate pattern of admission since then. The same applies to non-White ethnic minorities elsewhere – Native Americans in the US and Canada, Aborigines in Australia, Maoris in New Zealand. There are inherent relationships between race, poverty, oppression, and the interpretation of the degree of risk in mental ill health.

Carers in Anglo-Saxon countries seem to welcome community treatment orders as providing much needed structure and support. In fact, organisations such as NAMI in the US have led the demand for them. Yet the largest British carers' organisation – Rethink (formerly the National Schizophrenia Fellowship) has opposed the latest proposal to allow preventive hospital detention for people with personality disorders as a step too far in the deprivation of civil liberties.

Risk taking: value and theory framework

Although a cliché, it is worth repeating that it is virtually impossible to live by adhering only to *risk avoidance* as a major strategy for living, without the utilisation of *risk taking* as a complementary framework. This applies to the most banal risks such as crossing the road, extending to the more serious risks such as choosing a partner, or whether to be operated on when seriously ill. Some would go further to say that life is not worth living if it does not have some elements of risk taking; it is this which puts the spice of excitement into it. While a desire for risk taking can underlie non-conforming or even illegal behaviour, most risk taking behaviour is within the narrow boundaries of the law, and also the wider ones of social conformity – perhaps choosing to do something that is 'nice, but naughty' or 'frightening, but exciting', or even being prepared to 'risk it all' for something that would otherwise be unattainable.

As a society we worship some types of risk taking, ranging from mountain climbing, through car racing to business gambles which have paid off; or falling in love. Yet we dislike, and at times express contempt, towards those who dared to take a risk and failed. While by definition it is not possible to take risk without entertaining the possibility of failure, as a society we give the message that *the right to fail* has been suspended.

This right is also a part of the legacy of social work, having been recognised as a principle subsumed under the right to self-determination in social work. Sawyer (1975) argued that it is both difficult and unrealistic to expect clients to grow and develop without taking calculated risks, and without failing from time to time. I am not aware of any other helping profession which accepts failure as a right, rather than as an inevitable, regrettable, price we may have to pay when our calculated risk taking strategy has failed. This recognition within social work does not mean that social workers always enable this right to be enacted; but it does imply that the issue is acknowledged and at times debated and acted upon. In the original discussion, Sawyer looked at the underlying reasons which prevent social workers from enabling service users to exercise this right. These include:

- the wish to protect the service user from new failure, given that many of them would come with a history of failures
- the wish to protect one's professional reputation as someone who fosters success and prevents failure
- the fear that the service user will collapse if s/he fails yet again.

All of these reasons are highly relevant within the field of mental health.

The *right to fail* comes from a wider perspective within social work which has come to prominence, especially in working with disabled people, namely the *strengths approach*. This approach begins from a very different set of assumptions than that of the risk avoidance philosophy (Rapp, 1998; Saleebey, 1992); they include:

- focusing on the individual's strengths rather than pathology
- user–worker relationships are primary and essential
- interventions are based on user self-determination
- the community is viewed as an oasis of resources, not as an obstacle
- aggressive outreach is the preferred mode of intervention
- people suffering from severe mental illness can continue to learn, grow and change.

Everyday practice consequences to these assumptions entail the enhancement of the individualisation of service users, the facilitation of partnerships, fostering empowerment and blending societal, programmatic and service users' goals.

The need to cope with risk in everyday life in late modernity, where risk also provides *the promise of a new opportunity*, and not only an obstacle, is well analysed by Ferguson (2001). Interested in emancipatory politics, he looks at how the lack of permanency in life in late modernity offers us also more diverse options, such as different types of intimate relationships, work, leisure and communication. All of these choices necessitate a greater degree of personal responsibility. For him, accepting that life has become more risky for most people implies that this takes place together with more options becoming real possibilities.

It could be argued that the increase in possibilities also leads to increased stress levels, and inevitably to an increase in mental ill health, as it undermines the coherence we need in order to live at peace with ourselves and others. Yet we know from the world of work that taking risk while *being in control* enables people to do more, do it better and be more able to innovate (Murphy, 1999).

When we apply this understanding to users of mental health services, it makes sense to assume that they are more vulnerable due to their previous life experience, and therefore require more support in making life choices. However, we tend to assume, most of the time, that they cannot cope with the combination of high risk, choice and personal responsibility, and move them in the direction of the *least challenging* choice, which invariably tends to be the most boring one too. Yet the evidence we have from people who have manic depression and those experimenting with drugs is that they are looking for excitement and challenge in their lives.

Life at the professional level has also become less secure. At one level professionals are asked to take into account and to handle issues in the lives of service users which have been socially swept under the carpet up to now, but which are not any more. These include:

- recognition and respect of minority sexual orientation
- the right of disabled people to a sexual life
- accepting that different types of abuse occur within close relationships (physical and sexual abuse of children, elder abuse), and require professional intervention
- accepting the existence of abuse in some institutional settings and the need to eradicate this type of abuse
- recognising the existence of discrimination on the basis of age, ethnicity and gender in our societies and its negative impact on individuals and communities as an issue which calls for everyday professional response, as well as for policy and legislative responses
- the existence of *New Users*: users as committee members, trainers, advocates, service providers and researchers
- the existence of *New Carers*: carers as committee members, trainers, advocates, service providers and researchers.

At the other level they are expected to fully comply with highly bureaucratic processes while reaching highly discretionary decisions.

When discussed, the current instability of professional life is usually attributed to the rapid pace of organisational change and the threat to professional autonomy, rather than to the implications these have for service users. It is likely that the prevalent bleak view of risk taking among professionals blocks them also from taking risk within the organisational changes in which they participate, whether willingly or unwillingly.

Types of risk taking

Risk taking is necessary in each aspect of mental health where the primary purpose is that of improving the quality of life of service users; yet each aspect brings with it somewhat different issues and considerations. A secondary purpose is that of improving the quality of the working life of frontline workers. Examples include positive life events (Alabaster, 2002; Holmes and Rahe, 1967), participatory strategy on promoting well-being in the workplace (Hecker, 1997; Ramon and Hart, 2003), user researchers (Castillo 2002; Ramon, 2003), homeless peer advocacy (Brandon and Morris, 2000), family group conferencing (Essex Social Services Department, 2002) and risk taking in clinical work. Due to space constraints only the latter will be looked at in this chapter.

Risk taking in clinical work

Although undeclared, professional work in mental health has elements of risk taking beyond decisions not to use compulsion. In the following examples I shall not be using people's real initials.

Caterina Corbacio (2004), a psychiatrist from Turin, responsible for a supported housing scheme, has described how it was decided within a group home to prevent P, a young man in his twenties, from continuing with his prolonged series of ritual steps every morning, even though these were essential for his well-being from his perspective. The decision seems to have been motivated by staff shortages which meant that it became difficult to have a staff member at the disposal of only this young man during the performance of the rituals. Yet the staff also took into account that:

- the young man may regress even further if the rituals are obstructed
- his mother, who felt rejected due to his attempt to gain autonomy, may retaliate
- he may gain as a result in rational autonomy and be more optimistic about his life
- the staff would be able to offer him support for a more open-ended lifestyle.

The strategy worked successfully. He not only gave up the morning rituals for the purpose of going out to town with a support worker, but also asked that his mother's visits would be stopped, at least temporarily.

Stopping the mother's visits was another risk taking step, as it clearly hurt the mother, created tension in the relationships between the mother and the supported housing scheme, and could have led to a further regression and breakdown. Yet this risk taking change in direction offered the young man an opportunity to move to become a young adult, who takes responsibility for his relationships with significant others, and enabled the staff to encourage him to move in the direction of other, more mature, relationships.

The Barnet Crisis Intervention Team has worked since 1974 in North London in a multidisciplinary team focused on quick responses to a mental health crisis, mostly at the service user's home. Focusing on family dynamics of exclusion, the team has been committed to preventing hospitalisation in a crisis, and to a lesser extent also the medicalisation of such an event (Mitchell, 1993). The team has been largely successful in preventing hospitalisation, in enabling families to work through a crisis without the need to expel and exclude family members, using a variety of medical, psychosocial, and bio-feedback methods. In particular they have demonstrated the value of *being with* the service user and her/his family for as long as is necessary to enable the family to work through the first phase of the crisis. Although in existence and with a proven track record for more than 25 years, the focus on a psychosocial, conceptual and practice-oriented framework has not endeared the team to the psychiatric establishment, and its achievements are hardly recognised, let alone celebrated.

H is an articulate, middle-class, English woman in her thirties, who had numerous hospitalisations for self-harming, culminating in an 18-month stay in a medium secure unit, where she survived an attempt to strangulate her by another patient. Following the discharge to an empty flat, she was supported by a voluntary organisation on issues she selected, at times and places of her choice. She has since worked as a research assistant, is now reading for a PhD on the consequences of personality disorder, has been compensated for the strangulation episode by the secure unit, lives in a stable partnership, and is active in the user movement. She does not think that the time spent in the secure unit was of any use – in part because she was bored out of her mind, and in part because it confirmed her exclusionary status from society. She found the support by the voluntary organisation invaluable, as well as the contact with a user lecturer who stimulated her intellectually and who believed in her ability to go back to intellectually demanding work.

N is a young man who has remained in a secure unit for the last 20 years, since the age of 13, due to serious and repetitive attempts at suicide and self-harm. A ward of court, he was in psychotherapy all of these years in which more than one staff member had to be with him around the clock to restrain him from self-harm. He has published two books of short stories and poetry, won a prize for one of them, has began recently to visit his family, and is due to become a voluntary patient soon. He realises that becoming a voluntary patient is not going to change much in his current style of living, but that it will add dignity to his life.

S is a young woman in her twenties who has a history of hospitalisation, institutional living and abuse, and occasional explosive behaviour, with mental illness, multiple personalities and learning disability as attributed diagnoses. Largely due to the efforts of a militant therapist who was angered by the level of neglect and abuse apparent in this case, she is now living in the community with a team of 20 helpers in different part-time roles around the clock, inclusive of intensive psychotherapy, singing lessons, shopping, and a holiday abroad for the first time in her life.

Some would see this last vignette as an example of irresponsible and wasteful use of public funding; others would see it as a necessity with which to compensate for – and rebuild – a life of neglect and abuse.

All five examples have in common a strategy which includes both risk avoidance with considerable levels of *calculated*, phased, risk taking by professionals, family members and friends in working with people who clearly posed a risk – albeit mainly to themselves – but who also wanted more from life than being a docile patient. They have been fortunate enough to have the support of both professionals and lay people who cared much about them, and to have personal qualities which other people have found attractive, without condoning their harmful behaviours. For these life histories to come such a long way committed providers from more than one discipline were needed, as well as the equally committed, largely unconditional though highly emotionally charged, support of non-professionals.

This chapter has raised a number of issues related to *risk avoidance* and *risk taking* within the context of multidisciplinary work, attempting to outline what is meant by each concept, and its implications for different stakeholders and for policy, practice and research. The text reflects that good quality risk work in mental health, be it focused on risk avoidance and/or risk taking, requires a multidisciplinary approach. However, the type of multidisciplinary work necessary for such a success is not the traditional, medically dominated, multidisciplinary framework, but one impacted by a framework in which psychological and social factors, as well as psychosocial interventions, are at the forefront.

References

Alabaster, M. (2002) 'Post natal depression, making a difference: success to date.' In S. Ramon (ed.) *European Perspectives of Mental Health Promotion: First Steps.* Cambridge: Anglia Polytechnic University.

Barnes, M., Bowl, R. and Fisher, M. (1990) *Sectioned.* London: Routledge.

Beck, U. (1992) *The Risk Society.* London: Sage.

Benson, A., Secker, J. and Balfe, E., Lipsedge, M. Robinson, S. and Walker, J. (2003) 'Discourses of blame: accounting for aggression and violence on an acute mental health inpatient unit.' *Social Science and Medicine 57,* 5, 917–926.

Bowers, L. (2002) *Dangerous and Severe Personality Disorder: Response and Role of the Psychiatric Team.* London: Routledge.

Bracken, P. and Thomas, P. (1998) 'Safety and psychiatry.' *Open Mind 91,* May/June.

Brandon, D. (1991) 'Implications of normalisation work for professional skills.' In S. Ramon (ed.) *Beyond Community Care: Normalisation and Integration Work.* Basingstoke: Mind Macmillan.

Brandon, D. and Morris, L. (2000) 'Towards social inclusion: peer advocacy with homeless people.' In S. Ramon (ed.) *A Stakeholder's Approach to Innovation in Mental Health: A Reader for the Twenty-First Century.* Brighton: Pavilion Publishing.

Brennan, J. (2000) 'The cycle of opportunities and obstacles – setting up a safe house.' In S. Ramon (ed.) *A Stakeholder's Approach to Innovation in Mental Health: A Reader for the Twenty-First Century.* Brighton: Pavilion Publishing.

Brophy, L., Campbell, J. and Healy, B. (2003) 'Dilemmas in the case manager's role: implementing involuntary treatment in the community.' Special Edition on Psychiatry, Psychology and Law of the *Journal of the Australian and New Zealand Association of Psychiatry, Psychology and Law 10,* 1, 154–163.

Castillo, H. (2002) *Personality Disorder: Trauma or Temperament?* London: Jessica Kingsley.

Corbacio, C. (2004) 'Risk taking with Roberto.' In L. Sapouna (ed.) *Challenging Accepted Knowledge in Mental Health.* Dublin: Nova Publishing.

Essex Social Services Department (2002) *Essex Family Group Conference in Mental Health.* Chelmsford: Essex County Publications.

Ferguson, H. (2001) 'Social work, individualisation and life politics.' *British Journal of Social Work 31,* 41–55.

Foster, N. (2001) 'Involuntary outpatient commitment: managing mental health risks the New Hampshire way.' *Journal of Mental Health and Learning Disabilities Care 4,* 11.

Furedi, F. (1997) *Culture of Fear: Risk-taking and the Morality of Low Expectation.* London: Cassell.

Giddens, A. (1991) *Modernity and Self-identity.* Cambridge: Polity Press.

Hecker, R. (1997) 'Participatory action research as a strategy for empowering Aboriginal health workers.' *Australian and New Zealand Journal of Public Health 21,* 778–784.

Hiday, V.A. and Scheid-Cook, T.L. (1989) 'A follow-up of chronic patients committed to outpatient treatment.' *Hospital and Community Psychiatry 40*, 4, 52–58.

Holmes, T.H. and Rahe, R.H. (1967) 'The social readjustment scale.' *Journal of Psychosomatic Research 11*, 213–218.

Home Office and the Department of Health (1999) *Managing Dangerous People with Severe Personality Disorder: Proposal for Policy Development.* London: HMSO.

Lewis, G. and Appleby, L. (1988) 'Personality disorder: the people psychiatrists dislike.' *British Journal of Psychiatry 153*, 44–49.

Lowe, T. (1992) 'Characteristics of effective nursing interventions in the management of challenging behaviour.' *Journal of Advanced Nursing 17*, 10, 1226–1232.

May, R., Hartley, J. and Knight, T. (2003) 'Making the personal political.' *The Psychologist 16*, 4, 182–183.

Mental Health Media (2003) *What Women Want: Mainstreaming Women's Mental Health.* Mental Health Media (www.media.com).

Merton, R. (1958) *Social Theory and Social Structure.* Glencoe: The Free Press.

Mitchell, R. (1993) *Crisis Intervention in Practice: The Multidisciplinary Team and the Mental Health Social Worker.* Adlershot: Avebury.

Murphy, L. (1999) 'Organisational interventions to reduce stress in health care professionals.' In J. Firth-Cozens and R. Payne (ed.) *Stress in Health Professionals.* Chichester: Wiley.

Pilgrim, D. and Rogers, A. (1996) 'Two notions of risk in mental health debates.' In T. Heller and J. Reynolds (ed.) *Mental Health Matters.* Buckingham: Open University.

Ramon, S. (2003) (ed.) *Users Researching Health and Social Care: An Empowering Agenda?* Birmingham: Venture Press.

Ramon, S. and Hart, C. (2003) 'Promoting mental wellbeing in the workplace: a British case study.' *International Journal of Mental Health Promotion 5*, 2, 37–44.

Ramon, S. and Savio, M. 'A scandal of the 80s and 90s: media representation of mental health issues in Britain and Italy.' In S. Ramon (ed.) *A Shareholder's Approach to Innovation in Mental Health: A Reader for the 21st Century.* Brighton: Pavilion Publishing.

Rapaport, J. (2003) *A Relative Affair.* Unpublished PhD dissertation, Anglia Polytechnic University, Cambridge.

Rapp, C.A. (1998) *The Strengths Model: Case Management with People Suffering from Severe and Persistent Mental Illness.* Oxford: Oxford University Press.

Rose, N. (2000) *Powers of Freedom: Reframing Political Thought.* Cambridge: Cambridge University Press.

Saleebey, D. (ed.) (1992) *The Strengths Approach in Social Work Practice.* New York: Longman.

Sawyer, P. (1975) 'The right to fail.' In R. McDermott (ed.) *Self Determination in Social Work.* London: Routledge and Kegan Paul.

Schafer, T. (2003) 'Researching empowerment.' In S. Ramon (ed.) *Users Researching Health and Social Care: An Empowering Agenda.* Birmingham: Venture Press.

Shera, W., Healy, B., Aviram, U. and Ramon, S. (2002) 'Mental health policy and practice: a multi-country comparison.' *Journal of Health and Mental Health Social Work 35*, 1–2, 547–575.

Taylor, P. and Gunn, J. (1999) 'Homicides by people with mental illness: myth and reality.' *British Journal of Psychiatry 174*, 9–14.

Thomas, C.S., Stone, K., Osborn, M., Thomas, P. and Fisher, M. (1993) 'Psychiatric morbidity and compulsory admission among UK-born Europeans, Afro-Caribbeans and Asians in Central Manchester.' *British Journal of Psychiatry 163*, 91–99.

Weijers, R. and Manders, R. (2002) 'A territorial approach to constraint in clinical psychiatry.' Paper given at the Eighth International Network for Psychiatric Nursing Research, 18–20 September.

CHAPTER 11

Recovery from Mental Breakdown

Jan Wallcraft

Introduction

People on the receiving end of mental health services have been organising for many years now to call for significant changes. Many have argued that psychiatric diagnoses and the negative predictions about the patient's future that tend to go with a diagnosis make them feel hopeless. As Repper and Perkins (2003) point out, our existing mental health system has focused on deficits and dysfunctions, which has led to interventions designed to address illness symptoms rather than to enable people to 'use and develop their skills, make the most of their assets and pursue their aspirations' (p.11). This focus on a person's lack of competence may serve to reinforce an existing lack of self-worth and encourage dependence on services. Most physical treatments in psychiatry, including ECT and medication, have adverse effects that, along with the stigma and discrimination attached to mental illness diagnoses, make it hard for people to get back into employment. As one ex-patient activist said:

> The psychiatric system far from being a sanctuary and a system of healing was…a system of fear and continuation of illness for me. Like so many others recovery was a process that I did not encounter within the system, indeed…it was not until I left the system that the recovery process really got underway in my life. It was as if the system had no expectation of me recovering, instead the emphasis was on maintenance. I am not saying that those who worked in the system did not care for me, they did. They clothed me, fed me, housed me and ensured that I took my medication. What they did not do was consider the possibility that I could return to being the person I once was. (Coleman, 1999 p.5)

There are signs that concerted pressure on the 'deficit model' of mental illness from service users and their supporters, including socially oriented professionals, is beginning to make a difference. One concept in particular has wrought a powerful change in people's views of what is possible in mental health, and that is 'recovery'.

Anthony (2000) says that the 'recovery vision' resulted from consumers writing their own stories of recovery from mental illness and from the empirical work of Harding and her associates (Harding 1994) who carried out long-term outcome studies and reviewed a number of other long-term studies. Harding found that a deteriorating course for severe mental illness is not the norm, and that it is likely that chronic illness has less to do with the disorder itself and more to do with complex interactions between the person and their social environment.

Other writers such as Warner (1994) have also argued that recovery from severe mental illness is far more common than has been supposed, because most research is too short term to be able to trace people's individual journeys of recovery. Recovery research would ideally need to follow people's lives over the course of years, not months. Warner's (1994) analysis of long-term outcome studies shows that recovery rates from schizophrenia seem more closely related to economic factors such as high unemployment than to modern psychiatric medicine.

This realisation that most people, even those who have suffered the most severe and crippling mental illnesses, can and do recover and return to a life in the community, has led to new possibilities in research and service innovation. Increasingly researchers are asking what strategies are most helpful in enabling people regain a fulfilling life. Those who have recovered have a major role to play in guiding this work and keeping it user-centred in its conception of what 'recovery' means to the individual. The concept of 'recovery' is now part of the language of national policy. The recent Department of Health publication entitled *The Journey to Recovery – The Government's Vision for Mental Health Care* spells out how attitudes to mental health need to change to enable recovery:

> Historically, people with mental illness were often not expected to recover. For example, people with schizophrenia were generally perceived as having a poor outlook, having to live their life in a uniformly downward spiral of persistent symptoms. This perception has influenced the public view of people diagnosed as having a mental illness, as being ultimately unable to take control of their lives and to recover. Services of the future will talk as much about recovery as they do about symptoms and illness. We need to

create an optimistic, positive approach to all people who use mental health services. The vast majority have real prospects of recovery – if they are supported by appropriate services, driven by the right values and attitudes. The mental health system must support people in settings of their own choosing, enable access to community resources including housing, education, work, friendships – or whatever they think is critical to their own recovery. (Department of Health, 2001 p.24)

Along with this statement of intent, the National Institute of Mental Health in England is involving a wide range of stakeholders, including service users, in developing a framework of values to underpin mental health services. This exercise offers an opportunity to challenge the prevailing biomedical emphasis on scientific research using what is claimed to be neutral and value-free methodology. Biomedical claims of scientific neutrality in psychiatric research disguise a range of implicit value judgements about the meaning of the signs and symptoms of 'mental illness'. In Chapter 4, Jerry Tew suggests that scientific discourse defines as symptoms of 'illness' behaviours which might threaten the core social values of modernity. According to Fernando (1991) the stereotypical thinking underpinning western psychiatry is Eurocentric and permeated with racist ideology. It fails to take into account different cultural norms and values even within the dominant western culture. Attitudes towards homosexuality, for instance, continue to be somewhat unenlightened, as Sarah Carr argues in Chapter 9, pointing out that references to homosexuality as a disease were only 'finally removed from the British central database of mental illnesses in 1994'. My own research (Wallcraft, 2002) showed that people are being asked intrusive and inappropriate questions about their sexuality as part of the diagnostic assessment while actual concerns patients have about sexual issues are not well handled by professionals.

If the invisible assumptions behind psychiatric medicine are rendered more explicit this can help to balance existing psychiatric knowledge with other types of evidence, taking more account of the lived experiences and values of service users and their families and friends, and of frontline mental health workers. It is then possible to think rationally about what kind of value base we want our mental health research and service provision to adopt in the twenty-first century.

However, the concept of 'recovery' is still controversial and often misunderstood, arousing suspicion on the part of many mental health researchers, workers and service users. This chapter will explore some of the meanings of the term and look at how a shared understanding of recovery might lead to fundamental changes in service provision.

Defining 'recovery'

The literature on recovery generally describes it as a complex, individual and self-defined process concerned with regaining hope and independence (Turner-Crowson and Wallcraft, 2002). In service users' writings about recovery, the most common themes are: recovering hope; developing a perspective on the past in order to move on; taking control of one's own life; repairing or developing new valued relationships and social roles; developing new meaning and purpose in life; and persevering in spite of reverses and ongoing problems. Many people have written personal accounts of their own journeys through mental health problems and recovery (Barker, Campbell and Davidson, 2000; Coleman, 1999; Curtis *et al.*, 2000; Deegan, 1988; Pegler, 2002; Read, 2002).

According to the definitions evolved by service users, recovery does not necessarily mean being free of all symptoms, as Deegan, a clinical psychologist in the US describes:

> My journey of recovery is still ongoing. I still struggle with symptoms, grieve the losses that I have sustained...I am also involved in self help and mutual support and I still use professional services including medications, psychotherapy, and hospitals. However, now I do not just take medications or go to the hospital. I have learned to use medications and to use the hospital. This is the active stance that is the hallmark of the recovery process. (Deegan, 1996)

Recovery is best described as an ongoing journey or a process, rather than as a finite goal. People need to have the chance to talk about their lives, the bad as well as the good aspects, and to reflect on their life journey. Grieving over losses and painful experiences is a necessary part of recovery, as Lafond argues:

> Consciously grieving mental illness can bring healing to many, even all, aspects of our lives; it can help us become aware of the coping skills we already have and how to use them better. It can also help us develop new ways of coping, reduce stress and boost our self-esteem. (2002 p.xix)

Mental health workers can help in this process if they are willing to be open and use their qualities as fellow human beings, rather than hiding behind professional roles. Repper and Perkins (2003) have developed a model of professional practice to encourage mental health workers to support social inclusion and recovery by valuing and believing in their clients and helping them take control over their lives and gain access to social roles, relationships, activities and material resources. Professionals can be 'holders of hope' (Glover, 2001) for service users whose ability to hope and dream for themselves has been eroded by their illness and by negative messages from others.

'Hope', like 'recovery', has been seen by mental health researchers as an elusive concept that is difficult to use in evaluating services, and this has led to arguments that the 'recovery movement' is evangelical rather than evidence-based. However, there have been attempts to define the characteristics of hope and to show its connection to recovery. Dufault and Martocchio see it as a 'multidimensional dynamic life-force characterized by a confident yet uncertain expectation of achieving a personally significant goal' (1985 p.380). Russinova describes how hope and lack of hope interact with recovery in the context of relationships with service providers:

> The presence of a supportive other is particularly important at the early stages of recovery, when people with psychiatric disabilities tend to feel more hopeless and discouraged. Ironically, consumers often hear the most despairing and discouraging messages from mental health providers when first diagnosed with a serious mental illness. A supportive relationship instilling hope slowly breaks the closed circle of despair that tends to stagnate the person and limit involvement in recovery-promoting activities. (1999 p.52)

Other researchers have created measurement scales for hope and empowerment (Rogers *et al.*, 1997; Snyder *et al.*, 1991). So far, most of this work has been done in the US.

Recovery from what?

Before exploring what helps people recover there is a prior question that service providers and researchers should be asking, that is, what is it that people with mental health problems and diagnoses of mental illness are recovering from? Repper and Perkins suggest that this includes: the multiple and often recurring traumas of the symptoms, treatment and its side effects, stigma of psychiatric treatment, negative attitudes of professionals, the lack of appropriate professional skills to enable recovery, social exclusion and lack of opportunities for valued activities (2003 pp.48–49).

I argue that people should be allowed to define for themselves the particular complex of traumas and problems from which they are recovering. If there is disagreement between the practitioner and the patient about the origin of the problems, this is bound to impact on the therapeutic alliance, and make it less likely that the patient will feel understood and motivated to accept the diagnosis and treatment. Whatever the diagnosis given, listening to the service user's own views of what led up to the problems would help to indicate recovery strategies which take into account the person's social situation and stress factors.

Recovery strategies based on such a dialogue would be more likely to be accepted by the service user. Research shows that people rarely attribute their mental ill health to a pathological disease process:

> [Most patients] shrug off all references to any illness in the first place… They rarely use professional diagnostic terms, and when they do, it is generally in a critical sense. (Prior, 1993 p.160)

It is all too easy for medically trained professionals to dismiss this failure to recognise one's 'illness' as 'lack of insight'. Such an approach has arguably led to the widespread dissatisfaction with the attitudes of mental health professionals and their failure to listen and engage with service users which is evidenced in almost every study of mental health service users' views (Mental Health Foundation, 2000; Rogers, Pilgrim and Lacey, 1993).

I found (Wallcraft, 2002) that people talked about the onset of their first breakdown using everyday language such as 'stress', 'burnout', 'depression', 'anxiety' and 'trauma' and medical concepts in everyday use such as 'paranoia' rather than talking about the onset of a mental illness. Some interviewees accepted and used a biomedical diagnosis while in fact telling a more complex story of the onset of their mental health crisis in which life events figured largely. Other research supports my finding that people see their breakdown as related to their life circumstances. Briere (1999) found that over 80 per cent of patients admitted in a crisis have experienced childhood or adult interpersonal violence, though he reports that staff in psychiatric emergency services rarely ask the questions to uncover these histories of trauma. Sally Plumb, in Chapter 6, has set out some theories as to how abuse and trauma can lead to mental distress.

Once a person has been diagnosed and treated, they also have to recover from the effects of the psychiatric system and the social stigma attached to the diagnosis:

> People with mental illness may have to recover from the stigma they have incorporated into their very being; from the iatrogenic effects of treatment settings; from lack of recent opportunities for self-determination; from the negative side effects of unemployment; and from crushed dreams. (Anthony, 1993)

Some people, arguably a minority, do experience their illness as happening almost 'out of the blue', are convinced that their symptoms are completely unrelated to their circumstances, and believe that there may be a physical or genetic cause. For this group, I found that diagnosis could sometimes help them make sense of their experiences, though it was not always welcome at first (Wallcraft, 2002).

Whatever people's views of their diagnosis and treatment, there are well-documented adverse effects from drug treatment and ECT, and the majority of people with severe mental illness diagnoses do not find it easy to get back into employment. According to Martin Webber (Chapter 5), 'the employment rate of people receiving treatment and support from the mental health services rarely reaches more than 10 per cent and, when working, they work fewer hours and earn only two thirds of the national average hourly rate'.

Psychiatric treatment may be part of what helps people recover, but it can also inhibit and prevent recovery. While anti-depressants were found helpful by 67 per cent of the respondents in the 'Knowing Our Own Minds' survey (Mental Health Foundation 1997), 10 per cent of respondents found anti-depressants harmful: 'Side effects of dizziness and confusion [from anti-depressants] led to losing a job in 1993' (p.32). Major tranquillisers were seen as harmful by 21 per cent of respondents: 'They do not cure the causes of conditions, they make you unnaturally doped, enormously fat' (p.33). ECT was regarded as damaging by 47 per cent of those in the survey who had received it: 'It made me into a cabbage and destroyed great chunks of my memory – I had a real struggle to get back to my former self' (p.37). Stigma and discrimination in society also impede recovery: 'If I mention schizophrenia I won't get the job. If I don't tell them and become ill later, I might be fired' (Warner, 2000 p.89).

> We have an employment project trying to retrain people to get them back into employment. We have quite good contacts in business and industry, but

we haven't been able to place people at all easily. There is still so much fear.
(Dunn, 1999 p.12)

Unemployment and racism are implicated as causal factors in mental health problems in young Black men (Dunn, 1999 p.33). Unemployment leads to poverty, which further impedes recovery. The Well-Being Project (Campbell, 1989) found that 33 per cent of Caucasian and 44 per cent of Black mental health clients said that poverty was the main source of their psychological or emotional problems.

Recognition by service providers that people with mental health problems are the primary experts on the causes of their own distress and on what helps would lead to a more listening and patient-centred approach and, I believe, increase patient empowerment and engagement with services and make recovery more likely.

What helps recovery?

My research (Wallcraft, 2002) showed that the factors which help recovery include: good relationships; finding the right treatments and therapies; enjoyable activities; financial security and satisfying work; personal growth and development; self-management of problems; the right living environment; speaking out for others; care available for future crises; and developing one's own cultural or spiritual perspective.

I found the key aspects of relationships that were most helpful in recovery were those of respectful listening, closeness, love and support. The Strategies for Living project (Mental Health Foundation, 2000) also found good relationships to be the top of the list of what helps people cope. They list the key helping factors in good relationships as emotional support, companionship and friendship, bringing meaning and purpose to life, and practical support. On the other hand, damaged or poor relationships can be a factor making recovery difficult.

I found (Wallcraft, 2002) that family and intimate relationships were mentioned as important, but equally often valued were relationships with friends and fellow members of support groups, drop-ins and day centres. Those who felt isolated and lacking in support saw the lack of personal relationships as a reason for their continued problems. The Well-Being project (Campbell, 1989) found that 53 per cent of mental health clients value friendships because their friends listen to them and consider what they say to be valid and important. Mutual support, understanding and acceptance feature again and again as a central plank of recovery. Black voluntary sector projects clearly provide a vital system of support for Black service users who encounter the double discrimination of racism as well as that related to their diagnosis:

> There's a family togetherness…sometimes I think 'Oh, if it was a white establishment I wouldn't want to go', but because it's a black establishment, you know, people who've got the same illness as you've got yourself, you obviously want to come and mix with people who've got the same illness…in a white establishment, they don't understand. (Mental Health Foundation, 2000)

Relationships with voluntary and statutory workers were the next most commonly mentioned sources of support in my research (Wallcraft, 2002) though some people complained of the unwillingness or inability of workers to listen and to help their recovery. The qualities valued in these relationships are similar to those valued in family and friends. People want to be understood, believed and to receive non-judgemental listening. However, from professionals they also may hope for an explanation of their problems and an opportunity to let go of responsibility during the period of mental health crisis. In the longer term people want and need to be helped to rebuild their lives in the community, rather than to remain ill and dependent, and this I found did not often happen for the people I interviewed.

Personal control over one's life is a key factor in recovery. The Strategies for Living research (Mental Health Foundation, 2000) found that most people wished to play an active role in treatment decisions, to have full information about side effects and the opportunity to try alternatives – either different drugs or non-drug treatments such as talking therapies and complementary therapies.

> My GP will give me valium when I ask for it, because I very rarely do…he knows it will last me ages… I would not want to rely on things like that – every 3 months I take one – even when I was ill I hardly took them.

Finding the right treatment or making one's own decisions about treatment were important in recovery to most of the people I interviewed. A quarter believed that medication helped them stay out of hospital but an equal number found their medication unhelpful or irrelevant to recovery: 'they keep saying "take this pill try this pill try this pill"… I keep saying "well it's not about pills, it's other things"' (Wallcraft, 2002). Some said they did not begin to recover until they stopped taking medication. Some had found other treatments including talking treatment and spiritual healing that helped. The

Strategies for Living research (Mental Health Foundation, 2000) also found a wide variety of therapies helped people cope, including talking treatments, complementary therapies and development of spirituality. Another major area of help is found in enjoyable activities, such as reading, listening to music, sport and exercise, walking, and creative activities (Mental Health Foundation, 2000; Wallcraft, 2002).

Finally, being able to find paid or voluntary work or education and training towards a new career is highly valued in recovery. I found (Wallcraft, 2002) that those who were seeking work wanted it because of financial security, social status, acceptance, structure and meaning in life, or because work was intrinsically satisfying. 'I wanted to get back to work... I don't want to go into hospital any more... I prefer to become a...respected citizen again and get on with my life' (Wallcraft, 2002). Being more in control of one's own life and managing one's own mental health is the key to regaining self-respect and self-esteem, another major plank of recovery. Campbell (1989) found that self-esteem is importantly related to how people rate their mental and physical well-being. Low self-esteem goes with more self-reported physical illness and with disturbances such as insomnia, anxiety and depression.

In my study (Wallcraft, 2002), a quarter of the interviewees described how they had learned to manage their own problems, with or without the use of medication. Several user-led organisations now provide information, training and support in self-management of ongoing problems. The Manic Depression Fellowship run a programme of supporting self-management, and have found that people who self-manage have less frequent and less severe mood swings, more tolerance of stress, fewer hospital visits, and are more able to hold down a job. The Self-Harm Network offer information and training on how to hurt oneself less, and the Hearing Voices Network offer self-help groups and information on working with voices. Voices Forum at Rethink are developing self-management training for people with schizophrenia. These approaches are valued by service users because they find mutual understanding and acceptance in working with others in a similar position:

> A fellow voice-hearer at my very first hearing voices group asked me if I heard voices and when I replied that I did, told me they were real...that one sentence has been a compass showing me the direction I needed to travel and underpinning my belief in the recovery process. (Coleman, 1999)

Hospital services are part of recovery but only in so far as they provide an environment that enables people to regain their ability to control and manage their own lives. I found (Wallcraft, 2002) that medication was accepted if it was perceived as keeping the person well. What people valued most about hospital-based treatment was the prevention of relapse, good relationships with staff, talking treatments, opportunities to make choices and decisions, and the assurance of care being available for future crises. In most cases, I found that people felt they needed the protection of a hospital ward in the immediate crisis phase. Few, however, once through the worst of their crisis, found their recovery well served by being in a medical environment, with staff who failed to listen, lack of activities and talking therapies, the adverse effects of medication, poorly handled discharge, and lack of support for a return to independent living.

I found that community mental health and social services were seen as helpful when they offered good listening and support, practical solutions such as housing and advice, and help with medication. They were seen as unhelpful when they failed to provide practical support, or were seen as resembling in-patient services. A need was expressed for services that can meet the specific needs of women and gay people, and for non-medical community-based crisis services.

Outside the medical and social services, my study showed that people found help in increasing self-knowledge, self-management of their problems, relationships and support, work and activities, opportunities to use their own crisis experiences to help others, and spiritual and cultural development. Isolation and lack of support to achieve recovery goals, along with bad living conditions, were major factors inhibiting recovery for some people.

Implementing the recovery concept as part of mental health policy and practice

Rehabilitation services have for many years been the main means of support for reintegrating people into society after a breakdown. These services are often situated within psychiatric hospitals. They tend to include help with personal relationships, regaining or learning new occupational skills, leisure and recreational activities, education and help with finding suitable housing.

For rehabilitation services to fit with a service user-defined notion of recovery, clients should be able to choose the skills they want to develop, set their own goals and be able to use the service to recover in their own time. They need assurance that if they drop out because of a relapse in their recovery, they can come back when they are ready. This may mean the delivery of rehabilitation services needs to change to give more power to service users.

Farkas (1999) set up a committee including service users to review reha-bilitation programmes around the world. Key standards they sought in good services included: programmes designed to maximise natural supports and empower patients and family members, programmes that are integrated into a network of other services, resources and supports, and access to clinical ser-vices without the service necessarily being located in hospitals.

Access to satisfying work helps self-esteem and independence, and is a key part of recovery, but currently only 13 per cent of people with serious mental illnesses are employed (Warner, 2000). People without work or the prospect of obtaining work have no choice but to be on welfare benefits. But the benefits system does not have the flexibility to cater for those people whose mental health problems fluctuate, and who may not be able to work full time. People risk losing stable levels of benefit that they can manage on if they try to take on a full-time job and have to give it up when their problems become worse again. This is a risk many, perhaps most, are reluctant to take.

New schemes to provide individual 'back to work' support packages and 'joined-up' rehabilitation schemes are currently being proposed by the Department of Work and Pensions (DWP) to start to break down the barriers preventing people on benefits from taking jobs. Such schemes may help, but a major structural rethink of policy on benefits and employment for people with mental health problems to create the flexibility people need is essential if government policy is to support rather than prevent recovery from mental ill health. There are recent hopeful signs that the DWP has understood the prob-lem and changes may be forthcoming in the near future.

Community building is another policy initiative that is much needed. The various regeneration schemes that have been part of the present government's programme have not often had a mental health focus. However, the NHS Plan to provide 500 community development workers over the forthcoming year may be an important step towards meeting this need.

Finally, mental health workers have a vital role to play in helping people recover, and their views and concerns must be taken into account. Recovery cannot simply be imposed as yet another task they have to accomplish with-out some retraining and re-organisation of their work roles. The new local Support, Time and Recovery (STR) workers who are currently being recruited may provide a major new resource in aiding recovery and social inclusion, especially as the experience of using mental health services is seen as an asset in this work. There is no central guidance on how these STR workers will be trained however, and each authority is designing its own training programmes. A recovery training course for mental health workers has been designed by a leading service user consultant in New Zealand (Mental Health Commission, 2001) and something similar would be helpful in this country.

Measuring recovery

A recovery-oriented mental health system would need to be measured and evaluated in terms of recovery. A number of attempts have been made in the US to develop service user-oriented outcome measures. One set of criteria developed after many interviews and focus groups with mental health service users found that recovery is a process of (1) overcoming 'stuckness' (2) discovering and fostering self-empowerment (3) learning and self-redefinition (4) returning to basic functioning and (5) improving quality of life (Young and Ensing 1999).

A system of outcome measures linked to recovery has been developed and is being used in Ohio (Ohio Department of Mental Health, 2000), though it is not yet being used in this country. It has been discussed within the NIMHE Experts by Experience group which I currently facilitate, and has been adapted to make it more relevant to a British context. The measures cover clinical status, quality of life (life satisfaction, fulfilment and empowerment), functional status, safety and health. There are forms to be completed by service users, family members of young people and workers/clinicians. The information can be recorded on a computer and measured at various intervals to compare progress. The language used is easy to understand and relevant to service users, for example:

How do you feel about:

- the amount of friendship in your life
- the amount of money you get
- the amount of meaningful activity in your life
- the amount of freedom you have
- the way you and your family act toward each other
- your personal safety
- how often do you have the opportunity to spend time with people you really like?

The Department of Health are currently piloting a major programme of outcome measurement in mental health services. This is planned to extend to all in-patient and community mental health services over the next few years.

This work is at an early stage but has the potential to transform the ethos of psychiatry by putting patients at the centre of the services. There is a recognition by the Department that the forms of outcome measurement should incorporate user-identified recovery and empowerment goals, and ensure patients and service users are able to put across their views of how well services are working for them in terms of their quality of life.

Dangers of a professional-led recovery agenda

I have had discussions in the course of my work with a number of mental health service users who are wary of the term 'recovery'. Some see it as a medical term, implying getting over an illness. Not all service users accept the notion of 'mental illness' or see themselves as ill in the first place. The literature on recovery is in fact open on the question of illness. Accepting that one has an illness is not generally seen as a necessary part of the recovery process. It is however seen as important to recognise and understand one's problems. Repper and Perkins take a pragmatic view of this ideological debate:

> A recovery vision is not limited to a particular theory about the nature and causes of mental health problems... [It] does not commit one to a social, a psychological, a spiritual or an organic understanding of distress and disability, nor to the use or non-use of medical interventions. Whatever understanding of their situation a person comes to, recovery is an equally important process. (2003 p.47)

Some service users have raised concerns that the 'recovery model' will be defined by mental health workers and policy makers who are more concerned with saving money by getting people out of services and off benefits. I believe there are grounds for this concern. Professionally defined recovery goals could theoretically result in those who do not recover according to plan being seen to have failed or not tried hard enough, and perhaps mean loss of support and benefits. A focus on recovery could shift scarce resources for valued services such as talking treatments away from those seen as less able or willing to recover.

Some service users argue that it would be better to continue developing concepts such as 'coping strategies' and 'self-management' techniques, which do not imply that a person should be able to dispense with mental health services and become fully independent. At times in people's lives, recovery may seem a step too far. I argue however that the notion of recovery is a logical next step from coping strategies and self-management. It offers a vision that there is something more to be hoped for than merely surviving. Recovery can never be imposed on a person, but for many, the belief that recovery is possible can provide the hope and motivation to take the first step. Each person must have the right to define his or her own recovery vision. This does not have to include total independence from services. Long-term use of services is not incompatible with recovery. Services must to be designed to allow the flexibility for recovery to become possible. Recovery must never be owned and defined by service providers, otherwise the anxieties service users have expressed about the concept being taken over and used against them are likely to be confirmed.

Evaluating services in terms of how successful they are in helping patients to recover may shift the main focus of psychiatric services away from defining and treating illness towards promoting good mental health and enabling recovery. This would mean that much greater resources are needed to support and educate families and communities. Service user groups can be part of the solution, in providing mutual support and in helping to provide training on understanding what causes or exacerbates mental distress and how to enable recovery. Families and friends also may need help to recover. Positive mental health and recovery is primarily a social, not a medical, responsibility.

References

Anthony, W. (1993) 'Recovery from mental illness: the guiding vision of the mental health service system.' *Innovations and Research 2*, 3, 17–25.

Anthony, W. (2000) 'A recovery-oriented service system: setting some system level standards.' *Psychiatric Rehabilitation Journal 24*, 2, 159–168.

Barker, P., Campbell, P. and Davidson, B. (2000) *From the Ashes of Experience: Reflections on Madness, Survival and Growth.* London: Whurr Publications.

Briere, J. (1999) 'Psychological trauma and the psychiatric emergency service: new developments in emergency psychiatry.' *New Directions for Mental Health Services 82*, 43–51.

Campbell, J. (1989) *In Pursuit of Wellness: The Well-Being Project: Mental Health Clients Speak For Themselves. Vol. 6.* California Department of Mental Health (unpublished report).

Coleman, R. (1999) *Recovery: An Alien Concept.* Gloucester: Handsell Publishing.

Curtis, T., Dellar, D., Leslie, E. and Watson, B. (eds) (2000) *Mad Pride: A Celebration of Mad Culture.* London: Spare Change Books.

Deegan, P. (1988) 'Recovery: the lived experience of rehabilitation.' *Psychosocial Rehabilitation Journal 11*, 4, 11–19.

Deegan, P. (1996) 'Recovery as a journey of the heart.' *Psychiatric Rehabilitation Journal 19*, 3, 91–97.

Department of Health (2001) *The Journey to Recovery – The Government's Vision for Mental Health Care.* London: Department of Health.

Dufault, K. and Martocchio, B. (1985) 'Hope, its spheres and dimensions.' *Nursing Clinics of North America 20*, 2, 379–391.

Dunn, S. (1999) *Creating Accepting Communities*. London: Mind.

Farkas, M. (1999) (ed.) *International Practice in Psychosocial Psychiatric Rehabilitation*. World Association of Psychosocial Rehabilitation (unpublished report).

Fernando, S. (1991) *Mental Health, Race and Culture*. London: Macmillan.

Glover, H. (2001) *A Series of Thoughts on Personal Recovery*. Centre for Mental Health Policy and Interdisciplinary Centre for Mental Health, University of Central England (unpublished paper).

Harding, C.M. (1994) 'An examination of the complexities in the measurement of recovery in severe psychiatric disorders.' In R.J. Ancill, S. Holliday and G.W. MacEwan (eds) *Schizophrenia: Exploring the Spectrum of Psychosis*. Chicester: J. Wiley and Sons.

Lafond, V. (2002) *Grieving Mental Illness*. Toronto: University of Toronto Press.

Mental Health Commission (2001) *Recovery Competencies for New Zealand Mental Health Workers*. wwwmhc.govt.nz

Mental Health Foundation (1997) *Knowing Our Own Minds*. London: Mental Health Foundation.

Mental Health Foundation (2000) *Strategies for Living: A Report of User-led Research into People's Strategies for Living with Mental Distress*. London: Mental Health Foundation.

Ohio Department of Mental Health (2000) *The Ohio Mental Health Consumer Outcomes System. Procedural Manual*. www.mh.state.oh.us/initiatives/outcomes/outcomes.html

Pegler, J. (2002) *A Can of Madness*. Brentwood: Chipmunka Publishing.

Prior, L. (1993) *The Social Organisation of Mental Illness*. London: Sage.

Read, J. (ed.) (2002) *Something Inside So Strong*. London: Mental Health Foundation.

Repper, J. and Perkins, R. (2003) *Social Inclusion and Recovery: A Model for Mental Health Practice*. London: Baillière Tindall.

Rogers, A., Pilgrim, D. and Lacey, R. (1993) *Experiencing Psychiatry*. London: Mind/Macmillan.

Rogers, E.S., Chamberlin, J., Ellison, M.L. and Crean, T. (1997) 'A consumer-constructed scale to measure empowerment among users of mental health services.' *Psychiatric Services 48*, 8, 1042–1047.

Russinova, Z. (1999) 'Providers' hope-inspiring competence as a factor optimizing psychiatric rehabilitation outcomes.' *Journal of Rehabilitation 64*, 4, 50–57.

Snyder, C.R., Harris, C., Anderson, J.R., Halleran, S.A., Irving, L.M., Sigmon, S.T., Yoshinobu, L., Gibb, G., Langelle, C. and Harney, P. (1991) 'The will and the ways: development and validation of an individual-differences measure of hope.' *Journal of Personality and Social Psychology 60*, 4, 570–595.

Turner-Crowson, J. and Wallcraft, J. (2002) 'The recovery vision for mental health services and research: a British perspective.' *Psychiatric Rehabilitation Journal 25*, 3, 245–254.

Wallcraft, J. (2002) *Turning Towards Recovery? A Study of Personal Narratives of Mental Health Crisis and Breakdown*. Unpublished PhD thesis, South Bank University.

Warner, R. (1994) *Recovery from Schizophrenia – Psychiatry and Political Economy*. London: Routledge.

Warner, R. (2000) *The Environment of Schizophrenia*. London: Routledge.

Young, S.L. and Ensing, D.S. (1999) 'Exploring recovery from the perspective of people with psychiatric disabilities.' *Psychiatric Rehabilitation Journal 22*, 219–231.

CHAPTER 12

Social Perspectives

Towards a Framework for Practice

Jerry Tew

The ideas and approaches which have been explored in this book reflect a diverse range of starting points, from the situated knowledge of service users and of practitioners of various disciplines, to the application of social and psychological theories and research evidence. Brought together, they provide a set of intersecting perspectives, rather than a unitary social model. Nevertheless there may be seen to be substantial common ground, particularly in terms of underlying values and principles, and in terms of certain core ideas (see Chapter 1). The contributions contained in this book mark only the start of a process: there are significant gaps to be filled, and many ideas require to be developed further in order for their full potential to be realised.

The current practice context is one in which social model thinking still tends to be somewhat marginalised. It is not easy or effective to 'tack on' a few isolated social ideas around a practice discourse whose terms are defined by the biomedical model. Experience suggests that initial attempts at a synthesis of medical and social approaches may not have been entirely successful in underpinning a holistic approach to mental health: for example, the idea of the biopsychosocial model did not fully take account of issues of power, differences in value base and potentially fundamental differences in approaches to knowledge. If such issues are not addressed, the likely outcome in practice can be a tendency to revert to more conventional ways of working in which biomedical perspectives remain dominant – and a concern with the overall complexity of a situation can become lost in an over-emphasis on diagnosing and treating individual 'pathology'.

A more viable way forward may be to use 'higher level' integrative frameworks, through which it may be possible to see how social and medical perspectives may each contribute to the analysis of current difficulties and offer potentially relevant strategies towards their resolution. One starting point towards such a framework might be to use the stress/vulnerability model to identify physical *and* social factors that may contribute to people's distress (Zubin, Stuart and Condray, 1992; see Chapter 1). Another starting point might be the recovery paradigm which is designed to enable people to take charge of a co-ordinated plan of action to resolve or manage their distress which may involve both social *and* medical components (see Chapter 11). Whatever overall approach is to be used, it must be framed in such a way as not to give licence to professionals (of any discipline) to construct themselves as 'the experts', ignoring the meanings that people give to their own experiences and running roughshod over people's tentative visions of what may be the 'light at the end of the tunnel' for them.

As well as finding an overall way of thinking in mental health which allows medical and social approaches to talk to each other on an equal basis, it may be useful to lay out some more specific 'cornerstones' for establishing a social perspectives approach in practice.

Starting with lived experience and situated knowledge

As Peter Beresford argues in Chapter 2, professional and academic practice has a long history of systematically overlooking and over-ruling the knowledge and understanding that people may have of their own situations – although there is now at least a rhetoric that this needs to change.

Any process of getting to know what problems are, and what might be potential solutions, must be one of dialogue. Practitioners must be willing to treat service users, and their friends and family members, as valuable sources of situated knowledge, meaning and expertise in relation to their direct experience. It is they who have the capacity to be in touch with all the potentially confusing and conflicting elements that seem to be part of what is going on for them – and it is they who may have amassed considerable knowledge as to what coping strategies seem to work best, and in which circumstances. So it is they who may be in the best position to connect with those frameworks for understanding (social or otherwise) that provide the most useful 'pegs' on which to hang their experience.

What practitioners have to offer this dialogue are a range of ideas and perspectives which may help people to achieve a little distance from the immediacy of their distress, and make links and connections which may assist them in making more sense of what is going on. This may include working together to begin to decode what people may be expressing through forms of intermediary language, such as the meanings behind self-harming behaviours or how voices may relate to real people and real events or circumstances. From these new forms of understanding, people may be able to negotiate a way forward that is congruent with the ways in which they see reality.

Broadly speaking, such a dialogic approach corresponds to the 'exchange' model of assessment which has been developed within the wider context of care management – and is radically different from the 'questioning' or 'procedural' models which tend to characterise conventional professional practice and which can situate the professional, or their agency, as 'knowing best' (Smale *et al.*, 1998, 2000).

Being holistic

From critical psychiatry (see Chapter 3) to the expressed views of service users (see, for example, Chapter 7), there is a strong consensus in favour of a more holistic approach. It is important to step aside from the reductionist perspective of medical diagnosis with its inherent tendencies to individualise and pathologise. Instead, the focus needs to shift to the *person-in-their-context*. Biochemistry may then become one of a range of potentially valid and useful perspectives, but is no longer accorded the overall power to define.

At the heart of a holistic approach is an appreciation of the interconnectedness between the dynamics of what may be going on inside a person and what may be happening (or have happened in the past) in their social context. Although there is some common ground with the social model of disability – tackling damaging social responses to an impairment may be at least as important for many people as any medical interventions – a holistic understanding of mental distress is necessarily more complex. Not only may discriminatory and stigmatising attitudes impact upon people when they are showing signs of mental distress, but social factors may also be implicated in causing or exacerbating the distress itself (which cannot happen in the same sense in relation to a physical or learning impairment).

Whereas the concept of 'illness' leads to a primary focus on what may be going on inside a person, the concept of breakdown may lead to a broader understanding. It may allow an exploration not just of someone's distress patterns and coping mechanisms, but also of how their social and economic relationships may have been subject to some form of breakdown in their own right. Relationships with friends or family may be fraught or abusive – or have dwindled into non-communication. Losing one's job may involve the fracturing of a range of economic relationships and social statuses. In this way, we may understand that people may experience a breakdown of their social and economic life that is potentially just as significant as the breakdown of aspects of their mental or emotional functioning – and a recognition of this may be crucial in finding effective ways of supporting their recovery.

What is equally important, from a holistic perspective, is a focus on what has not broken down: both people's strengths and capabilities, and the aspects of their family and social networks that are (or could be) supportive and empowering. Alongside this, there is a need to explore potentially untapped resources that may be out there within the person's social environment: how people may currently, and in the future, be able to access new forms of economic, social and cultural capital (see Chapter 5). Again, these perspectives are ones that are easily lost if situations are viewed through the narrow lens of medical diagnosis and treatment.

Crucial to a holistic approach is acknowledging and working with the social and cultural contexts in which people live. It may be important to understand the nuances of meaning and expectation which come with particular backgrounds, before seeking to make sense of particular manifestations of distress (see Chapters 7 to 9). There may need to be not just a commitment to learn about the generalities of a particular context (whether defined by, say, culture, gender or sexual orientation), but also a sensitivity to the specific ways in which a person (and their family and community) may negotiate their identities within and around this. Such an awareness needs to take seriously the possible impacts of social discrimination, such as racism, sexism or heterosexism. It is not acceptable for professionals, however inadvertently, to work from assumptions based on their own social or cultural background, or to impose stereotypes derived from their own limited understanding of the culture and world view of 'others'.

Finally, service systems themselves need to be viewed as part of the holistic context in which people are trying to live their lives – and potentially these may be just as much part of 'the problem' as they are part of 'the solution'. There are powerful tendencies within mental health practice (and not just medical practice) which separate people from their family, friends and social environment – and undermine what may be already somewhat fragile connections. Typical responses to crisis situations may involve removing a person to hospital and offering little meaningful support to friends and relatives who may be frightened and confused, and unsure how to (or whether to) retain contact. Very little attention may be paid to supporting, renegotiating or strengthening key relationships, or working through tensions, conflicts or dislocations within them. Even more modern alternatives, such as home treatment, can be delivered in ways that focus almost exclusively on 'the patient'.

Particularly damaging can be an over-individualised and pathologising approach to risk in which people are seen as inherently dangerous because of their 'illness', and insufficient attention is paid to the dynamics of their social situation and what may be stressful or potentially damaging within this (see Chapter 10). Crucial to achieving a more holistic understanding of what may promote people's safety must be an engagement with (and a valuing of) the situated knowledge of those whose experience of mental distress is most direct. However, recent research indicates that, in England, meaningful service user involvement in risk assessment and risk management is yet to take place in any systematic way (Langan and Lindow, 2004).

It must be recognised that a holistic perspective runs counter to the training and working culture of the majority of mental health professions – and embracing it may mean moving outside the narrow 'comfort zone' of perceived professional expertise. In terms of practice, this implies an assessment process which is centred around the person who is experiencing distress, and which seeks to engage in a dialogue that covers *all* aspects of their situation, from the content and possible meanings of what they may be expressing (through words or actions), to their interrelationships with significant others, their social and cultural context, their access to social and economic opportunities, their experiences of powerlessness or subjection to oppressive or collusive forms of power, their potential needs for safety and protection, and their actual or potential access to more productive forms of personal and social power.

Recognising the limiting and productive operation of power

As was explored in Chapter 4, the operation of power in its different forms may be the 'unseen hand' that can influence people's experience of mental distress, societal and professional responses to that distress, and people's possibilities for recovery. Underlying the different experiences of women, lesbian and gay people, Black people and those who are survivors of abuse – and impacting on all relationships between practitioners and service users – are questions of power and how it is used (see Chapters 6 to 9). Although the operation of power may be understood in different ways, the centrality of its impact is widely recognised.

For many, the story starts with being rendered powerless in the face of (often systematic) forms of discrimination, abuse or deprivation – the deployment of oppressive forms of power by those privileged on the basis of their age, status, gender, 'race', sexual orientation or other factors. Very often, such issues of power may be seen to be bound up with people's subsequent experiences of distress and breakdown.

It is unfortunately all too rare within the current organisation of mental health services for people to be given the opportunity of having this acknowledged (see Chapter 8). On the contrary, people all too frequently report that, in subtle and not so subtle ways, the deployment of professional power and the organisation of services can deny or marginalise such aspects of their experience. Worse still, some people report instances in which services re-victimise them or compound their experiences of powerlessness, exclusion and subordination – particularly when treatment is delivered on the basis of compulsion (see, for example, Barnes, Davis and Tew, 2000).

It can feel hard for individual practitioners to go against the flow of services that seem implicitly designed to force people to 'keep a lid on' their experiences of oppression or abuse. However, with the support of colleagues, and preferably with access to a supervision process that is not dominated by a defensive agenda of accountability and risk management, it is possible to act as an enlightened witness to such issues. For many people, being listened to and taken seriously is the crucial first step on their journey to empowerment and recovery. For some people, the most potent 'therapy' comes not so much through any professional input, but through discovering shared experiences with other service users and developing forms of co-operative power through support networks or informal friendships.

The tentacles of limiting social power relations may also be seen behind the processes of stigmatisation, exclusion and vilification that the social mainstream can impose on people who become marked out as showing the signs of mental distress. Although, as Peter Beresford acknowledges in Chapter 2, there has been some reticence among people experiencing mental distress to establish common cause with those with physical or other disabilities (and vice versa), there is the potential for some 'joined-up' campaigning that can use levers such as the Disability Discrimination Act and the Human Rights Act to start to break down barriers and challenge social attitudes. Central to the social model of disability is a challenge to existing oppressive power relations.

Developing out of an awareness of the oppressive impact of power is the need to negotiate or overcome a range of potential 'us' and 'them' social barriers – whether based on wider social divisions (such as gender) or on the stigmatisation of people with the 'mental illness' label, or inhering within the structuring of relationships between service users and practitioners. This issue is particularly prominent in relation to the highly charged issue of risk where, rather than working together to provide an adequate net of safety and support, there is a polarisation between 'normal' society and the 'mentally ill', in which the latter are constructed as inherently dangerous and lacking capacity to be an equal party to decision making.

As well as a focus on the negative impacts of power, it is important to identify ways in which power can be deployed to protect people when they are vulnerable, as in the appropriate use of professional authority (see Chapter 7). Protecting people from harm, abuse or exploitation can, if it is done in a respectful and non-patronising way, open up new possibilities for them to take power for themselves. An important source of power for many people may involve establishing opportunities for mutual support or co-operative action through formal and informal networks. Co-operative power may also be realised through the experience of working in genuine partnership with practitioners, where real efforts are made to acknowledge and work across power issues that may potentially be divisive or oppressive (see Chapter 4).

Social capital, social inclusion and recovery

A focus that is easily lost within an 'illness' service is that of mental health promotion. Approaches such as the stress/vulnerability model (Zubin *et al.*, 1992), together with the evidence around the potential impact of trauma, abuse and discrimination (see Chapters 6 to 9), offer a framework for targeting activity towards those individuals and social groups who may be most vulnerable. Offering counselling or other forms of individual support may be important, but equally valuable may be a community development and capacity building approach which aims to foster the development of social capital and challenge discriminatory and exclusionary social barriers.

While the current interest in promoting a social inclusion agenda within mental health is to be applauded, there is a concern that, as with the emphasis on 'normalisation' in relation to services for people with learning difficulties, there can be an underlying expectation that people who may be seen as 'different' should be encouraged (or even required) to fit in with the social mainstream. Although there may be a very positive focus on identifying and removing barriers to participation – some of which may be the inadvertent consequences of professional practice or government policy (as in the case of the 'benefits trap') – there may nevertheless be little recognition of the power relations of the mainstream and how these may need to change if there is to be a more genuinely inclusive social order.

With its acknowledgement of issues of power, and its analysis of inter-locking social, cultural and symbolic forms of capital within specific communities and societies, Bourdieu's conception of social capital may be helpful in informing practice – although further work needs to be done to bring his relatively abstract ideas to bear on the particular contexts in which people with mental health difficulties may be living (see Chapter 5). In supporting people's recovery, it can be helpful to look explicitly at strategies for enabling them to access (or develop) more effective forms of social capital as a means of achieving a greater degree of social inclusion. This may involve net-working and other activities that involve not just service users, but also other members of people's communities, from relatives and neighbours to commu-nity leaders and opinion formers. This perspective does not put all the onus on the individual to have to 'fit in' or assimilate within existing forms of social organisation, but suggests more of a balance between individual change, social networking, community development and political, legal or other activ-ity aimed at challenging stigmatising or discriminatory attitudes and practices within the mainstream.

Although it is important not to conflate the two, there is much compatibil-ity between an emphasis on the social aspects of people's lives and recent developments in recovery thinking that have come primarily from service user movements (see Chapter 11). Without a recovery perspective, social model thinking may tend to remain focused on explaining some of the factors which may influence why people may be suffering mental distress – for example, poverty or discrimination – rather than harnessing such insights in any practi-cal way in helping people take more charge of their lives. Similarly, where there is a tendency for recovery thinking to become somewhat introverted – seeing recovery as a journey of healing that primarily depends on inner strengths and resources – a social perspective may be useful in seeing that it may be interpersonal relationships and social networks, just as much as individuals, that need to recover.

Action planning

The final cornerstone to underpin the practical implementation of a social perspectives approach is a shift away from the conventional ideologies of 'care' or 'treatment' which currently dominate the ways in which professional interventions are planned and organised. Each of these tends to rest on a fundamental imbalance of power: people with mental distress are automatically placed in a 'one-down' situation, constructed as essentially passive and helpless, lacking capacity or capability to do things for themselves and requiring 'experts' to control and treat them, or 'normal' others to take charge of their daily living. For many, this can feel infantilising, and for some it can erode their sense of self in a more profound and damaging way than the experience of distress itself, particularly when implicit or explicit forms of compulsion are used (Deegan, 1996). Such paradigms may be seen to construct and reinforce a process of 'othering' which meshes insidiously with wider social processes of inferiorisation and stigmatisation, and which may compound experiences of discrimination, oppression or abuse which may have contributed to people's distress in the first place.

The concept of 'care' underpins an approach to practice which is forever about 'doing to' or 'doing for' inferiorised others – it does not sit easily with any philosophy of partnership in which 'doing together' would be seen as the norm. There is nothing implicit in the concept of 'care' that suggests that recovery is possible – there is an assumption of ongoing disability and an inherent inability of people fully to take charge of their lives again. In England, this ideology is enshrined in the Care Programme Approach which has no provision for an exit strategy – people are assumed to be risky and needy for ever. While 'treatment' holds out the hope that people may get better, they are constructed as passive recipients of the 'doing to' interventions undertaken by expert professionals: it is not a paradigm that gives people charge of their recovery in any meaningful sense.

Within some parts of service provision in the social care sector, there is a shift of language towards planning 'support' rather than care. This term has been found more acceptable within the recovery movement: people may potentially take charge and identify what support they need in order to achieve their goals in terms of lifestyle and other aspirations (Deegan, 1992). And, in England, this has now become more practically possible through the introduction of Direct Payments schemes in which people can take charge of organising and purchasing their own personal assistance. However, this still leaves a planning and decision-making process which is somewhat unbalanced. There remains a tendency to assume ongoing disability, as it is a model that has essentially been borrowed from other areas of disability where levels of impairment are relatively fixed and predictable. What it does not focus on is what people may be able to do, with the assistance or intervention of others, to reduce the impact of, or even resolve, their mental distress.

An alternative approach, which is much more explicitly oriented towards change and empowerment, is that of Action Planning – as in, for example, the Wellness Recovery Action Planning process devised by Mary Ellen Copeland (1997). The implications of this are significantly different from those of more conventional paradigms of mental health intervention. Action Planning rests on principles of working in partnership, with leadership coming, as far as is possible, from the person experiencing the mental distress. It is focused, however distantly, on the prospect of a form of personal and social 'recovery' that is meaningful to the person, in terms of (re)claiming a sense of self, personal relationships and preferred lifestyle (this may or may not involve complete remission of 'symptoms'). It builds on a person's strengths and capacities while recognising areas of difficulty or vulnerability, and seeks to capitalise on their own situated knowledge, both in terms of what they feel may be wrong, and in terms of what seems to work best in terms of strategies to deal with this. There is a more genuine commitment to avoid or minimise compulsion than is characteristic of current services.

An Action Planning approach does not seek to impose standardised forms of intervention. Potential solutions are devised jointly on the basis of the knowledges available to service user and practitioner. There is no presupposition that medical treatment, or social care, are going to be relevant or effective courses of action – although these may be valuable options that work for some people in managing particular forms of experience. Other actions, such as forming a support group, resolving difficult family relationships or accessing education, may be equally important, particularly in promoting longer-term recovery.

Out of an assessment process that is based on dialogue rather than prescription, courses of action may emerge which focus on the person *and* their social situation. There can be a false dichotomy between looking *either* at internalisations of problematic social experiences, in the form of damaging or self-limiting beliefs, irrational thinking and discordant emotions, *or* at current realities of social exclusion, stressful or abusive interpersonal relationships, and so on. In practice, for most people, these are inextricably interlinked, with each impacting on the other. Often they may interact in the form of an increasingly damaging vicious circle or downward spiral, with internal and external processes reinforcing one another, and no way out seeming to be available.

An Action Plan may be a concerted strategy whereby to break out of such spirals. It may involve 'talking time' to help the person to accept, make sense of, and start to change patterns of thinking and emotion which may have previously seemed overwhelming and confusing. This time may be with workers, friends or other service users. It may also involve, as a part of the same plan, tasks, activities and supports which are about accessing social networks or economic resources, challenging social attitudes and practices (where these are stigmatising or exclusionary), or renegotiating the terms of abusive or damaging interpersonal relationships. It may include advance directives and/or relapse plans to identify and agree what would be appropriate forms of support, protection and treatment as and when crises may re-occur. It may include strategies for flexible and discretionary use of medication so as to maintain it at the minimum effective level. And it may involve sorting out practicalities such as housing, food and personal hygiene. Most crucially, it must contain some, perhaps tentative, statement of recovery goals or desired outcomes that arise from the aspirations of the person (and not the professional system).

An Action Planning process may be seen to take place within a specific social and cultural context – with its associated complexities of power relations and accepted ways of doing things. If it is to be effective, it must be sensitive to issues such as those of race, gender and sexual orientation (including the identities of practitioners). Capitalising on the situated knowledge that people may have about their social and cultural context may be crucial in devising courses of action that will actually work. Seeking to impose an externally validated 'evidence-based' approach may well be ineffective or even disastrous.

Action plans may need to include strategies for balancing needs for external support or intervention, in order to ensure short-term safety and protection, with longer-term needs for people to regain the ability to trust themselves and build up effective support systems of their own. However well-intentioned, excessive deployment of protective power can be disabling rather than enabling. Too great an emphasis on safety can trap people within the current configuration of their distress – having the courage to move on may be seen to require a degree of risk taking by both the person and those around them – including professionals (see Chapter 10).

And finally…

Significant parts of this framework of holistic assessment and Action Planning may be familiar to many practitioners – and may, to some extent, already be incorporated within current practice. Nevertheless, taken as a whole, it marks a radical departure from the norms of current mental health practice in the UK. It is only by introducing and working within such a broader and more user-centred framework that it becomes possible to incorporate social perspectives, as a basis for understanding and action, in anything other than a tokenistic or piecemeal fashion.

References

Barnes, M., Davis, A. and Tew, J. (2000) 'Valuing experience: users' experiences of compulsion under the 1983 Mental Health Act.' *Mental Health Review 5*, 3, 11–14.

Copeland, M. E. (1997) *Wellness Recovery Action Plan.* Brattleboro, Vermont: Peach Press.

Deegan, P. (1992) 'The independent living movement and people with psychiatric disabilities: taking back control over our own lives.' *Psychosocial Rehabilitation Journal 15*, 3, 3–19.

Deegan, P. (1996) 'Recovery as a journey of the heart.' *Psychiatric Rehabilitation Journal 19*, 3, 91–97.

Langan, J. and Lindow, V. (2004) *Living with Risk: Mental Health Service User Involvement in Risk Assessment and Management.* Bristol: Policy Press.

Smale, G., Tuson, G., Biehal, N. and Marsh, P. (1998) *Empowerment, Assessment, Care Management and the Skilled Worker (Second Edition).* London: National Institute for Social Work.

Smale, G., Tuson, G. and Statham, D. (2000) *Social Work and Social Problems: Working Towards Social Inclusion and Change.* Basingstoke: Macmillan.

Zubin, J., Stuart, R. and Condray, R. (1992) 'Vulnerability to relapse in schizophrenia.' *British Journal of Psychiatry 161*, 13–18.

Contributors

Peter Beresford is Professor of Social Policy and Director of the Centre for Citizen Participation at Brunel University. He is Chair of Shaping Our Lives, the national independent user-controlled organisation, Visiting Fellow of the School of Social Work and Psychosocial Science at the University of East Anglia and a long-term user of mental health services.

Sarah Carr is a research analyst at the Social Care Institute for Excellence (SCIE), leading some of the organisation's user participation projects. She previously worked as a Research and Information Officer at the National Institute for Social Work (NISW). She was involved with developing the National Electronic Library for Mental Health and was a researcher for a Department of Health commissioned literature review on social work assessment for older people with mental health problems. Sarah has also worked for Oxleas NHS Trust and at the Sainsbury Centre for Mental Health where she researched and co-edited a practice manual on developing assertive outreach and home treatment services. Alongside her professional interest lies Sarah's personal interest in social perspectives, as she is a mental health service user herself. She is now a trustee of PACE, a London-wide organisation which responds to the emotional, mental and physical health needs of lesbians and gay men in the Greater London Area.

Duncan Double is a consultant psychiatrist and Honorary Senior Lecturer, Norfolk and Waveney Mental Health Partnership NHS Trust and University of East Anglia. He is the website editor of the Critical Psychiatry Network (www.criticalpsychiatry.co.uk).

Peter Ferns is an independent training consultant with a wide experience of working in public and not-for-profit organisations. He also undertakes leadership training and teamworking in the commercial sector. He has been involved in the participatory development of community-based services and is committed to the creation of anti-discriminatory and holistic mental health services. He has co-authored 'Letting Through Light' a training package for practitioners on race and culture in mental health. Peter has a particular interest in mental health, learning disabilities, advocacy, equality issues, social work education and service quality issues. He can be contacted at ferns@dsl.pipex.com.

Sally Plumb worked as a mental health social worker and approved social worker (ASW) for 12 years in a multi-cultural, inner-city area of Birmingham. For ten years of this time she facilitated a self-help group for women who had been sexually abused. From 2001 until July 2004 she was the Mental Health (ASW) Training Officer for Birmingham Social Care and Health Directorate, designing and managing the delivery of two ASW training programmes.

She is now an independent trainer, specialising in mental health law and practice, in particular issues around women and mental health and the impact of sexual abuse experiences on people's mental well-being. Sally has for some time been involved in a voluntary organisation that provides support and counselling to people who have experienced rape and sexual violence.

Shulamit Ramon is Professor of Inter-professional Health and Social Studies at Anglia Polytechnic University, based in Cambridge. She is a social worker and chartered clinical psychologist, who has extensively researched de-institutionalisation and resettlement, as well as community mental health. Shulamit teaches and researches mental health in West and East Europe, and more recently has focused on involving mental health service users in research. She has published eight books and numerous articles, including her latest book, *Users Researching Health and Social Care: An Empowering Agenda?*

Jerry Tew is a senior lecturer in Social Work at the University of Central England with substantial previous experience as an Approved Social Worker, manager and training officer within the mental health sector. Over recent years, he has worked in collaboration with service user colleagues in developing training programmes for mental health practitioners, and in conducting mental health research. He has been a member of the Social Perspectives Network from the outset, and currently convenes the Research Sub-group. He is also the subject adviser for social work for the Mental Health in Higher Education Project – an initiative to develop learning and teaching in mental health across the subject centres of medicine, psychology, health sciences and social work.

Jan Wallcraft is currently Fellow for Experts by Experience (service users and carers) at the National Institute for Mental Health in England, and a Senior Researcher on user-focussed research at the Sainsbury Centre for Mental Health. Her current areas of research are the national service user/survivor movement, service user-led research and developing a survivor discourse of mental health.

Martin Webber is a qualified social worker with over six years' experience of working with adults with mental health problems or learning disabilities. He is currently researching the role of social capital in recovery from depression for his PhD and contributes to the MSc in Mental Health Social Work programme at the Institute of Psychiatry.

Jennie Williams is a clinical psychologist and Director of Inequality Agenda. This organisation supports mental health staff – through training and consultancy – to be mindful of the effects of social inequalities on mental health and service provision. She is a part-time senior lecturer in mental health at the Tizard Centre, University of Kent, and contributes through Department of Health committees to the implementation of the National Women's Mental Health Strategy and to getting equality issues on the agenda of workforce planning.

Subject Index

Author Index